Solutions Manual

Prepared by
BIJAN RAFAILZADEH

Elements of Econometrics

SECOND EDITION

Jan Kmenta

Ann Arbor
THE UNIVERSITY OF MICHIGAN PRESS

First published by the University of Michigan Press 1997
Second edition copyright © by Macmillan Publishing Company 1987
Earlier edition copyright © by Jan Kmenta 1971

ISBN 0-472-08476-3
Library of Congress Catalog Card No. 97-060800
Published in the United States of America by
The University of Michigan Press
Manufactured in the United States of America

2000 1999 1998 1997 4 3 2 1

To Ghodsian and Rafailzadeh families

ACKNOWLEDGEMENTS

I would like to thank a number of people and institutions for their help in preparing this solutions manual: Dr. Jan Kmenta (the University of Michigan), who has edited the entire manual, has provided many comments, corrections, and suggestions, and has provided access to his computer account, Dr. Joann Fenton and Dr. Frank Billes (the California State University, Dominguez Hills), who have jointly approved funds for two essential trips to the University of Michigan, Dr. E. P. Howrey (the University of Michigan), who has provided comments on solutions to exercises (9-6), (9-8), and (12-4), Dr. Gerry Musgrave and Mr. Chul-Ho Jung, who have provided numerical solutions to exercises (11-9-b) and (c), Mr. Sepehr Sarchar, who has carefully read the first six chapters and has provided many suggestions, the University of Michigan for providing computer time, and the California State University, Dominguez Hills, for providing funds for the two trips.

I would also like to thank the Ghodsian and the Rafailzadeh families, whose support and patience were a great source of energy and endurance for me. Especially my wife, Nora, and my children, Padideh and Neema, who suffered from my diverted attention to the preparation of the Manual, deserve my utmost gratitude and appreciation.

TABLE OF CONTENTS

INTRODUCTION

This solutions manual is processed using TEXTEDIT, a text processing program developed by the Statistical Research Laboratory, the University of Michigan. In preparing the manual much attempt has been made to employ the same notation as used in the text, *Elements of Econometrics*, as far as capabilities of TEXTEDIT allows.

Computations are made using SHAZAM, Version 5, an econometrics computer program developed by the University of British Columbia. Accuracy of computations are checked by MINITAB, a general purpose statistical system developed by the Minitab Inc. and the Pennsylvania State University. Calculations are generally carried to more than four decimal places. However, in most cases only four decimal places are presented by omitting the rest if the fifth decimal place were 0, 1, 2, 3, and 4, and by adding one to the fourth decimal place otherwise. In few cases where six decimal places are presented, the above convention is applied to the seventh decimal place.

As for the numbering of the solutions to the exercises,

1-8-a.

...

(ii) ...

means chapter 1, exercise 8, part a, sub-part (ii). Further, when we intend to refer to solution to an earlier part of an exercise, only reference to that part will be given. However, when referring to solution to an exercise in the same chapter, reference to exercise number and part will be given. For instance, both

1-5-e.

Referring to part (a), ...

and

1-7-b.

Referring to (5-a), ...

refer to the solution to the exercise **1-5-a.**

In presentation of the mathematical operations the following conventions are used

$$a \pm b/c = a \pm \frac{b}{c},$$

$$(a \pm b)/c = \frac{a \pm b}{c},$$

and

$$(a/b)/(c/d) = \frac{a/b}{c/d}.$$

However, superscripts and subscripts are presented as follows

$$X^{a\pm b},$$

and

$$Y_{a\pm b}.$$

Further, matrices and vectors are presented as follows

$$\begin{bmatrix} a\pm b & c\pm d \\ e\pm f & g\pm h \end{bmatrix}, \quad \text{and} \quad \begin{bmatrix} a\pm b \\ c\pm d \end{bmatrix}.$$

Mathematical expectation (E), logarithm (log), limit (lim), probability limit (plim), and exponential (exp) of expressions are presented within parentheses, brackets, or braces. For instance,

$$E[X - E(X)],$$

$$\log(\frac{a}{b - c}),$$

$$\lim_{n\to\infty}\{\frac{a[b/n - c(d/n + e)]}{f}\},$$

$$\text{plim}[\Sigma(X_i - \bar{X})^2/n],$$

and

$$\exp[f(X)].$$

The order in which parentheses, brackets, and braces appear in an expression is as follows

$$\{ \cdots [\cdots (\cdots) \cdots] \cdots \}.$$

Matrices and column vectors are presented by boldface upper and lower case letters, respectively. Row vectors are presented as transpose of column vectors. Matrices or vectors of observations in the form of deviations about the mean are presented with an under-bar. For instance,

$\mathbf{X}$	$\mathbf{Y}$	$\mathbf{Z}$	are matrices,
$\mathbf{x}$	$\mathbf{y}$	$\mathbf{z}$	are column vectors,
$\mathbf{x}'$	$\mathbf{y}'$	$\mathbf{z}'$	are row vectors,
$\underline{\mathbf{X}}$	$\underline{\mathbf{y}}$	$\underline{\mathbf{z}}'$	are matrices or vectors in the form of deviation about the mean.

In presentation of mathematical expressions involving matrices and/or vectors an entire expression except scalars is given in boldface if the expression involves more than one relation, otherwise if the expression involves only one relation only those parts of the expression which are in matrix and/or vector form are given in boldface. Thus,

$$\mathbf{a} = b(\mathbf{A}'\mathbf{A})^{-1}\mathbf{c} + 3d\mathbf{Be},$$

implies that **A**, **A'**, and **B** are matrices, **a**, **c**, and **e** are column vectors, and b and d are scalars, whereas

$$a = 2(\mathbf{b}'\mathbf{A}\mathbf{b})^{-1} + 5\mathbf{c}'\mathbf{c}/(12 - d),$$

implies that **A** is a matrix, **b** and **c** are column vectors, **b'** and **c'** are row vectors, and a and d are scalars.

CHAPTER 1

1-1-a.

$$\bar{x} = \sum_{i=1}^{10} x_i/n = 60/10 = 6.$$

1-1-b.

$$SD = \sqrt{(\Sigma x_i^2 - n\bar{x}^2)/n} = \sqrt{[396 - 10(6^2)]/10} = 1.8974.$$

1-1-c.

$$\Sigma(x_i - \bar{x})/SD = 0/SD = 0.$$

1-1-d.

$$\begin{aligned} \Sigma 2(x_i - 5) &= 2\Sigma(x_i - 5) \\ &= 2\Sigma x_i - 2\Sigma 5 \\ &= 2(60) - 2(10)(5) \\ &= 20. \end{aligned}$$

1-1-e.

$$\begin{aligned} \bar{z} &= \Sigma z_i/n \\ &= \Sigma[x_i - (x_i - \bar{x})/SD]/10 \\ &= [\Sigma x_i - \Sigma(x_i - \bar{x})/SD]/10 \\ &= (60 - 0)/10 \\ &= 6. \end{aligned}$$

1-2-a.

The frequency distribution is presented in figure 1-1.

FIGURE 1-1

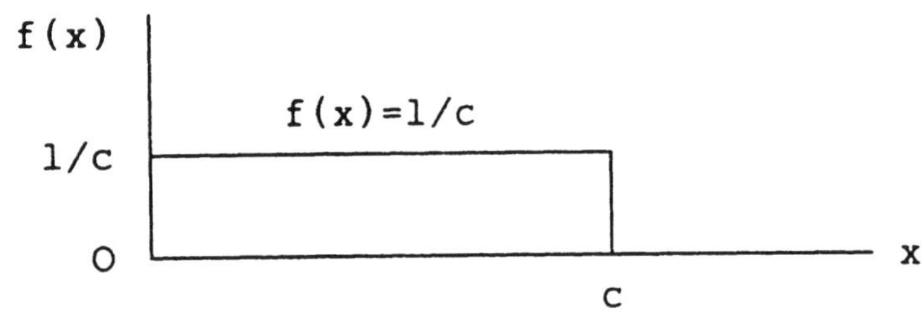

where c is a constant.

1-2-b.

The frequency distribution is presented in figure 1-2.

FIGURE 1-2

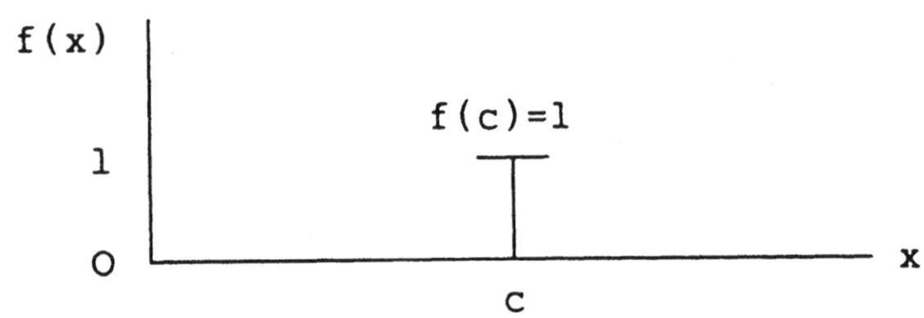

where x assumes the value of c at each observation.

1-2-c.

The frequency distribution is presented in figure 1-3.

FIGURE 1-3

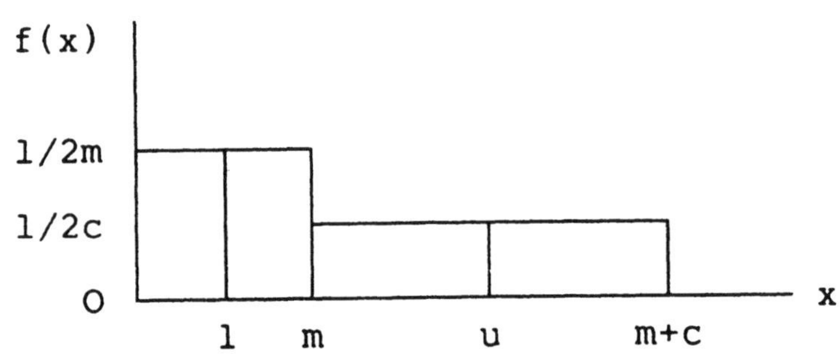

where l, m, and u denote lower quartile, median and upper quartile, respectively, and c is a positive constant.

1-2-d.

The graph is the same as that of part (b).

1-2-e.

The frequency distribution is presented in figure 1-4.

FIGURE 1-4

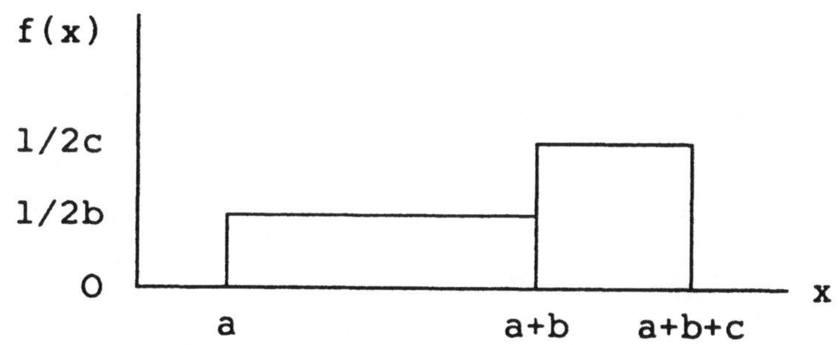

where a, b, and c are constants such that (b > c > 0). Here,

$$a < \text{mean} < (a + b) \le \text{mode} \le (a + b + c).$$

1-3.

Let x_i and y_i, $(i = 1, \ldots, n)$, denote the true and the census ages of the i-th individual, respectively. Then

$$\sum_{i=1}^{n} x_i = \sum_{i=1}^{n} y_i + 1(n/4) - 2(n/4),$$

or

$$\sum_{i=1}^{n} x_i = \sum_{i=1}^{n} y_i - n/4.$$

Dividing both sides by n, we obtain

$$\bar{x} = \bar{y} - 0.25,$$

or

$$\text{true mean age} = \text{census mean age} - 0.25.$$

1-4-a.

(i) Consider

$$\frac{1}{12}\sum_{i=1}^{12} x_i = \frac{1}{11}\sum_{i=1}^{11} x_i,$$

$$\sum_{i=1}^{12} x_i = \frac{12}{11}\sum_{i=1}^{11} x_i,$$

$$\sum_{i=1}^{11} x_i + x_{12} = \frac{12}{11}\sum_{i=1}^{11} x_i,$$

or

$$x_{12} = \frac{1}{11}\sum_{i=1}^{11} x_i = \bar{x}_{11} = \bar{x}.$$

(ii) Consider

$$\frac{1}{12}\sum_{i=1}^{12} x_i = \frac{11}{12}\left(\frac{1}{11}\sum_{i=1}^{11} x_i\right),$$

$$\sum_{i=1}^{12} x_i = \sum_{i=1}^{11} x_i,$$

or

$$x_{12} = 0.$$

(iii) Consider

$$\frac{1}{12}\sum_{i=1}^{12} x_i = x_{12},$$

$$\sum_{i=1}^{11} x_i + x_{12} = 12x_{12},$$

or

$$x_{12} = \frac{1}{11}\sum_{i=1}^{11} x_i = \bar{x}_{11} = \bar{x}.$$

1-4-b.

Since $x_{12} = \bar{x}$, then

$$SD_{12}^2 = \frac{1}{12}\sum_{i=1}^{12}(x_i - \bar{x})^2 = \frac{1}{12}\sum_{i=1}^{11}(x_i - \bar{x})^2,$$

and since $\bar{x}_{11} = \bar{x}$, then

$$SD_{11}^2 = \frac{1}{11}\sum_{i=1}^{11}(x_i - \bar{x}_{11})^2 = \frac{1}{11}\sum_{i=1}^{11}(x_i - \bar{x})^2.$$

Thus

$$SD_{12}^2 < SD_{11}^2,$$

and

$$SD_{12} < SD_{11}.$$

1-5-a.

Let $y_i = (x_i + c)$, $(i = 1, \ldots, n)$, where $c > 0$. Then

$$\begin{aligned}\bar{y} &= \sum_{i=1}^{n} y_i/n \\ &= \Sigma(x_i + c)/n \\ &= \bar{x} + c.\end{aligned}$$

$$\begin{aligned}SD_y &= \sqrt{\Sigma(y_i - \bar{y})^2/n} \\ &= \sqrt{\Sigma(x_i + c - \bar{x} - c)^2/n} \\ &= SD.\end{aligned}$$

$$\begin{aligned}(a_3)_y &= [\Sigma(y_i - \bar{y})^3/n]/SD_y^3 \\ &= [\Sigma(x_i - \bar{x})^3/n]/SD^3 \\ &= a_3.\end{aligned}$$

1-5-b.

Let $z_i = 2x_i$, $(i = 1, \ldots, n)$. Then

$$\bar{z} = \Sigma z_i/n$$

$$= \Sigma 2x_i/n$$

$$= 2\Sigma x_i/n$$

$$= 2\bar{x}.$$

$$SD_z = \sqrt{\Sigma(z_i - \bar{z})^2/n}$$

$$= \sqrt{\Sigma(2x_i - 2\bar{x})^2/n}$$

$$= \sqrt{4\Sigma(x_i - \bar{x})^2/n}$$

$$= 2SD.$$

$$(a_3)_z = [\Sigma(z_i - \bar{z})^3/n]/SD_z^3$$

$$= [\Sigma(2x_i - 2\bar{x})^3/n]/(2SD)^3$$

$$= 8[\Sigma(x_i - \bar{x})^3/n]/8SD^3$$

$$= a_3.$$

1-5-c.

Let $w_i = \bar{x}$, $(i = 1, \ldots, n)$. Then

$$\bar{w} = \Sigma w_i/n$$

$$= \Sigma\bar{x}/n$$

$$= \bar{x}.$$

$$SD_w = \sqrt{\Sigma(w_i - \bar{w})^2/n}$$

$$= \sqrt{\Sigma(\bar{x} - \bar{x})^2/n}$$

$$= 0.$$

$$(a_3)_w = [\Sigma(w_i - \bar{w})^3/n]/SD_w^3$$

$$= [\Sigma(\bar{x} - \bar{x})^3/n]/0$$

$$= 0/0 \quad \text{(undefined)}.$$

1-5-d.

Let $u_i = x_i/\bar{x}$, $(i = 1, \ldots, n)$. Then

$$\bar{u} = \Sigma u_i/n$$

$$= \Sigma x_i/n\bar{x}$$

$$= 1.$$

$$SD_u = \sqrt{\Sigma(u_i - \bar{u})^2/n}$$

$$= \sqrt{\Sigma(x_i/\bar{x} - 1)^2/n}$$

$$= \sqrt{\Sigma[(x_i - \bar{x})/\bar{x}]^2/n}$$

$$= SD/\bar{x}.$$

$$(a_3)_u = [\Sigma(u_i - \bar{u})^3/n]/SD_u^3$$

$$= \{\Sigma[(x_i - \bar{x})/\bar{x}]^3/n\}/(SD/\bar{x})^3$$

$$= [\Sigma(x_i - \bar{x})^3/n\bar{x}^3]/(SD^3/\bar{x}^3)$$

$$= a_3.$$

1-5-e.

Referring to part (a), let $c = -\bar{x}$. Then

$$y_i = x_i + c = x_i - \bar{x}.$$

Now

$$\bar{y} = \bar{x} + c = 0,$$

$$SD_y = SD,$$

and

$$(a_3)_y = a_3.$$

1-5-f.

Let $v_i = (x_i - \bar{x})/SD$, $(i = 1, \ldots, n)$. Then

$$\bar{v} = \Sigma v_i/n$$

$$= \Sigma(x_i - \bar{x})/nSD$$

$$= 0.$$

$$SD_v = \sqrt{\Sigma(v_i - \bar{v})^2/n}$$

$$= \sqrt{\Sigma[(x_i - \bar{x})/SD]^2/n}$$

$$= \sqrt{\Sigma(x_i - \bar{x})^2/nSD^2}$$

$$= 1.$$

$$(a_3)_v = [\Sigma(v_i - \bar{v})^3/n]/SD_v^3$$

$$= \Sigma[(x_i - \bar{x})/SD]^3/n$$

$$= \Sigma(x_i - \bar{x})^3/nSD^3$$

$$= a_3.$$

1-6.

The relationship between Fahrenheit (F) and Celsius (C) degrees is

$$C_i = (5F_i - 160)/9.$$

Then

$$\bar{C} = \sum_{i=1}^{10} C_i/10$$

$$= \Sigma(5F_i - 160)/90$$

$$= (5\bar{F} - 160)/9$$

$$= [5(50) - 160]/9$$

$$= 10.$$

Further,

$$SD_C = \sqrt{\Sigma(C_i - \bar{C})^2/10}$$

$$= \sqrt{\Sigma[(5F_i - 160 - 5\bar{F} + 160)/9]^2/10}$$

$$= \sqrt{(5/9)^2\Sigma(F_i - \bar{F})^2/10}$$

$$= (5/9)\sqrt{\Sigma(F_i - \bar{F})^2/10}$$

$$= 5SD_F/9$$

$$= 5(6)/9$$

$$= 10/3.$$

1-7-a.

Let x_i and $y_i = x_i^2$ denote the length and the area of the i-th room, respectively. The average area of a room ($\bar{y}$) can be calculated as

$$\bar{y} = \sum_{i=1}^{100} y_i/100 = \Sigma x_i^2/100 = SD^2 + \bar{x}^2 = 2^2 + 16^2 = 260.$$

The number of square feet of carpeting needed for all 100 rooms can be calculated as

$$n\bar{y}^2 = 100(260) = 26{,}000.$$

1-7-b.

Referring to (**5-a**), let c = -1. Then

$$\text{correct mean length} = \bar{x} - 1 = 15,$$

and

$$\text{correct SD} = \text{SD} = 2.$$

1-8-a.

(**i**) The result is uncertain, and depends on whether the changed distribution (1) has a different range than that of the original distribution, and (2) is bell-shaped, mound-shaped, uniform, u-shaped, bimodal, etc. (For instance, if the changed distribution is bell-shaped and has the same range as the original distribution, the proportion of poor families will decrease.)

(**ii**) No change. Such an increase would only change the unit of measurement used along the horizontal axis without affecting the distribution.

1-8-b.

Let m < c denote median, where c is a constant. In the following three figures, uniform distribution is assumed for segments of the positively skewed income distribution.

(i) The income distribution is presented in figure 1-5.

FIGURE 1-5

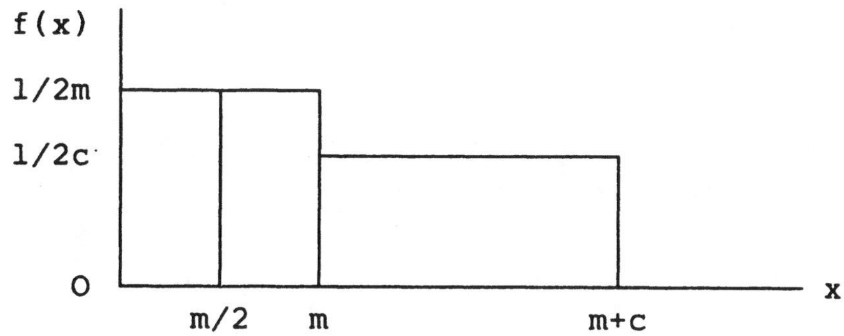

(ii) The income distribution is presented in figure 1-6.

FIGURE 1-6

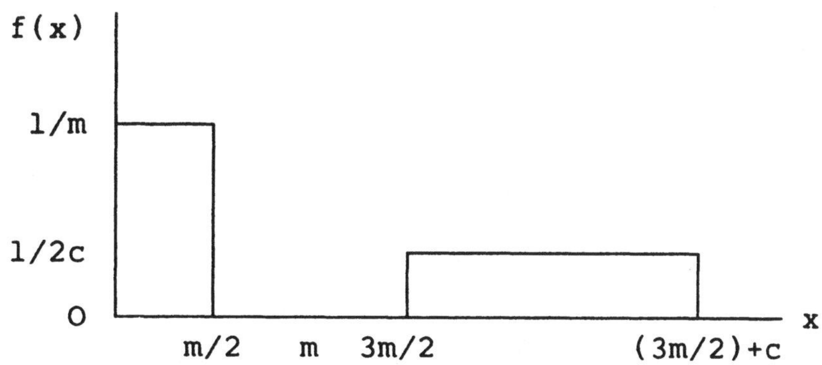

(iii) The income distribution is presented in figure 1-7.

FIGURE 1-7

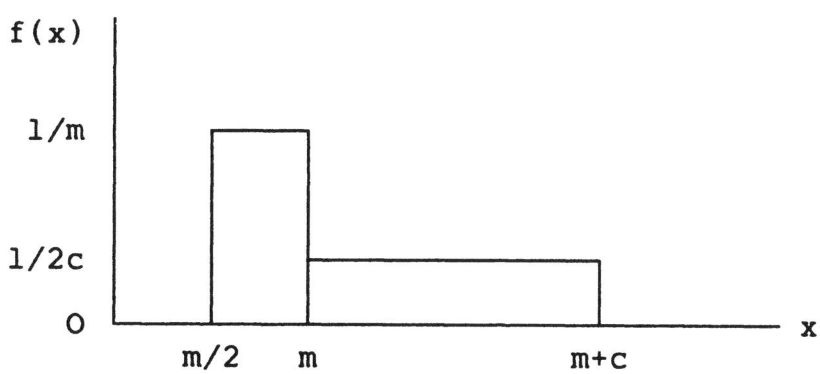

1-9.

Let m and f denote the number of the male and the female students, respectively. Furthermore, let M_i and F_j denote the score of the i-th male and the j-th female student, respectively. Then

$$\sum_{i=1}^{m} M_i = 62m,$$

and

$$\sum_{j=1}^{f} F_j = 80f.$$

Now

$$(\sum_i M_i + \sum_j F_j)/(m + f) = 65,$$

$$(62m + 80f)/(m + f) = 65,$$

or

$$f/(m + f) = 1/6.$$

Thus the proportion of female students was 1/6.

CHAPTER 2

2-1.

An experimental sampling distribution of the proportion of heads for samples of 4 tosses of a coin is given in table 2-1.

TABLE 2-1

Successes		Frequency	
Number	Proportion: $\hat{\pi}$	Absolute	Relative: $f(\hat{\pi})$
0	0.00	5	0.05
1	0.25	21	0.21
2	0.50	32	0.32
3	0.75	37	0.37
4	1.00	5	0.05

The mean, the variance, and the standard deviation (SD) of the distribution can be calculated as

$$\text{Mean} = \Sigma\hat{\pi}_i f(\hat{\pi}_i)$$

$$= 0.00(0.05) + \cdots + 1.00(0.05)$$

$$= 0.54,$$

$$\text{Variance} = \Sigma(\hat{\pi}_i - 0.54)^2 f(\hat{\pi}_i)$$

$$= (0.00 - 0.54)^2(0.05) + \cdots$$

$$= 0.0597,$$

and

$$\text{SD} = 0.2442.$$

An experimental sampling distribution of the proportion of heads for samples of 16 tosses of a coin is given in table 2-2.

TABLE 2-2

Successes		Frequency	
Number	Proportion: $\hat{\pi}$	Absolute	Relative: $f(\hat{\pi})$
0	0.0000	0	0.0000
1	0.0625	0	0.0000
2	0.1250	0	0.0000
3	0.1875	1	0.0100
4	0.2500	1	0.0100
5	0.3125	7	0.0700
6	0.3750	17	0.1700
7	0.4375	13	0.1300
8	0.5000	21	0.2100
9	0.5625	11	0.1100
10	0.6250	14	0.1400
11	0.6875	10	0.1000
12	0.7500	3	0.0300
13	0.8125	1	0.0100
14	0.8750	1	0.0100
15	0.9375	0	0.0000
16	1.0000	0	0.0000

The mean and the standard deviation are

$$\text{Mean} = 0.5094,$$

and

$$\text{SD} = 0.1337.$$

The results of these two experiments are consistent with those of the two experiments under case (A), section (2-1) of the text.[1] This implies that $\hat{\pi}$ is an unbiased and a consistent estimator of π, that its sampling distribution tends to become more symmetrical as sample size increases, and that its SD changes in inverse proportion to the square root of the sample size.

[1] Pp. 21-4.

2-2-a.

There are $3^3 = 27$ different samples of size 3 that can be drawn from this population. These are 111, 112, 113, ..., 333, or in general ijk, where (i, j, and k = 1, 2, 3). The sample mean, then, is (i + j + k)/3, and the sample median is equal to the middle number where i, j and k are arranged in order of magnitude. The distributions of sample mean and sample median are presented in table 2-3.

TABLE 2-3

Distribution of Sample Mean		Distribution of Sample Median	
Sample Mean	Frequency	Sample Median	Frequency
3/3	1/27		
4/3	3/27	1	7/27
5/3	6/27		
6/3	7/27	2	13/27
7/3	6/27		
8/3	3/27	3	7/27
9/3	1/27		

Mean of means = 2. Mean of medians = 2.

SD of means = 0.4714. SD of medians = 0.7201.

2-2-b.

There are $3^4 = 81$ different samples of size 4 that can be drawn from this population. These are 1111, 1112, 1113, ..., 3333. The distributions of sample mean and sample median are presented in table 2-4.

TABLE 2-4

Distribution of Sample Mean		Distribution of Sample Median	
Sample Mean	Frequency	Sample Median	Frequency
1.00	1/81	1.00	1/9
1.25	4/81		
1.50	10/81	1.50	2/9
1.75	16/81		
2.00	19/81	2.00	3/9
2.25	16/81		
2.50	10/81	2.50	2/9
2.75	4/81		
3.00	1/81	3.00	1/9

Mean of means = 2.

SD of means = 0.4082.

Mean of medians = 2.

SD of medians = 0.5774.

The ratio of the SD of the mean to that of the median for sample size 3 is 0.6547 and for sample size 4 is 0.7071.

2-3-a.

An experimental sampling distribution of the proportion of times that one gets two heads and a tail in ten tosses of three coins of equal denomination based on 100 samples is presented in table 2-5.

2-3-b.

The mean and the standard deviation of the proportion of successes are

$$\text{Mean} = 0.00(0.00) + \cdots + 1.00(0.00) = 0.3790,$$

and

$$\text{SD} = [(0.00 - 0.3790)^2(0.00) + \cdots]^{1/2} = 0.1551.$$

TABLE 2-5

Successes		Frequency	
Number	Proportion: $\hat{\pi}$	Absolute	Relative: $f(\hat{\pi})$
0	0.00	0	0.00
1	0.10	7	0.07
2	0.20	15	0.15
3	0.30	21	0.21
4	0.40	24	0.24
5	0.50	21	0.21
6	0.60	7	0.07
7	0.70	4	0.04
8	0.80	1	0.01
9	0.90	0	0.00
10	1.00	0	0.00

2-4.

In order to construct an empirical sampling distribution of sample mean for samples of size 5 drawn from a normal population with mean of zero and variance of one, obtain five numbers from a computer program for generating random normal deviates and calculate the value of sample mean. Repeat this 100 times as an approximation to large number of times. Arrange the resulting 100 sample means in a frequency distribution. The resulting distribution is an empirical sampling distribution of sample mean. Unless the experiment is repeated large number of times, the resulting sampling distribution based on 100 repetitions will be different from experiment to experiment. The result of one such experiment is given in table 2-6.

TABLE 2-6

Empirical Sampling Distribution of Sample Mean				
Value of Sample Mean			Frequency	
Interval		Midpoint	Absolute	Relative
-1.5000	-1.2500	-1.3750	1	0.0100
-1.2499	-1.0000	-1.1250	0	0.0000
-0.9999	-0.7500	-0.8750	3	0.0300
-0.7499	-0.5000	-0.6250	15	0.1500
-0.4999	-0.2500	-0.3750	16	0.1600
-0.2499	0.0000	-0.1250	20	0.2000
0.0001	0.2500	0.1250	18	0.1800
0.2501	0.5000	0.3750	19	0.1900
0.5001	0.7500	0.6250	5	0.0500
0.7501	1.0000	0.8750	3	0.0300

The mean and the standard deviation of the distribution are -0.0690 and 0.4300 which are approximately equal to zero (or the population mean) and $1/\sqrt{5} = 0.4472$ (or the population standard deviation divided by $\sqrt{5}$), respectively.

2-5-a.

$$S = \{1 \text{ and } 1,\ 1 \text{ and } 3,\ 3 \text{ and } 1,\ 3 \text{ and } 3\}.$$

2-5-b.

Let X denote all possible samples of size two that can be drawn from this population. All equally likely values of X, $\bar{X}$,

$$\hat{a}_1 = \bar{X}^2,$$

and

$$\hat{a}_2 = (X_1^2 + X_2^2)/2,$$

are given in table 2-7.

TABLE 2-7

All Equally Likely Values of			
X	$\bar{X}$	$\hat{a}_1$	$\hat{a}_2$
1 and 1	(1 + 1)/2 = 1	1	(1 + 1)/2 = 1
1 and 3	(1 + 3)/2 = 2	4	(1 + 9)/2 = 5
3 and 1	(3 + 1)/2 = 2	4	(9 + 1)/2 = 5
3 and 3	(3 + 3)/2 = 3	9	(9 + 9)/2 = 9

The sampling distributions of $\hat{a}_1$ and $\hat{a}_2$ are presented in table 2-8.

TABLE 2-8

Sampling Distribution of $\hat{a}_1$		Sampling Distribution of $\hat{a}_2$	
$\hat{a}_1$	$P\{\hat{a}_1\}$	$\hat{a}_2$	$P\{\hat{a}_2\}$
1	0.25	1	0.25
4	0.50	5	0.50
9	0.25	9	0.25

Mean of $\hat{a}_1$ = 4.50 Mean of $\hat{a}_2$ = 5.00

2-5-c.

Neither of the two estimators is unbiased, and hence neither is efficient.

2-6-a.

Both estimators are unbiased since the mean of each one is equal to the median number of children in a family, or

$$\text{Mean of } \tilde{X} = \text{Mean of } \bar{X} = 1.$$

2-6-b.

(i)

$$P\{\tilde{x} = 1\} = 44/64.$$

(ii)

$$P\{\bar{x} = 1\} = 20/64.$$

2-6-c.

(i)

$$P\{\tilde{x} > 1\} = P\{\tilde{x} = 2\} = 10/64.$$

(ii)

$$P\{\bar{x} > 1\} = P\{\bar{x} \geq 4/3\} = 22/64.$$

2-6-d.

Sample mean is a better estimator of population median since it has a smaller variance, i.e.,

$$\text{Var}(\bar{X}) = 32/192 < \text{Var}(\tilde{X}) = 60/192.$$

CHAPTER 3

3-1-a.

Let W and R stand for getting a white ball and a red ball, respectively, in drawing (with replacement) two balls from an urn containing 7 white and 3 red balls. The sample space corresponding to this experiment is

$$S = \{WW, WR, RW, RR\}.$$

3-1-b.

Let H and T stand for getting a head and a tail in a flip of a coin, respectively. The sample space corresponding to the experiment of flipping the coin and, provided a head appears, rolling a six-sided die (if a tail appears, the experiment is stopped) is

$$S = \{H1, H2, H3, H4, H5, H6, T\}.$$

3-1-c.

Let F and N stand for getting a face and a non-face (number) card, respectively, when drawing cards from a pack of 52 cards. The sample space corresponding to this experiment is

$$S = \{F, NF, NNF, \ldots, N\cdots NF\},$$

where the last element in S consists of forty N's and one F.

3-2-a.

$$P\{n\} = 1/n, \qquad P\{S_1\} = 1/2,$$

$$P\{S_2\} = 1/2, \qquad P\{S_3\} = 1/3.$$

3-2-b.

$$S_1 \cap S_3 = \{3, 9, \ldots, n-3\},$$

$$P\{S_1 \cap S_3\} = 1/6.$$

3-2-c.

$$S_2 \cap S_3 = \{6, 12, \ldots, n\},$$

$$P\{S_2 \cap S_3\} = 1/6.$$

3-2-d.

$$S_1 \cup S_2 = S,$$

$$P\{S_1 \cup S_2\} = 1.$$

3-2-e.

$$S_1 \cup S_3 = \{1, 3, 5, 6, \ldots, n\},$$

$$P\{S_1 \cup S_3\} = 2/3.$$

3-2-f.

$$S_2 \cup S_3 = \{2, 3, 4, 6, \ldots, n\},$$

$$P\{S_2 \cup S_3\} = 2/3.$$

3-2-g.

$$S_1 \cup (S_2 \cap S_3) = \{1, 3, 5, 6, \ldots, n\},$$

$$P\{S_1 \cup (S_2 \cap S_3)\} = 2/3.$$

3-3-a.

The solution to this exercise can be facilitated by using a Venn diagram such as figure (3-1), section (**3-1**) of the text.[1] Also a two way table such as table 3-1 may be of some help.

TABLE 3-1

Joint and Marginal Probabilities			
	S_2	$\bar{S}_2$	
S_1	$P\{S_1 \cap S_2\}$	$P\{S_1 \cap \bar{S}_2\}$	$P\{S_1\}$
$\bar{S}_1$	$P\{\bar{S}_1 \cap S_2\}$	$P\{\bar{S}_1 \cap \bar{S}_2\}$	$P\{\bar{S}_1\}$
	$P\{S_2\}$	$P\{\bar{S}_2\}$	1

Using the above table, we have

$$\begin{aligned} P\{\bar{S}_1 \cup \bar{S}_2\} &= P\{\bar{S}_1\} + P\{\bar{S}_2\} - P\{\bar{S}_1 \cap \bar{S}_2\} \\ &= 1 - P\{S_1\} + 1 - P\{S_2\} - 1 + P\{S_1 \cup S_2\} \\ &= 1 - P\{S_1\} - P\{S_2\} + P\{S_1\} + P\{S_2\} - P\{S_1 \cap S_2\} \\ &= 1 - P\{S_1 \cap S_2\}. \end{aligned}$$

3-3-b.

$$\begin{aligned} P\{\bar{S}_1 \cap \bar{S}_2\} &= 1 - P\{S_1 \cup S_2\} \\ &= 1 - P\{S_1\} - P\{S_2\} + P\{S_1 \cap S_2\}. \end{aligned}$$

[1]P. 35.

3-3-c.

$$P\{\bar{S}_1 \cap S_2\} = P\{S_2\} - P\{S_1 \cap S_2\}.$$

3-3-d.

$$\begin{aligned} P\{\bar{S}_1 \cup S_2\} &= P\{\bar{S}_1\} + P\{S_2\} - P\{\bar{S}_1 \cap S_2\} \\ &= 1 - P\{S_1\} + P\{S_2\} - P\{S_2\} + P\{S_1 \cap S_2\} \\ &= 1 - P\{S_1\} + P\{S_1 \cap S_2\}. \end{aligned}$$

3-4-a.

The solution to this exercise can best be obtained by constructing a two way table such as table 3-2.

TABLE 3-2

Joint and Marginal Probabilities			
	B	$\bar{B}$	
A	0.30	0.10*	0.40
$\bar{A}$	0.20*	0.40*	0.60*
	0.50	0.50*	1.00

where the values without * are given and the ones with * are calculated using the fact that for each row or column the sum of the first two values is equal to the third one. Now

$$\begin{aligned} P\{A \cup B\} &= P\{A\} + P\{B\} - P\{A \cap B\} \\ &= 0.40 + 0.50 - 0.30 \\ &= 0.60. \end{aligned}$$

3-4-b.

$$P\{A \cap \bar{B}\} = 0.10.$$

3-4-c.

$$P\{\bar{A} \cap B\} = 0.20.$$

3-4-d.

$$P\{\bar{A} \cap \bar{B}\} = 0.40.$$

3-5-a.

(i) Since A and B are mutually exclusive, then

$$P\{A \cap B\} = 0.$$

Thus

$$P\{A \cup B\} = P\{A\} + P\{B\} - P\{A \cap B\} = 0.25 + 0.40,$$

or

$$P\{A \cup B\} = 0.65.$$

(ii)

$$P\{\bar{A} \cap \bar{B}\} = 1 - P\{A \cup B\} = 1 - 0.65 = 0.35.$$

3-5-b.

(i) Since A and B are independent, then

$$P\{A|B\} = P\{A\} = 0.20.$$

(ii) Since A and B are independent, then

$$P\{A \cap B\} = P\{A\} \cdot P\{B\} = 0.09.$$

Thus

$$P\{A \cup B\} = 0.20 + 0.45 - 0.09 = 0.56.$$

(iii)

$$P\{\bar{A} \cap \bar{B}\} = 1 - 0.56 = 0.44.$$

3-6-a.

The joint probability distribution of X and Y is presented in table 3-3.

TABLE 3-3

Joint Probability Distribution of X and Y	
x,y	f(x,y)
0,0	0.1250 + 0.1250 = 0.2500
0,1	0.1000 + 0.1500 = 0.2500
1,0	0.0800 + 0.1200 = 0.2000
1,1	0.0900 + 0.2100 = 0.3000

3-6-b.

The marginal probability distributions of X, Y, and Z are presented in table 3-4.

TABLE 3-4

Marginal Probability Distributions of X, Y, and Z					
x	f(x)	y	f(y)	z	f(z)
0	0.5000	0	0.4500	0	0.3950
1	0.5000	1	0.5500	1	0.6050

3-6-c.

Mean of X = E(X) = $\Sigma xf(x)$ = 0.50.

$$\text{Var}(X) = E[X - E(X)]^2$$

$$= (0 - 0.50)^2(0.50) + (1 - 0.50)^2(0.50)$$

$$= 0.25.$$

3-6-d.

The conditional probability distribution of $X|Z$ is presented in table 3-5.

TABLE 3-5

Conditional Probability Distribution of X|Z	
$x\|0$	$f(x\|0)$
0	0.57
1	0.43

where the conditional probabilities are calculated as

$$f(0|0) = \frac{f(0,0)}{f(0)} = \frac{0.1250 + 0.1000}{0.3950} = 0.57,$$

and

$$f(1|0) = 1 - f(0|0) = 1 - 0.57 = 0.43.$$

Now

$$E(X|Z) = \Sigma(x|z)f(x|z) = 0.43.$$

3-6-e.

The probability distribution of W is presented in table 3-6.

TABLE 3-6

Probability Distribution of W	
w	f(w)
0	0.1250
1	0.3050
2	0.3600
3	0.2100

3-6-f.

The probability distribution of V is presented in table 3-7.

TABLE 3-7

Probability Distribution of V	
v	f(v)
0	0.70
1	0.30

$$E(V) = 0.30.$$

3-7.

Let the random variables X and Y = (0.25 - X) denote the prize and the profit per throw of a dart, respectively. Their probability distributions are presented in table 3-8.

TABLE 3-8

Probability Distributions of X and Y			
x	f(x)	y	f(y)
0.00	0.50	0.25	0.50
0.05	0.20	0.20	0.20
0.10	0.15	0.15	0.15
0.25	0.10	0.00	0.10
1.00	0.05	-0.75	0.05

The expected profit on 400 throws is calculated as

$$\begin{aligned} E(400Y) &= 400\Sigma yf(y) \\ &= 400[0.25(0.50) + \cdots + (-0.75)(0.05)] \\ &= \$60. \end{aligned}$$

3-8-a.

$$P\{x < 1\} = P\{-1 < x < 1\} = 0.50.$$

3-8-b.

$$P\{x < -0.50\} = P\{-1 < x < -0.50\} = 0.1250.$$

3-8-c.

$$P\{0 < x < 1\} = 0.25.$$

3-8-d.

$$P\{x < 0 \text{ or } x > 1\} = 1 - P\{0 < x < 1\} = 0.75.$$

3-8-e.

$$P\{|x| < 0.50\} = P\{-0.50 < x < 0.50\} = 0.25.$$

3-8-f.

$$P\{|x - 1| < 0.50\} = P\{0.50 < x < 1.50\} = 0.3750.$$

3-8-g.

$$P\{x = 1\} = 0.$$

3-8-h.

Median of X = 1.

In order to calculate the mean of X, consider

$$f(x) = \begin{cases} 0.25 & \text{if } -1 < x < 1, \\ 0.50 & \text{if } 1 < x < 2. \end{cases}$$

Then

$$\text{Mean of X} = \int_{-1}^{1} 0.25x\,dx + \int_{1}^{2} 0.50x\,dx = 0.75.$$

3-9-a.

Let M, F, and E denote observations of a male student, a female student, and an economics major, respectively. Then

$$\begin{aligned} P\{E\} &= P\{E\cap M\} + P\{E\cap F\} \\ &= P\{E|M\}\cdot P\{M\} + P\{E|F\}\cdot P\{F\} \\ &= 0.20(0.50) + 0.05(0.50) \\ &= 0.1250. \end{aligned}$$

3-9-b.

$$P\{M\cap E\} = P\{E|M\}\cdot P\{M\} = 0.10.$$

3-9-c.

$$P\{M|E\} = P\{M\cap E\}/P\{E\} = 0.10/0.1250 = 0.80.$$

3-10-a.

All equally likely outcomes of the experiment and the values of X and Y are presented in table 3-9.

TABLE 3-9

Equally Likely Outcomes of the Experiment and Values of X and Y

Outcome	x	y
TTT	0	0
TTH	1	1
THT	1	2
HTT	1	1
THH	2	1
HTH	2	2
HHT	2	1
HHH	3	0

Thus the sample space corresponding to this experiment is

$$S = \{00, 11, 12, 21, 22, 30\}.$$

The marginal probability distributions of X and Y are presented in table 3-10.

TABLE 3-10

Marginal Probability Distributions of X and Y			
x	f(x)	y	f(y)
0	0.1250	0	0.2500
1	0.3750	1	0.5000
2	0.3750	2	0.2500
3	0.1250		

3-10-b.

The joint probability distribution of X and Y is presented in table 3-11.

TABLE 3-11

		Values of X			
		0	1	2	3
Values of Y	0	0.1250	0	0	0.1250
	1	0	0.2500	0.2500	0
	2	0	0.1250	0.1250	0

3-10-c.

$$
\begin{aligned}
E(X) &= \Sigma x f(x) \\
&= 1(0.3750) + 2(0.3750) + 3(0.1250) \\
&= 1.50,
\end{aligned}
$$

$$
\begin{aligned}
\text{Var}(X) &= E[X - E(X)]^2 \\
&= \Sigma(x - 1.50)^2 f(x) \\
&= (0 - 1.50)^2(0.1250) + \cdots + (3 - 1.50)^2(0.1250) \\
&= 0.75,
\end{aligned}
$$

$$E(Y) = 1,$$

$$\text{Var}(Y) = 0.50,$$

and

$$
\begin{aligned}
\text{Cov}(X,Y) &= E[X - E(X)][Y - E(Y)] \\
&= \sum_{y}\sum_{x}(x - 1.50)(y - 1)f(x,y) \\
&= (0 - 1.50)(0 - 1)(0.1250) + \cdots \\
&= 0.
\end{aligned}
$$

3-11-a.

Let X denote the duration of unemployment (in weeks) of applicants for unskilled jobs. For the last entry of X, mid-point of 10.50 is assumed. Then

$$E(X) = 0(0.25) + \cdots + 10.50(0.06) = 2.69.$$

3-11-b.

$$\text{Var}(X) = (0 - 2.69)^2(0.25) + \cdots = 8.1189.$$

$$SD = 2.8494.$$

$$a_3 = [(0 - 2.69)^3(0.25) + \cdots]/(2.8494)^3 = 1.3138.$$

3-12.

Consider $E(X) = \mu$, and $E(X - \mu)^2 = \sigma^2$. Now

$$\begin{aligned} E(Z) &= E[X - (X - \mu)/\sigma] \\ &= E(X) - E(X - \mu)/\sigma \\ &= \mu - [E(X) - \mu]/\sigma \\ &= \mu, \end{aligned}$$

and

$$\begin{aligned} Var(Z) &= E[Z - E(Z)]^2 \\ &= E[X - (X - \mu)/\sigma - \mu]^2 \\ &= E[(1 - 1/\sigma)(X - \mu)]^2 \\ &= (1 - 1/\sigma)^2 E(X - \mu)^2 \\ &= (1 - 1/\sigma)^2 \sigma^2 \\ &= (\sigma - 1)^2. \end{aligned}$$

3-13.

Consider

$$E(X - \mu)^2 < E(X - b)^2,$$

$$E(X - \mu)^2 < E(X - \mu + \mu - b)^2,$$

$$E(X - \mu)^2 < E[(X - \mu)^2 + 2(X - \mu)(\mu - b) + (\mu - b)^2],$$

$$E(X - \mu)^2 < E(X - \mu)^2 + (\mu - b)^2,$$

or

$$0 < (\mu - b)^2 \qquad \text{Q.E.D.}^1$$

[1]Q.E.D. stands for "quod erat demonstrandum," meaning "which was to be demonstrated."

3-14-a.

$$\begin{aligned} \mathrm{Var}(X + a) &= E[X + a - E(X + a)]^2 \\ &= E[X + a - E(X) - a]^2 \\ &= \mathrm{Var}(X). \end{aligned}$$

3-14-b.

Substituting Y for X and b for a in part (a), we get

$$\mathrm{Var}(Y + b) = \mathrm{Var}(Y).$$

3-14-c.

$$\begin{aligned} \mathrm{Cov}(X+a,Y+b) &= E[X + a - E(X + a)][Y + b - E(Y + b)] \\ &= \mathrm{Cov}(X,Y). \end{aligned}$$

3-15-a.

$$\begin{aligned} E(X_i^2) &= E(X_i - \mu + \mu)^2 \\ &= E[(X_i - \mu)^2 + 2\mu(X_i - \mu) + \mu^2] \\ &= E(X_i - \mu)^2 + 2\mu E(X_i - \mu) + \mu^2 \\ &= \sigma^2 + \mu^2. \end{aligned}$$

3-15-b.

$$\begin{aligned} E(X_i\bar{X}) &= E(X_i \Sigma X_i/n) \\ &= E(X_iX_1 + \cdots + X_i^2 + \cdots + X_iX_n)/n \\ &= [E(X_i)E(X_1) + \cdots + E(X_i^2) + \cdots + E(X_i)E(X_n)]/n \\ &= (\mu\cdot\mu + \cdots + \mu^2 + \sigma^2 + \cdots + \mu\cdot\mu)/n \\ &= \mu^2 + \sigma^2/n. \end{aligned}$$

3-15-c.

$$E(\bar{X}^2) = E(\bar{X}\Sigma X_i/n)$$

$$= [E(X_1\bar{X}) + \cdots + E(X_n\bar{X})]/n$$

$$= (\mu^2 + \sigma^2/n + \cdots + \mu^2 + \sigma^2/n)/n$$

$$= \mu^2 + \sigma^2/n.$$

3-15-d.

$$E[X_i(X_i - \bar{X})] = E(X_i^2 - X_i\bar{X})$$

$$= E(X_i^2) - E(X_i\bar{X})$$

$$= \mu^2 + \sigma^2 - (\mu^2 + \sigma^2/n)$$

$$= \sigma^2(1 - 1/n).$$

3-15-e.

$$E[\bar{X}(X_i - \bar{X})] = E(X_i\bar{X} - \bar{X}^2)$$

$$= E(X_i\bar{X}) - E(\bar{X}^2)$$

$$= \mu^2 + \sigma^2/n - (\mu^2 + \sigma^2/n)$$

$$= 0.$$

3-15-f.

$$E[X_i(X_j - \bar{X})] = E(X_iX_j - X_i\bar{X})$$

$$= E(X_iX_j) - E(X_i\bar{X})$$

$$= \mu^2 - (\mu^2 + \sigma^2/n)$$

$$= -\sigma^2/n.$$

3-15-g.

$$\begin{aligned}\mathrm{Cov}(X_i,\bar{X}) &= E[X_i - E(X_i)][\bar{X} - E(\bar{X})] \\ &= E(X_i - \mu)(\bar{X} - \mu) \\ &= E(X_i\bar{X} - \mu X_i - \mu\bar{X} + \mu^2) \\ &= E(X_i\bar{X}) - \mu E(X_i) - \mu E(\bar{X}) + \mu^2 \\ &= \mu^2 + \sigma^2/n - \mu\cdot\mu - \mu\cdot\mu + \mu^2 \\ &= \sigma^2/n.\end{aligned}$$

3-15-h.

Consider

$$\begin{aligned}E(X_i - \bar{X}) &= E(X_i - \Sigma X_i/n) \\ &= E(X_i) - E(\Sigma X_i/n) \\ &= \mu - \Sigma E(X_i)/n \\ &= \mu - \Sigma\mu/n \\ &= 0.\end{aligned}$$

Now

$$\begin{aligned}\mathrm{Var}(X_i - \bar{X}) &= E[X_i - \bar{X} - E(X_i - \bar{X})]^2 \\ &= E(X_i - \bar{X})^2 \\ &= E(X_i^2 - 2X_i\bar{X} + \bar{X}^2) \\ &= E(X_i^2) - 2E(X_i\bar{X}) + E(\bar{X}^2) \\ &= \mu^2 + \sigma^2 - 2(\mu^2 + \sigma^2/n) + \mu^2 + \sigma^2/n \\ &= \sigma^2(1 - 1/n).\end{aligned}$$

3-15-i.

$$
\begin{aligned}
\mathrm{Cov}(X_i-\bar{X},\bar{X}) &= E[X_i - \bar{X} - E(X_i - \bar{X})][\bar{X} - E(\bar{X})] \\
&= E(X_i - \bar{X})(\bar{X} - \mu) \\
&= E(X_i\bar{X} - \mu X_i - \bar{X}^2 + \mu\bar{X}) \\
&= E(X_i\bar{X}) - \mu E(X_i) - E(\bar{X}^2) + \mu E(\bar{X}) \\
&= \mu^2 + \sigma^2/n - \mu\cdot\mu - (\mu^2 + \sigma^2/n) + \mu\cdot\mu \\
&= 0.
\end{aligned}
$$

3-15-j.

$$
\begin{aligned}
\mathrm{Cov}(X_i-\bar{X},X_j-\bar{X}) &= E(X_i - \bar{X})(X_j - \bar{X}) \\
&= E(X_iX_j - X_i\bar{X} - X_j\bar{X} + \bar{X}^2) \\
&= E(X_iX_j) - E(X_i\bar{X}) - E(X_j\bar{X}) + E(\bar{X}^2) \\
&= E(X_iX_j) - E(X_i\bar{X}) \\
&= \mu^2 - (\mu^2 + \sigma^2/n) \\
&= -\sigma^2/n.
\end{aligned}
$$

3-16-a.

The marginal probability distributions of X and Y are presented in table 3-12.

3-16-b.

The conditional probability distributions of $X|Y$ are presented in table 3-13.

TABLE 3-12

Marginal Probability Distributions of X and Y			
x	f(x)	y	f(y)
-2	0.10		
-1	0.20	10	0.80
0	0.35		
1	0.30	20	0.20
2	0.05		

TABLE 3-13

Conditional Probability Distributions of X|Y			
x|20	f(x|20)	x|10	f(x|10)
-2	0.0500	-2	0.1125
-1	0.2500	-1	0.1875
0	0.4000	0	0.3375
1	0.2500	1	0.3125
2	0.0500	2	0.0500

where conditional probability of $-2|20$ is calculated as

$$f(-2|20) = f(-2,20)/f(20) = 0.01/0.20 = 0.05.$$

Other conditional probabilities are calculated similarly.

3-16-c.

Consider

$$E(XY) = -2(10)(0.09) + \cdots + 2(20)(0.01) = 0,$$

$$E(X) = -2(0.10) + \cdots + 2(0.05) = 0,$$

$$E(Y) = 10(0.80) + 20(0.20) = 12,$$

and

$$\text{Cov}(X,Y) = E(XY) - E(X)E(Y) = 0.$$

Since $\text{Cov}(X,Y) = 0$, it follows that X and Y are uncorrelated.

3-16-d.

Consider

$$P\{-2,10\} = 0.09,$$

and

$$P\{-2\}\cdot P\{10\} = 0.10(0.80) = 0.08.$$

Since the necessary and sufficient condition for independence is

$$f(x,y) = f(x)\cdot f(y),$$

and since

$$P\{-2,10\} = 0.09 \neq 0.08 = P\{-2\}\cdot P\{10\},$$

it follows that X and Y are not independent.

3-17.

Let X and Y = $(X^2 - 4)$ denote number of heads observed in a toss of four coins and the amount of gain, respectively. Their probability distributions are presented in table 3-14.

TABLE 3-14

Probability Distributions of X and Y			
x	f(x)	y	f(y)
0	0.0625	-4	0.0625
1	0.2500	-3	0.2500
2	0.3750	0	0.3750
3	0.2500	5	0.2500
4	0.0625	12	0.0625

The expected gain, then, is

$$E(Y) = -4(0.0625) + \cdots + 12(0.0625) = \$1.$$

3-18.

Let p denote the probability of either project being successful. Then

$$20{,}000p - 2{,}000(1 - p) = 25{,}000p - 5{,}000(1 - p),$$

or

$$p = 0.3750.$$

CHAPTER 4

4-1.

Let X denote number of people who use brand D soap out of 10 people in the elevator. The probability distribution of X may be calculated by the following formula

$$f(x) = \binom{n}{x}\pi^{x}(1 - \pi)^{n-x},$$

where n = 10, π = 0.20, (1 - π) = 0.80, and (x = 0, ..., 10), and is presented in table 4-1.

TABLE 4-1

Probability Distribution of X	
x	f(x)
0	0.1074
1	0.2684
2	0.3020
3	0.2013
4	0.0881
5	0.0264
6	0.0055
7	0.0008
8	0.0001
9	0.0000
10	0.0000

For instance

$$f(0) = \binom{10}{0}(0.20)^{0}(0.80)^{10-0} = 0.1074.$$

4-2.

Let π and $\rho = (1 - \pi)$ denote population proportions of heads and tails in repeated tosses of the coin, respectively. Assuming the coin is fair, $\pi = \rho = 0.50$. The best linear unbiased estimator of π based on a sample of n observations is $\hat{\pi}$, or the sample proportion of heads, and has the following binomial distribution

$$\hat{\pi} \sim B(\pi = 0.50,\ \pi\rho/n = 0.25/n).$$

The probability that the proportion of heads will lie between 0.40 and 0.60 to be at least 95 percent is presented as

$$P\{0.40 < \hat{\pi} < 0.60\} \geq 0.95.$$

Using normal approximation to binomial, we get

$$P\{\frac{0.40 - 0.50}{\sqrt{0.25/n}} < z < \frac{0.60 - 0.50}{\sqrt{0.25/n}}\} \geq 0.95,$$

$$P\{0 < z < \frac{0.10}{\sqrt{0.25/n}}\} \geq 0.4750,$$

$$\frac{0.10}{\sqrt{0.25/n}} \geq 1.96,$$

or

$$n \geq 96.04,$$

thus the coin should be tossed at least 97 times.

4-3.

Let X denote the number of successes in n trails. Thus it has the following binomial distribution

$$X \sim B[n\pi = 8,\ n\pi(1 - \pi) = 2^2].$$

Solving for n and π, we obtain

$$n = 16, \qquad \text{and} \qquad \pi = 0.50.$$

4-4.

Since $(0 < X < 1)$ is a continuous uniform random variable, then

$$f(x) = \begin{cases} 1 & \text{if } 0 < x < 1, \\ 0 & \text{otherwise.} \end{cases}$$

Now

$$E(X) = \int_0^1 xf(x)dx$$

$$= \int_0^1 xdx$$

$$= 0.50.$$

$$E(X - 0.50)^2 = \int_0^1 (x - 0.50)^2 f(x)dx$$

$$= 1/3(x - 0.50)^3$$

$$= 1/3[(1 - 0.50)^3 - (0 - 0.50)^3]$$

$$= 1/12.$$

Thus

$$X \sim U(0.50,\ 1/12).$$

Now according to the Central Limit Theorem and based on n = 20,

$$\bar{X} \sim N(0.50,\ \frac{1/12}{20} = \frac{1}{240}).$$

The probability that the mean of 20 observations will lie between 0.40 and 0.60 is

$$P\{0.40 < \bar{x} < 0.60\} = P\{\frac{0.40 - 0.50}{\sqrt{1/240}} < z < \frac{0.60 - 0.50}{\sqrt{1/240}}\}$$

$$= P\{-1.5492 < z < 1.5492\}$$

$$= 0.8787.$$

4-5.

Let X and Y = X/3 denote the number and the proportion of white balls in a sample of three drawn without replacement from an urn containing five white and five red balls, X = 0, 1, 2, 3, respectively. The sample space corresponding to this experiment is

$$S = \{RRR, RRW, RWR, RWW, WRR, WWR, WWW\},$$

where R and W denote drawing red and white balls, respectively. The sampling distribution of Y is presented in table 4-2.

TABLE 4-2

Sampling Distribution of Y		
sample	y	f(y)
RRR	0	1/12
RRW, RWR, WRR	1/3	5/12
RWW, WRR, WWR	2/3	5/12
WWW	1	1/12

where f(0), or the probability that y = 0, is calculated as

$$f(RRR) = f(R)\cdot f(R|R)\cdot f(R|RR) = (5/10)(4/9)(3/8) = 1/12.$$

Other probabilities are calculated similarly.

Alternatively, the sampling distribution of Y, known as hypergeometric probability distribution, can be calculated using the following formula

$$f(y) = \binom{5}{x}\binom{5}{3-x}/\binom{10}{3} \qquad (x = 0, \ldots, 3).$$

For instance

$$f(0) = \binom{5}{0}\binom{5}{3}/\binom{10}{3} = 1(10)/120 = 1/12.$$

4-6.

Let X denote rate of profit of companies within the industry. Then

$$X \sim N(16,\ 4^2).$$

The probability of making a profit of at least 22% is

$$P\{x > 22\} = P\{z > \frac{22 - 16}{4}\} = P\{z > 1.50\} = 0.0668.$$

4-7-a.

$$P\{6 < x < 10\} = P\{-0.50 < z < 0.50\} = 0.3830.$$

4-7-b.

$$P\{10 < x < 12\} = P\{0.50 < z < 1\} = 0.1500.$$

4-7-c.

$$P\{x < 0\} = P\{z < -2\} = 0.0228.$$

4-7-d.

$$P\{x > 20\} = P\{z > 3\} = 0.0013.$$

4-7-e.

$$P\{x_1 < x < x_2\} = 0.5000,$$

$$P\{\frac{x_1 - 8}{4} < z < \frac{x_2 - 8}{4}\} = 0.5000.$$

However, from the Z table

$$P\{-0.6745 < z < 0.6745\} = 0.5000.$$

Thus $\frac{x_1 - 8}{4} = -0.6745, \quad \frac{x_2 - 8}{4} = 0.6745,$

and $x_1 = 5.3020, \quad x_2 = 10.6980,$

or $P\{5.3020 < x < 10.6980\} = 0.5000.$

4-8-a.

Given

$$X \sim N(\mu_X = 590,\ \sigma_X^2 = 80^2),$$

and

$$Y \sim N(\mu_Y = 620,\ \sigma_Y^2 = 60^2),$$

then

$$X - Y \sim N(\mu_X - \mu_Y = -30,\ \sigma_X^2 + \sigma_Y^2 = 100^2).$$

The probability that the in-state student has a higher score than the out-state can be calculated as

$$\begin{aligned} P\{x > y\} &= P\{x - y > 0\} \\ &= P\{z > \frac{0 - (-30)}{100}\} \\ &= P\{z > 0.30\} \\ &= 0.3821. \end{aligned}$$

4-8-b.

Given

$$X_1 \sim N(590,\ 80^2),$$

and

$$X_2 \sim N(590,\ 80^2),$$

then

$$X_1 - X_2 \sim N(590 - 590 = 0,\ 80^2 + 80^2 = 12{,}800).$$

The probability that scores of two in-state freshmen will differ by more than 50 points is

$$\begin{aligned} P\{|x_1 - x_2| > 50\} &= P\{x_1 - x_2 > 50\} + P\{x_1 - x_2 < -50\} \\ &= P\{z > \frac{50 - 0}{\sqrt{12{,}800}}\} + P\{z < \frac{-50 - 0}{\sqrt{12{,}800}}\} \\ &= P\{z > 0.4419\} + P\{z < -0.4419\} \\ &= 0.6586. \end{aligned}$$

4-8-c.

Since the best guess is 590, the probability that it is correct to within ±20 points can be calculated as

$$P\{590 - 20 < x < 590 + 20\} = P\{570 < x < 610\}$$
$$= P\{\frac{570 - 590}{80} < z < \frac{610 - 590}{80}\}$$
$$= P\{-0.25 < z < 0.25\}$$
$$= 0.1974.$$

This is the highest probability for any $(c - 20) < x < (c + 20)$, where c is any guess. The expected gain of the game, thus, is

$$\$10(0.1974) + \$0(0.8026) = \$1.97,$$

which is the maximum amount one would be willing to pay as a fee to play this game.

4-8-d.

Given the distributions of X and Y in part (a), according to the Central Limit Theorem and based on a sample of size n = 25,

$$\bar{X} \sim N(\mu_{\bar{X}} = \mu_X = 590,\ \sigma^2_{\bar{X}} = \sigma^2_X/n = 80^2/25 = 16^2),$$

and $$\bar{Y} \sim N(\mu_{\bar{Y}} = \mu_Y = 620,\ \sigma^2_{\bar{Y}} = \sigma^2_Y/n = 60^2/25 = 12^2).$$

The distribution of $(\bar{X} - \bar{Y})$, then, is

$$\bar{X} - \bar{Y} \sim N(590 - 620 = -30,\ 16^2 + 12^2 = 20^2).$$

The probability that the sample mean score of the in-state freshmen exceeds that of the out-state freshmen, then, is

$$P\{\bar{x} - \bar{y} > 0\} = P\{z > \frac{0 - (-30)}{20}\}$$
$$= P\{z > 1.50\}$$
$$= 0.0668.$$

4-9.

The frequency distribution of X = log(Y) is presented in table 4-3.

TABLE 4-3

Frequency Distribution of X = log(Y)

Interval: y		Midpoint: y	x = log(y)	f(x)
Under	5,000	2,500	3.3979	0.0820
5,000	6,999	6,000	3.7782	0.0610
7,000	9,999	8,500	3.9294	0.0970
10,000	11,999	11,000	4.0414	0.0680
12,000	14,999	13,500	4.1303	0.0990
15,000	24,999	20,000	4.3010	0.3140
25,000	49,999	37,500	4.5740	0.2430
50,000	over	100,000	5.0000	0.0360

The mean, variance, and standard deviation of the distribution are

$$\mu_X = \Sigma x_i f(x_i)$$

$$= 3.3979(0.0820) + \cdots + 5.0000(0.0360)$$

$$= 4.2160,$$

$$\sigma_X^2 = \Sigma(x_i - 4.2160)^2 f(x_i)$$

$$= (3.3979 - 4.2160)^2(0.0820) + \cdots$$

$$= 0.1329,$$

and

$$\sigma_X = 0.3645.$$

Next, transform X_i to $Z_i = (X_i - 4.2160)/0.3645$. The normal probabilities for Z are presented in table 4-4.

TABLE 4-4

Normal Probabilities for Z				
Interval: x		Interval: z		f(z)
$-\infty$	3.6989	$-\infty$	-1.4187	0.0780
3.6990	3.8450	-1.4186	-1.0178	0.0760
3.8451	4.0000	-1.0177	-0.5926	0.1220
4.0000	4.0791	-0.5925	-0.3756	0.0770
4.0792	4.1761	-0.3755	-0.1095	0.1030
4.1761	4.3979	-0.1094	0.4990	0.2350
4.3979	4.6990	0.4991	1.3251	0.2160
4.6990	∞	1.3252	∞	0.0930

Since $f(x_i)$ differs from $f(z_i)$ substantially, the distribution of X is not normal, even by approximation.

4-10-a.

Let X be the weights of people using the elevator. Then

$$X \sim N(\mu = 162.50,\ \sigma^2 = 22^2 = 484).$$

Now, sum of weights of a random group of 10 people, ΣX_i, is a linear combination of X's, and therefore, has a normal distribution. The mean and the variance of the distribution is calculated in part (**b**). Thus

$$\Sigma X_i \sim N(10\mu = 1{,}625,\ 10\sigma^2 = 4{,}840).$$

The probability that the sum of weights of a random group of 10 people will exceed the capacity load limit of the elevator is

$$\begin{aligned} P\{\Sigma x_i > 1{,}800\} &= P\{z > \frac{1{,}800 - 1{,}625}{\sqrt{4{,}840}}\} \\ &= P\{z > 2.5154\} \\ &= 0.0059. \end{aligned}$$

4-10-b.

$$E(\Sigma X_i) = \Sigma E(X_i) = 10\mu = 1{,}625.$$

$$Var(\Sigma X_i) = \Sigma[Var(X_i)] = 10\sigma^2 = 4{,}840,$$

and, therefore, the standard deviation is 69.5701.

CHAPTER 5

5-1.

Under the null hypothesis and based on a sample of size 9,

$$\bar{X} \sim N(\mu = 10,\ \sigma^2/n = 81/9 = 3^2).$$

The critical value (CV), i.e., the value that separates acceptance from rejection region, for $\alpha = 5\%$ is calculated as

$$\begin{aligned} CV &= z_{0.05}(\sigma/\sqrt{n}) + \mu \\ &= 1.6449(3) + 10 \\ &= 14.9347. \end{aligned}$$

In order to find the power of the test, assign different values to μ and calculate

$$\text{Power} = 1 - P\{z > \frac{CV - \mu}{\sigma/\sqrt{n}}\}.$$

The power of the test for different values of μ is presented in table 5-1.

TABLE 5-1

Power of the Test			
μ	Power	μ	Power
10.00	0.05	18.00	0.85
10.50	0.07	19.50	0.94
12.00	0.16	21.00	0.98
13.50	0.32	22.50	0.99
15.00	0.51	24.00	1.00
16.50	0.70	25.50	1.00

The diagram of the power function is given in figure 5-1.

FIGURE 5-1

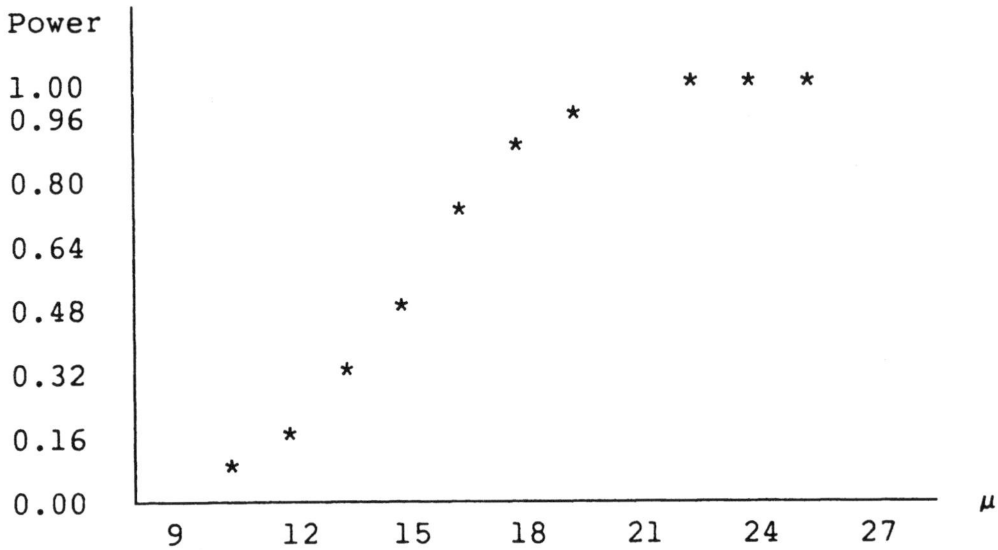

5-2-a.

Using subscripts c and s for city and suburb, let p_c and p_s denote food prices in the two areas, respectively. Their distributions are assumed to be

$$p_c \sim N(\mu_c, \sigma_c^2),$$

and

$$p_s \sim N(\mu_s, \sigma_s^2).$$

In absence of any information to the contrary, we assume that the two variances are the same, i.e., that $\sigma_c^2 = \sigma_s^2$.

Step 1: The null and the alternative hypotheses are

$$H_o: \mu_c - \mu_s = 0,$$

$$H_a: \mu_c - \mu_s \neq 0.$$

Steps 2 & 3: The test statistic and its distribution are

$$t = (\bar{p}_c - \bar{p}_s)/s\sqrt{1/n_c + 1/n_s} \sim t_{n_c+n_s-2},$$

where

$$s^2 = \frac{(n_c - 1)s_c^2 + (n_s - 1)s_s^2}{n_c + n_s - 2}.$$

Step 4: Do not reject the null hypothesis if

$$|t| < t_{\alpha/2,n_c+n_s-2} = t_{0.0250,30} = 2.0420,$$

otherwise reject it.

Step 5: The sample values are

$$\bar{p}_c = 12.60/14 = 0.9000.$$

$$\bar{p}_s = 14.96/18 = 0.8311.$$

$$(n_c - 1)s_c^2 = 14(1.68) - 0.90(12.60) = 12.1800.$$

$$(n_s - 1)s_s^2 = 18(1.96) - 0.8311(14.96) = 22.8466.$$

$$s^2 = \frac{12.1800 + 22.8466}{14 + 18 - 2} = 1.1676.$$

Thus the value of the test statistic is

$$t = \frac{0.9000 - 0.8311}{\sqrt{1.1676(1/14 + 1/18)}} = 0.1789.$$

Step 6: Since the value of the test statistic falls in the acceptance region, do not reject the null hypothesis. There is evidence to indicate that the mean prices in the two areas are the same.

5-2-b.

Step 1: The null and the alternative hypotheses are

$$H_o: \sigma_s^2/\sigma_c^2 = 1,$$

$$H_a: \sigma_s^2/\sigma_c^2 > 1.$$

Steps 2 & 3: The test statistic and its distribution are

$$F = s_s^2/s_c^2 \sim F_{n_s-1,n_c-1}.$$

Step 4: Do not reject the null hypothesis if

$$F < F_{\alpha,n_s-1,n_c-1} = F_{0.05,13,17} = 2.3567,$$

otherwise reject it.

Step 5: The value of the test statistic is

$$F = (22.8466/17)/(12.1800/13) = 1.4344.$$

Step 6: Since the value of the test statistic falls in the acceptance region, do not reject the null hypothesis. There is evidence to indicate that the dispersions of prices in the two areas are the same.

5-3-a.

The normal approximation to binomial distribution of the proportion of very satisfied customers of "pizza A" based on a sample of size n = 30 and $\pi = 0.75$ is

$$\hat{\pi} \sim N[\mu_{\hat{\pi}} = \pi = 0.75,\ \sigma_{\hat{\pi}}^2 = \pi\rho/n = 0.75(0.25)/30 = 0.0791^2].$$

Step 1: The null and the alternative hypotheses are

$$H_o: \pi \geq 0.75,$$

$$H_a: \pi < 0.75.$$

Steps 2 & 3: The test statistic and its distribution are

$$Z = (\hat{\pi} - \pi)/\sigma_{\hat{\pi}} \sim N(0,\ 1).$$

Step 4: Do not reject the null hypothesis if

$$z > -z_{\alpha} = -z_{0.05} = -1.6449.$$

otherwise reject it.

Step 5: The value of the test statistic is

$$z = (20/30 - 0.75)/0.0791 = -1.0541.$$

Step 6: Since the value of the test statistic falls in the acceptance region, do not reject the null hypothesis. There is no evidence that the population proportion of very satisfied customers of "pizza A" is *less* than 75%.

5-3-b.

Step 1: The null and the alternative hypotheses are

$$H_o: \pi \geq 0.75,$$

$$H_a: \pi < 0.75.$$

Step 2: The test statistic is X, the number of very satisfied customers of "pizza B," based on the sample of size 5.

Step 3: The distribution of X under the null hypothesis and based on a sample of size 5 is calculated using the following formula

$$f(x) = \binom{5}{x} 0.75^x 0.25^{n-x} \qquad (x = 0, \ldots, 5),$$

and is presented in table 5-2.

TABLE 5-2

Probability Distribution of X		
Region	x	f(x)
Rejection	0	0.0010
	1	0.0146
Acceptance	2	0.0879
	3	0.2637
	4	0.3955
	5	0.2373

Step 4: Do not reject the null hypothesis if

$$x > CV,$$

where CV is calculated as

$$P\{x \le CV\} \le 0.05,$$

or

$$CV = 1,$$

otherwise reject it.

Step 5: The value of the test statistic is 2.

Step 6: Since the value of the test statistic falls in the acceptance region, do not reject the null hypothesis. There is no evidence that the population proportion of very satisfied customers of "pizza B" is *less* than 75%.

5-4.

Using subscripts m and t for married men and teenagers (14-19 years), let X_m and X_t denote the employment rates of the two categories of labor, respectively. The distributions of the two employment rates are assumed to be

$$X_m \sim N(\mu_m, \sigma_m^2),$$

and

$$X_t \sim N(\mu_t, \sigma_t^2).$$

Since employment rate is a measure of demand for labor, a test that the cyclical fluctuations in the demand for teenage workers are greater than those in the demand for married males is the same as comparison of the two variances.

Consider the unemployment rates of the two categories of labor, $(1 - X_i)$, $(i = m, t)$. Their distributions are

$$1 - X_m \sim N(1 - \mu_m, \sigma_m^2),$$

and

$$1 - X_t \sim N(1 - \mu_t, \sigma_t^2).$$

Since the variances of the employment and the unemployment rates of each category of labor are the same, the above test could be conducted by comparison of the variances of the unemployment rates of the two categories of labor.

Step 1: The null and the alternative hypotheses are

$$H_o: \sigma_t^2/\sigma_m^2 = 1,$$

$$H_a: \sigma_t^2/\sigma_m^2 > 1.$$

Steps 2 & 3: The test statistic and its distribution are

$$F = s_t^2/s_m^2 \sim F_{n_t-1,n_m-1}.$$

Step 4: Do not reject the null hypothesis if

$$F < F_{\alpha,n_t-1,n_m-1} = F_{0.05,12,12} = 2.69,$$

otherwise reject it.

Step 5: The value of the test statistic is

$$F = 6.5124/1.5269 = 4.2651.$$

Step 6: Since the value of the test statistic falls in the rejection region, reject the null hypothesis. There is evidence to indicate that the cyclical fluctuations in the demand for teenage workers are greater than those in the demand for married males.

5-5.

Since the null hypothesis that the standard deviation is equal to 2,000 against the alternative hypothesis that it is more than 2,000 is not rejected and since the value of the test statistic is very close to the border line, it follows that the value must be smaller than but close to the value of χ^2 from the table, or

$$(n - 1)s^2/\sigma^2 < \chi^2_{0.05,2},$$

$$2s^2/4,000,000 < 5.9910,$$

$$s^2 < 11,982,000.$$

Therefore s must be smaller than but close to 3,461.5026.

Since the null hypothesis that the mean is equal to 40,000 against the alternative hypothesis that it is less than 40,000 is not rejected and since the value of the test statistic is very close to the border line, it follows that the value must be larger than but close to the value of t from the table, or

$$\sqrt{n}(\bar{x} - \mu)/s > -t_{0.05,2},$$

$$\sqrt{3}(\bar{x} - 40,000)/3,461.5026 > -2.9200.$$

Therefore $\bar{x}$ must be larger than but close to 34,164.3816.

5-6.

Let subscripts A and B denote farmer A and B, respectively. Using normal approximation to binomial, the distribution of the best linear unbiased estimator of proportion of defective peaches of farmer A is

$$\hat{\pi}_A \sim N[\pi_A = 0.05,\ \sigma^2_A = \pi_A\rho_A/n = 0.05(0.95)/100 = 0.0218^2],$$

and that of farmer B is

$$\hat{\pi}_B \sim N[\pi_B = 0.10,\ \sigma_B^2 = \pi_B\rho_B/n = 0.10(0.90)/100 = 0.03^2].$$

Consider the null and alternative hypotheses

H_o: Sample comes from farmer A $(\pi = 0.05)$,

H_a: Sample comes from farmer B $(\pi = 0.10)$.

Now assign different values to α, or probability of error type I, defined as

$$\alpha = P\{\text{Rejecting } H_o | H_o \text{ is true}\}$$
$$= P\{\text{Sample comes from farmer B} | \text{It comes from farmer A}\},$$

find the value of z_α from the Z table, calculate the critical value (CV), defined as

$$CV = \pi_A + z_\alpha \cdot \sigma_A = 0.05 + 0.0218 z_\alpha,$$

compute β, or the probability of error type II, defined as

$$\beta = P\{\text{Not rejecting } H_o | H_a \text{ is true}\}$$
$$= P\{\text{Sample comes from farmer A} | \text{It comes from farmer B}\}$$
$$= P\{\hat{\pi} < CV | 0.10\}$$
$$= P\{\hat{\pi} < 0.05 + 0.0218 z_\alpha | 0.10\}$$
$$= P\{z < (0.05 + 0.0218 z_\alpha - \pi_B)/\sigma_B\}$$
$$= P\{z < (-0.05 + 0.0218 z_\alpha)/0.03\},$$

and calculate E(L), or the expected loss, defined as

$$E(L) = 800\alpha + 1{,}000\beta.$$

The calculated values of CV, β, and E(L) for different assigned values of α and corresponding values of z_α are presented in table 5-3.

TABLE 5-3

Critical Value, Error Type II, and Expected Loss for Different Values of Error Type I

a	z_a	CV	β	E(L)
0.05	1.6449	0.0858	0.318568	358.57
0.10	1.2816	0.0779	0.230975	310.98
0.13	1.1264	0.0745	0.198118	302.12
0.14	1.0803	0.0735	0.188934	300.93
0.15	1.0364	0.0726	0.180433	300.43
0.16	0.9945	0.0717	0.172531	300.53
0.20	0.8416	0.0683	0.145657	305.66
0.25	0.6745	0.0647	0.119665	319.67

Therefore when $a = 0.15$, the expected loss is minimized at \$300.43, $\beta = 0.180433$, and CV = 0.0726.

5-7-a.

The two diagrams of the probability distributions of X under the null and the alternative hypotheses are presented in figure 5-2.

FIGURE 5-2

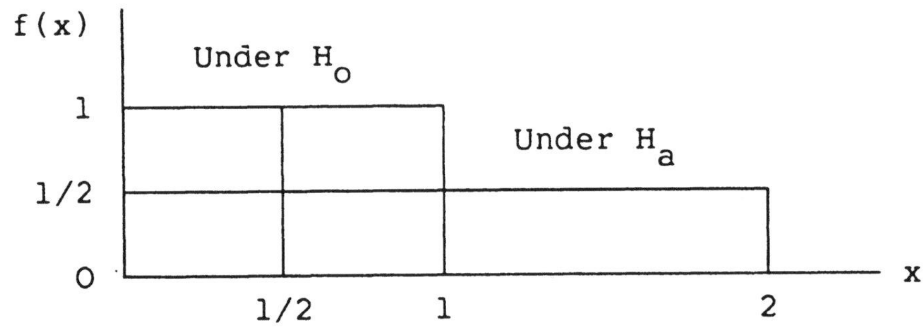

$$a = P\{x \geq 1/2 | H_o \text{ is true}\} = P\{x \geq 1/2 | f(x) = 1\} = 0.50.$$

$$\beta = P\{x < 1/2 | H_a \text{ is true}\} = P\{x < 1/2 | f(x) = 1/2\} = 0.25.$$

5-7-b.

$$\alpha = P\{1 \le x \le 2 | f(x) = 1\} = 0.$$

$$\beta = P\{x < 1 | f(x) = 1/2\} = 0.50.$$

5-8.

Let π denote the probability of getting a head in a toss of the suspected coin. The null and alternative hypotheses are

H_o: $\pi = 0.50$ (the coin is unbiased),

H_a: $\pi = 0.75$ (the coin is rigged).

Further let X denote the number of heads observed in 3 tosses of the coin. The probability distributions of X under the two hypotheses are presented in table 5-4.

TABLE 5-4

Conditional Probability Distributions of X Given			
Null Hypothesis		Alternative Hypothesis	
x|0.50	P{x|0.50}	x|0.75	P{x|0.75}
0	0.125000	0	0.015625
1	0.375000	1	0.140625
2	0.375000	2	0.421875
3	0.125000	3	0.421875

where $$P\{x|0.50\} = \binom{3}{x}(0.50)^x(0.50)^{3-x},$$

and $$P\{x|0.75\} = \binom{3}{x}(0.75)^x(0.25)^{3-x}.$$

Therefore

$$\alpha = P\{3|0.50\} = 0.1250.$$

$$\beta = 1 - P\{3|0.75\} = 0.578125.$$

5-9.

Step 1: The null and the alternative hypotheses are

$$H_o: \pi_c - \pi_n = 0,$$

$$H_a: \pi_c - \pi_n > 0,$$

where c and n denote college and non-college, respectively.

Steps 2 & 3: The test statistic and its distribution are

$$Z = (\hat{\pi}_c - \hat{\pi}_n)/\sqrt{\hat{\pi}\hat{\rho}(1/n_c + 1/n_n)} \sim N(0, 1),$$

where $\hat{\pi}_c$ and $\hat{\pi}_n$ are the sample proportions of the beer-drinking college and non-college males, respectively, and $\hat{\pi}$ is the "pooled" sample proportion of beer-drinking males.

Step 4: Do not reject the null hypothesis if

$$z < z_a = z_{0.05} = 1.6449,$$

otherwise reject it.

Step 5: The sample values are

$$\hat{\pi}_c = 60/100 = 0.6000,$$

$$\hat{\pi}_n = 120/260 = 0.4615,$$

$$\hat{\pi} = (60 + 120)/(100 + 260) = 0.50.$$

Thus the value of the test statistic is

$$z = \frac{0.6000 - 0.4615}{\sqrt{0.50(0.50)(1/100 + 1/260)}} = 2.3534.$$

Step 6: Since the value of the test statistic falls in the rejection region, reject the null hypothesis. There is evidence to indicate that the proportion of male college students who drink beer is greater than that of non-college males in the same age group.

CHAPTER 6

6-1.

Consider

$$E(\bar{X}_i) = \mu \qquad (i = 1, 2),$$

$$Var(\bar{X}_i) = \sigma^2/n_i,$$

and

$$Cov(\bar{X}_1,\bar{X}_2) = 0.$$

Let us examine properties of the estimators.

(i) *Unbiasedness*

$$E(\hat{\mu}) = E[(\bar{X}_1 + \bar{X}_2)/2]$$

$$= [E(\bar{X}_1) + E(\bar{X}_2)]/2$$

$$= \mu.$$

$$E(\tilde{\mu}) = E[(n_1\bar{X}_1 + n_2\bar{X}_2)/(n_1 + n_2)]$$

$$= [n_1E(\bar{X}_1) + n_2E(\bar{X}_2)]/(n_1 + n_2)$$

$$= \mu.$$

Thus both estimators are unbiased.

(ii) *Efficiency*

$$Var(\hat{\mu}) = Var[(\bar{X}_1 + \bar{X}_2)/2]$$

$$= [Var(\bar{X}_1) + Var(\bar{X}_2) + 2Cov(\bar{X}_1,\bar{X}_2)]/4$$

$$= [\sigma^2/n_1 + \sigma^2/n_2 + 2(0)]/4$$

$$= (n_1 + n_2)\sigma^2/4n_1n_2.$$

$$\begin{aligned}\mathrm{Var}(\tilde{\mu}) &= \mathrm{Var}[(n_1\bar{X}_1 + n_2\bar{X}_2)/(n_1 + n_2)] \\ &= [n_1^2\mathrm{Var}(\bar{X}_1) + n_2^2\mathrm{Var}(\bar{X}_2)]/(n_1 + n_2)^2 \\ &= (n_1^2\sigma^2/n_1 + n_2^2\sigma^2/n_2)/(n_1 + n_2)^2 \\ &= \sigma^2/(n_1 + n_2).\end{aligned}$$

Since the Cramer-Rao lower bound for the variance of an unbiased estimator of μ is $\sigma^2/(n_1 + n_2)$, and since

$$\mathrm{Var}(\hat{\mu}) > \mathrm{Var}(\tilde{\mu}),$$

because
$$(n_1 + n_2)\sigma^2/4n_1n_2 > \sigma^2/(n_1 + n_2),$$

or
$$(n_1 - n_2)^2 > 0,$$

it follows that $\hat{\mu}$ is not efficient, but $\tilde{\mu}$ is.

(iii) *BLUE*. Since $\hat{\mu}$ is not efficient and since $\tilde{\mu}$ is efficient and it also is a linear combination of the sample observations, it follows that $\hat{\mu}$ is not BLUE but $\tilde{\mu}$ is.

(iv) *Asymptotic unbiasedness*. Since both estimators are unbiased, it follows that they are asymptotically unbiased.

(v) *Consistency*. Since $\hat{\mu}$ is unbiased

$$\mathrm{MSE}(\hat{\mu}) = \mathrm{Var}(\hat{\mu}) = \sigma^2/4n_1 + \sigma^2/4n_2.$$

$$\lim_{n_1, n_2 \to \infty} [\mathrm{MSE}(\hat{\mu})] = 0.$$

$$\mathrm{MSE}(\tilde{\mu}) = \sigma^2/(n_1 + n_2).$$

$$\lim_{n_1, n_2 \to \infty} [\mathrm{MSE}(\tilde{\mu})] = 0.$$

Thus both estimators are consistent.

(vi) *Asymptotic efficiency*

$$(n_1 + n_2)\text{Var}(\hat{\mu}) = (n_1 + n_2)^2\sigma^2/4n_1n_2$$

$$= (n_1/4n_2 + 1/2 + n_2/4n_1)\sigma^2.$$

Now if $\lim_{n_1,n_2\to\infty} (n_1/n_2) = 1$, then

$$\text{Asympt. Var}(\hat{\mu}) = [1/(n_1 + n_2)] \lim_{n_1,n_2\to\infty} [(n_1 + n_2)\text{Var}(\hat{\mu})]$$

$$= [1/(n_1 + n_2)](1/4 + 1/2 + 1/4)\sigma^2$$

$$= \sigma^2/(n_1 + n_2)$$

$$= \text{Asympt. Var}(\tilde{\mu}),$$

and both estimators are asymptotically efficient since $\tilde{\mu}$ is efficient. Otherwise $\hat{\mu}$ is not asymptotically efficient. The above results are summarized in table 6-1.

TABLE 6-1

Properties	Estimator	
	$\hat{\mu}$	$\tilde{\mu}$
Finite sample		
Unbiasedness	No	Yes
Efficiency	No	Yes
BLUE	No	Yes
Asymptotic properties		
Unbiasedness	Yes	Yes
Consistency	Yes	Yes
Efficiency	Yes*	Yes

* Provided $\lim_{n_1,n_2\to\infty} (n_1/n_2) = 1$.

6-2.

It is suspected that an unbiased estimator of $Var(\hat{\pi})$ is proportional to $\hat{\pi}(1 - \hat{\pi})$. Taking the mathematical expectation, we get

$$\begin{aligned}
E[\hat{\pi}(1 - \hat{\pi})] &= E(\hat{\pi} - \hat{\pi}^2) \\
&= E(\hat{\pi}) - E(\hat{\pi}^2) \\
&= \pi - E(\hat{\pi} - \pi + \pi)^2 \\
&= \pi - E(\hat{\pi} - \pi)^2 - 2\pi E(\hat{\pi} - \pi) - \pi^2 \\
&= \pi - \pi(1 - \pi)/n - 2\pi(0) - \pi^2 \\
&= \pi(1 - \pi)(1 - 1/n) \\
&= (n - 1)Var(\hat{\pi}).
\end{aligned}$$

Adjusting for factor of proportionality, an unbiased estimator of $Var(\hat{\pi})$ is found to be

$$s_{\hat{\pi}}^2 = \hat{\pi}(1 - \hat{\pi})/(n - 1).$$

6-3-a.

Consider $X = \Sigma X_i$, $(i = 1, \ldots, n)$, where

$$X_i = \begin{cases} 1 & \text{if the i-th observation results in success,} \\ 0 & \text{if the i-th observation results in failure,} \end{cases}$$

and

$$f(x_i) = \pi^{x_i}(1 - \pi)^{1-x_i},$$

which means that X_i has a binomial distribution. This in turn implies that X also has a binomial distribution. The mean and the variance of X are presented in table (4-3), section (4-1) of the text.[1] Therefore

$$X \sim B[n\pi,\ n\pi(1 - \pi)].$$

Since $\hat{\pi}$ and $\tilde{\pi}$ are merely linear transformations of X, they too have binomial distributions. The mean and the variance of $\hat{\pi}$ are given in the same table, and those of $\tilde{\pi}$ are calculated as

$$\begin{aligned} E(\tilde{\pi}) &= E[(X + 1)/(n + 2)] \\ &= [E(X) + 1]/(n + 2) \\ &= (\pi + 1)/(n + 2), \end{aligned}$$

and

$$\begin{aligned} \text{Var}(\tilde{\pi}) &= [\text{Var}(X + 1)]/(n + 2)^2 \\ &= n\pi(1 - \pi)/(n + 2)^2. \end{aligned}$$

Thus

$$\hat{\pi} \sim B[\pi,\ \pi(1 - \pi)/n],$$

and

$$\tilde{\pi} \sim B[(\pi + 1)/(n + 2),\ n\pi(1 - \pi)/(n + 2)^2].$$

Let us examine properties of these estimators.

(i) *Unbiasedness*. Since the mean of $\hat{\pi}$ is equal to π but that of $\tilde{\pi}$ is not, the former is unbiased but the latter is not.

(ii) *Efficiency*. The Cramer-Rao lower bound is calculated as

$$\begin{aligned} l &= f(x_1, \ldots, x_n) \\ &= f(x_1)\cdots f(x_n) \qquad \text{(because of independence)} \\ &= \pi^{x_1}(1 - \pi)^{1-x_1}\pi^{x_2}(1 - \pi)^{1-x_2}\cdots\pi^{x_n}(1 - \pi)^{1-x_n} \\ &= \pi^X(1 - \pi)^{n-X}. \end{aligned}$$

---

[1] P. 82.

Now

$$L = X\log(\pi) + (n - X)\log(1 - \pi),$$

$$dL/d\pi = (X - n\pi)/\pi(1 - \pi),$$

$$d^2L/d\pi^2 = (2\pi X - X - n\pi^2)/\pi^2(1 - \pi)^2,$$

$$E(d^2L/d\pi^2) = [2\pi E(X) - E(X) - n\pi^2]/\pi^2(1 - \pi)^2 = -n/\pi(1 - \pi),$$

and

$$[-E(d^2L/d\pi^2)]^{-1} = \pi(1 - \pi)/n.$$

Since the Cramer-Rao lower bound for the variance of an unbiased estimator of π is $\pi(1 - \pi)/n$ and since $\hat{\pi}$ is unbiased with the same variance, it is efficient. However, $\tilde{\pi}$ is not efficient because it is biased.

(iii) *BLUE*. Since $\hat{\pi}$ is a linear function of the sample observations and since it is efficient, it is BLUE. However, $\tilde{\pi}$ is not BLUE because it is biased.

(iv) *Asymptotic unbiasedness*

$$\lim_{n\to\infty}[E(\tilde{\pi})] = \lim_{n\to\infty}[(\pi + 1/n)/(1 + 2/n)] = \pi.$$

Thus both estimators are asymptotically unbiased.

(v) *Consistency*

$$MSE(\hat{\pi}) = Var(\hat{\pi}) = \pi(1 - \pi)/n.$$

$$\lim_{n\to\infty}[MSE(\hat{\pi})] = 0.$$

$$\begin{aligned} MSE(\tilde{\pi}) &= Var(\tilde{\pi}) + [B(\tilde{\pi})]^2 \\ &= n\pi(1 - \pi)/(n + 2)^2 + [(n\pi + 1)/(n + 2) - \pi]^2 \\ &= [1 + (n - 4)\pi(1 - \pi)]/(n + 2)^2, \end{aligned}$$

where $B(\tilde{\pi})$ denotes bias of $\tilde{\pi}$. Now

$$\lim_{n\to\infty}[\text{MSE}(\tilde{\pi})] = \lim_{n\to\infty}\{[1 + (n - 4)\pi(1 - \pi)]/(n + 2)^2\}$$

$$= \lim_{n\to\infty}\left[\frac{1/n^2 + (1/n - 4/n^2)\pi(1 - \pi)}{(1 + 2/n)^2}\right]$$

$$= 0.$$

Thus both estimators are consistent.

(vi) *Asymptotic efficiency*

$$E(\sqrt{n}\{\tilde{\pi} - \lim_{n\to\infty}[E(\tilde{\pi})]\})^2 = E[\sqrt{n}(\tilde{\pi} - \pi)]^2$$

$$= n\{\text{Var}(\tilde{\pi}) + [B(\tilde{\pi})]^2\}$$

$$= \frac{1/n + (1 - 4/n)\pi(1 - \pi)}{(1 + 2/n)^2}.$$

$$\text{Asympt. Var}(\tilde{\pi}) = \left(\frac{1}{n}\right)\lim_{n\to\infty}\left[\frac{1/n + (1 - 4/n)\pi(1 - \pi)}{(1 + 2/n)^2}\right]$$

$$= \pi(1 - \pi)/n.$$

Thus both estimators are asymptotically efficient. The above results are summarized in table 6-2.

TABLE 6-2

Properties	Estimator	
	$\hat{\pi}$	$\tilde{\pi}$
Finite sample		
Unbiasedness	Yes	No
Efficiency	Yes	No
BLUE	Yes	No
Asymptotic properties		
Unbiasedness	Yes	Yes
Consistency	Yes	Yes
Efficiency	Yes	Yes

6-3-b.

$$\text{MSE}(\hat{\pi}) \lesseqqgtr \text{MSE}(\tilde{\pi}),$$

implies that

$$\pi(1 - \pi)/n \lesseqqgtr [1 + (n - 4)\pi(1 - \pi)]/(n + 2)^2,$$

or

$$\pi(1 - \pi) \lesseqqgtr 1/(8 + 4/n).$$

Since

$$n \geq 1,$$

it follows that

$$1/12 \leq 1/(8 + 4/n) \leq 1/8.$$

Therefore, a sufficient condition for $\text{MSE}(\hat{\pi}) < \text{MSE}(\tilde{\pi})$ is

$$\pi(1 - \pi) < 1/12,$$

or equivalently

$$\pi < 1/2 - 1/\sqrt{6} = 0.0918,$$

or

$$\pi > 1/2 + 1/\sqrt{6} = 0.9082.$$

A sufficient condition for $\text{MSE}(\hat{\pi}) > \text{MSE}(\tilde{\pi})$ is

$$\pi(1 - \pi) > 1/8,$$

or equivalently

$$1/2 - 1/\sqrt{8} = 0.1464 < \pi < 1/2 + 1/\sqrt{8} = 0.8536,$$

However, $\text{MSE}(\hat{\pi})$ may be greater than or less than $\text{MSE}(\tilde{\pi})$ even if the sufficient conditions are not met. For instance for a large n, $\text{MSE}(\hat{\pi}) < \text{MSE}(\tilde{\pi})$ as long as $\pi(1 - \pi) < 1/8$, or equivalently

$$\pi < 1/2 - 1/\sqrt{8} = 0.1464,$$

or

$$\pi > 1/2 + 1/\sqrt{8} = 0.8536.$$

6-4.

The likelihood function of k is presented in table 6-3.

TABLE 6-3

Likelihood Function of k										
k	1	2	...	8	9	10	11	...	k
$l(k)$	0	0	...	0	1/9	1/10	1/11	...	1/k

Since $l(k)$ is at maximum when k = 9, $l(9)$ is the MLE of k. The graph of likelihood function is presented in figure 6-1.

FIGURE 6-1

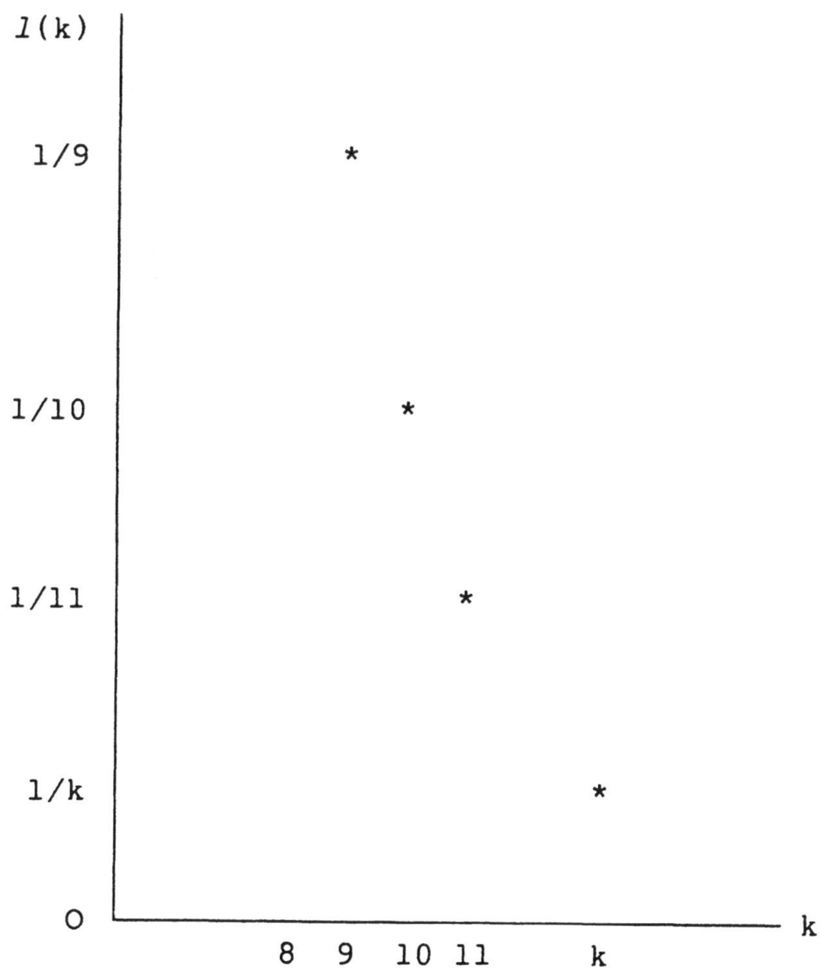

6-5.

Consider a set of n independently and identically distributed (i.i.d.) variables $X_1, \ldots, X_n$. The assumption of linearity requires

$$\mathring{\mu} = \Sigma a_i X_i .$$

Thus

$$E(\mathring{\mu}) = E(\Sigma a_i X_i) = \mu \Sigma a_i ,$$

$$B(\mathring{\mu}) = \mu - E(\mathring{\mu}) = \mu(1 - \Sigma a_i),$$

and

$$\mathrm{Var}(\mathring{\mu}) = \Sigma a_i^2 \mathrm{Var}(X_i) = \sigma^2 \Sigma a_i^2 .$$

Consider

$$H = \mathrm{Var}(\mathring{\mu})/\sigma^2 + [B(\mathring{\mu})]^2/\mu^2 = \Sigma a_i^2 + (1 - \Sigma a_i)^2 .$$

To minimize H, set the first partial derivatives equal to zero and solve for a_i, $(i = 1, \ldots, n)$.

$$\partial H/\partial a_i \equiv 2a_i + 2(1 - \Sigma a_i)(-1) = 0.$$

Summing over all i's, we get

$$2\Sigma a_i - 2n(1 - \Sigma a_i) = 0,$$

or
$$a_i = 1/(n + 1).$$

Checking for positive signs of the second partial derivatives, we get

$$\partial^2 H/\partial a_i^{\,2} = 4 > 0.$$

Therefore

$$\mathring{\mu} = \Sigma X_i/(n + 1) = n\bar{X}/(n + 1).$$

6-6-a.

Consider

$$s^2 = \Sigma(X_i - \bar{X})^2/(n - 1) = n\hat{\sigma}^2/(n - 1).$$

Thus

$$\text{Var}(s^2) = n^2\text{Var}(\hat{\sigma}^2)/(n - 1)^2 = 2\sigma^4/(n - 1).$$

Now

$$\text{Var}(\hat{\sigma}^2) < \text{Var}(s^2),$$

$$2\sigma^4(n - 1)/n^2 < 2\sigma^4/(n - 1),$$

or

$$(n - 1)^2 < n^2 \qquad \text{Q.E.D.}$$

6-6-b.

Since s^2 is an unbiased estimator of σ^2, we have

$$\text{MSE}(s^2) = \text{Var}(s^2) = 2\sigma^4/(n - 1).$$

Consider

$$E(\hat{\sigma}^2) = E(s^2)(n - 1)/n = \sigma^2(n - 1)/n.$$

$$B(\hat{\sigma}^2) = E(\hat{\sigma}^2) - \sigma^2 = -\sigma^2/n.$$

Thus

$$\begin{aligned} \text{MSE}(\hat{\sigma}^2) &= \text{Var}(\hat{\sigma}^2) + [B(\hat{\sigma}^2)]^2 \\ &= 2\sigma^4(n - 1)/n^2 + \sigma^4/n^2 \\ &= \sigma^4(2n - 1)/n^2. \end{aligned}$$

Now

$$\text{MSE}(\hat{\sigma}^2) < \text{MSE}(s^2),$$

$$\sigma^4(2n - 1)/n^2 < 2\sigma^4/(n - 1),$$

or

$$n > 1/3 \qquad \text{Q.E.D.}$$

6-6-c.

Consider

$$\lim_{n\to\infty}[\text{MSE}(\hat{\sigma}^2)] = \lim_{n\to\infty}[\sigma^4(2/n - 1/n^2)] = 0,$$

and

$$\lim_{n\to\infty}[\text{MSE}(s^2)] = \lim_{n\to\infty}[2\sigma^4/(n - 1)] = 0.$$

Thus both estimators are consistent.

6-6-d.

Since s^2 is an unbiased estimator of σ^2, then

$$\begin{aligned}\text{Asympt. Var}(s^2) &= (1/n)\lim_{n\to\infty}[(n)\text{Var}(s^2)] \\ &= (1/n)\lim_{n\to\infty}[2n\sigma^4/(n - 1)] \\ &= (1/n)\lim_{n\to\infty}[2\sigma^4/(1 - 1/n)] \\ &= 2\sigma^4/n.\end{aligned}$$

Further,

$$\begin{aligned}\text{Asympt. Var}(\hat{\sigma}^2) &= \text{Asympt. Var}[(n - 1)s^2/n] \\ &= (1/n)\lim_{n\to\infty}[n(n - 1)^2\text{Var}(s^2)/n^2] \\ &= (1/n)\lim_{n\to\infty}[2(1 - 1/n)^2\sigma^4/(1 - 1/n)] \\ &= 2\sigma^4/n.\end{aligned}$$

Thus both estimators are asymptotically efficient.

6-7-a.

Let $Y_i = (X_{2i-1} + X_{2i})/2$, $(i = 1, \ldots, n/2)$. Since

$$X \sim N(\mu, \sigma^2),$$

then

$$Y \sim N(\mu, \sigma^2/2).$$

An unbiased estimator of μ given the available information is

$$\bar{Y} = \Sigma Y_i/(n/2) \qquad (i = 1, \ldots, n/2),$$

whose distribution according to the Central Limit Theorem is

$$\bar{Y} \sim N[\mu, (\sigma^2/2)/(n/2) = \sigma^2/n].$$

Therefore

$$\mathrm{Var}(\bar{Y}) = \sigma^2/n.$$

6-7-b.

An unbiased estimator of $\mathrm{Var}(Y) = \sigma_y^2 = \sigma^2/2$ is

$$s_y^2 = \Sigma(Y_i - \bar{Y})^2/(n/2 - 1) \qquad (i = 1, \ldots, n/2).$$

Since $\mathrm{Var}(X) = \sigma^2 = 2\sigma_y^2$, then an unbiased estimator of σ^2 given the available information is

$$s^2 = 2s_y^2 = 2\Sigma(Y_i - \bar{Y})^2/(n/2 - 1).$$

Now from (**6-a**), we have

$$\mathrm{Var}(s_y^2) = 2(\sigma^2/2)^2/(n/2 - 1) = \sigma^4/(n - 2).$$

Therefore

$$\mathrm{Var}(s^2) = \mathrm{Var}(2s_y^2) = 4\mathrm{Var}(s_y^2) = 4\sigma^4/(n - 2).$$

6-8.

Let X denote the number of children of a married graduate student at a U.S. university. The probability distribution of X is presented in table 6-4.

TABLE 6-4

Probability Distribution of X	
x	$P\{x\}$
0	π_0
1	π_1
2	π_2

where $\pi_1 = 3\pi_2$ and $(\pi_0 + \pi_1 + \pi_2) = 1$. Combining the two we get $\pi_0 = (1 - 4\pi_2)$. Consider now the likelihood function

$$\begin{aligned} P\{1,2,0,1\} &= P\{1\}\cdot P\{2\}\cdot P\{0\}\cdot P\{1\} \\ &= (\pi_1)(\pi_2)(\pi_0)(\pi_1) \\ &= (3\pi_2)(\pi_2)(1 - 4\pi_2)(3\pi_2) \\ &= 9\pi_2^3 - 36\pi_2^4. \end{aligned}$$

Setting the first derivative equal to zero and putting a hat "^" on π_2 to indicate that we are solving for the maximum likelihood estimate of π_2, we get

$$dP\{1,2,0,1\}/d\pi_2 \equiv 27\hat{\pi}_2^2 - 144\hat{\pi}_2^3 = 0,$$

or equivalently $$\hat{\pi}_2 = \begin{cases} 0.1875, \\ 0, \end{cases}$$

where the second derivative

$$d^2P\{1,2,0,1\}/d\pi_2^2 = 54\hat{\pi}_2 - 432\hat{\pi}_2^2,$$

is equal to -5.0625 when $\hat{\pi}_2 = 0.1875$, and zero when $\hat{\pi}_2 = 0$. Since the function is maximized at $\hat{\pi}_2 = 0.1875$, it follows that

$$\hat{\pi}_1 = 3\hat{\pi}_2 = 0.5625,$$

$$\hat{\pi}_0 = 1 - 4\hat{\pi}_2 = 0.2500,$$

and $$P\{1,2,0,1\} = \hat{\pi}_1 \cdot \hat{\pi}_2 \cdot \hat{\pi}_0 \cdot \hat{\pi}_1 = 0.0148.$$

6-9-a.

Using hints (i) and (ii), we have

$$\begin{aligned} E(X^3) &= E(X - \mu)^3 + 3\mu E(X^2) - 3\mu^2 E(X) + \mu^3 \\ &= 0 + 3\mu(\mu^2 + \sigma^2) - 3\mu^2 \cdot \mu + \mu^3 \\ &= \mu^3 + 3\mu\sigma^2. \end{aligned}$$

Now

$$\begin{aligned} E(\hat{\mu}_1^3) &= E(\Sigma X_i^3/n) \\ &= \Sigma E(X_i^3)/n \\ &= \Sigma(\mu^3 + 3\mu\sigma^2)/n \\ &= \mu^3 + 3\mu\sigma^2, \end{aligned}$$

and

$$\begin{aligned} E(\hat{\mu}_2^3) &= E(\bar{X}^3) \\ &= E(\bar{X} - \mu)^3 + 3\mu E(\bar{X}^2) - 3\mu^2 E(\bar{X}) + \mu^3 \\ &= 0 + 3\mu(\mu^2 + \sigma^2/n) - 3\mu^2 \cdot \mu + \mu^3 \\ &= \mu^3 + 3\mu\sigma^2/n. \end{aligned}$$

Further,

$$B(\hat{\mu}_1^3) = E(\hat{\mu}_1^3) - \mu^3 = 3\mu\sigma^2,$$

and

$$B(\hat{\mu}_2^3) = 3\mu\sigma^2/n.$$

Therefore for $n > 1$, $\hat{\mu}_2^3$ is preferred if lesser bias is the criterion to be used.

6-9-b.

Since $\bar{X}$ and s^2 are independent and since $E(s^2) = \sigma^2$, where

$$s^2 = \Sigma(X_i - \bar{X})^2/(n - 1),$$

then an unbiased estimator of μ^3 is

$$\tilde{\mu}^3 = \bar{X}^3 - 3\bar{X}s^2/n.$$

6-10-a.

Consider

$$X \sim N(\mu, \sigma^2),$$

and

$$\bar{X} \sim N(\mu, \sigma^2/n).$$

For the given 20 observations the sample mean and the sample standard deviation are

$$\bar{X} = 0.3647, \quad \text{and} \quad s = 1.2833.$$

The 95% confidence interval for μ is

$$\bar{X} - t_{0.0250,19}s/\sqrt{n} < \mu < \bar{X} + t_{0.0250,19}s/\sqrt{n},$$

$$0.3647 - 2.0930(1.2833/\sqrt{20}) < \mu < 0.3647 + 2.0930(1.2833/\sqrt{20}),$$

or

$$-0.2359 < \mu < 0.9652.$$

6-10-b.

The 95% confidence interval for σ^2 is

$$(n - 1)s^2/\chi^2_{0.0250,19} < \sigma^2 < (n - 1)s^2/\chi^2_{0.9750,19},$$

$$19(1.2833)^2/32.8520 < \sigma^2 < 19(1.2833)^2/8.9070,$$

or

$$0.9525 < \sigma^2 < 3.5130.$$

Thus the 95% confidence interval for σ is

$$0.9759 < \sigma < 1.8743.$$

6-10-c.

From the example 2, section **(6-4)** of the text,[1] and assuming that $\sigma^2 = 1$, the likelihood function is

$$l(\mu) \propto \exp[-\Sigma(X_i - \mu)^2/2],$$

where "$\propto$" means "is proportional to." Now for n = 20,

$$\Sigma(X_i - \mu)^2/2 = \Sigma[X_i - \bar{X} - (\mu - \bar{X})]^2/2$$

$$= \Sigma[(X_i - \bar{X})^2 - 2(X_i - \bar{X})(\mu - \bar{X}) + (\mu - \bar{X})^2]/2$$

$$= \Sigma(X_i - \bar{X})^2/2 + 10(\mu - \bar{X})^2.$$

Therefore

$$l(\mu) \propto \exp[-10(\mu - \bar{X})^2],$$

since

$$\exp[-\Sigma(X_i - \bar{X})^2/2],$$

which does not involve μ, can be absorbed in the factor of

[1]Pp. 195-7.

proportionality. Since $\bar{X} = 0.3647$, the likelihood function of μ may be written as

$$l(\mu) \propto \exp\left[\frac{-(\mu - 0.3647)^2}{2(1/\sqrt{20})^2}\right],$$

which can be represented by a normal distribution with mean of 0.3647 and variance of 1/20. The graph of the likelihood function for selected values of the population mean is presented in figure 6-2.

FIGURE 6-2

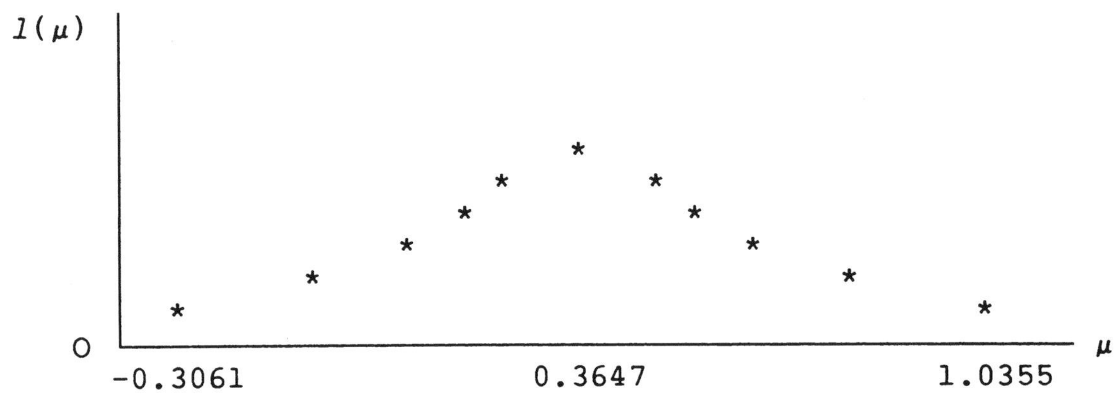

The maximum likelihood estimate (MLE) of μ is 0.3647.

6-11.

Since the 95% confidence interval for the population mean is

$$\bar{X} - 1.96(0.10/\sqrt{n}) < \mu < \bar{X} + 1.96(0.10/\sqrt{n}),$$

the length of the 95% confidence interval is

$$\bar{X} + 1.96(0.10/\sqrt{n}) - \bar{X} + 1.96(0.10/\sqrt{n}) \leq 0.10,$$

or

$$3.92(0.10/\sqrt{n}) \leq 0.10.$$

Therefore

$$n = 16.$$

6-12-a.

According to the example 1, section (**6-4**) of the text,[1] and considering $0 \le \pi \le 1$, $n = 5$ and $m = 3$

$$f(\pi|\text{data}) = C(1 - \pi)^{5-3}\pi^3 = C(\pi^3 - 2\pi^4 + \pi^5),$$

where C is a constant equal to the factor of proportionality. In order to calculate C, set the integral of the function equal to one, i.e.,

$$\int_0^1 C(\pi^3 - 2\pi^4 + \pi^5)d\pi = 1,$$

and evaluate the result between zero and one, i.e.,

$$C(\pi^4/4 - 2\pi^5/5 + \pi^6/6 + b)]_0^1 = 1,$$

where b is a constant. Calculating C, we obtain

$$C = 60.$$

Thus

$$f(\pi|\text{data}) = 60(\pi^3 - 2\pi^4 + \pi^5),$$

$$E(\pi) = \int_0^1 60\pi(\pi^3 - 2\pi^4 + \pi^5)d\pi$$

$$= 60(\pi^5/5 - \pi^6/3 + \pi^7/7 + b)]_0^1$$

$$= 4/7,$$

and

$$\text{Var}(\pi) = \int_0^1 60(\pi - 4/7)^2(\pi^3 - 2\pi^4 + \pi^5)d\pi$$

$$= 60(4\pi^4 - 88\pi^5/5 + 59\pi^6/2 - 22\pi^7 + 49\pi^8/8 + b)/49]_0^1$$

$$= 3/98.$$

---

[1] P. 195.

6-12-b.

Considering n = 5, m = 3 and $\alpha = \beta = 1$, we have

$$f(\pi|\text{data}) = C(1 - \pi)^{5-3+1}\pi^{3+1} = C(\pi^4 - 3\pi^5 + 3\pi^6 - \pi^7).$$

Following the same procedure as in part (a), we get

$$f(\pi|\text{data}) = 280(\pi^4 - 3\pi^5 + 3\pi^6 - \pi^7),$$

$$E(\pi) = 5/9,$$

and

$$\text{Var}(\pi) = 2/81.$$

6-13.

Let X denote the heights of adult males in the population. Given

$$X \sim N(\mu, \sigma^2 = 4),$$

the likelihood function according to the example 2, section (6-4) of the text,[1] is

$$l \propto \exp[-\Sigma(X - \mu)^2/2\sigma^2].$$

Since the prior distribution is informative and takes the form of

$$g(\mu) \sim N(\ldots, \sigma_0^2 = 1),$$

the posterior distribution of μ is

$$f(\mu|\text{data}) \sim N[\ldots, \sigma^2/(n + \sigma^2/\sigma_0^2) = 4/(n + 4)].$$

The smallest sample size to yield the variance of this distribution equal to 0.01 is

or $$4/(n + 4) = 0.01,$$

$$n = 396.$$

---

[1]Pp. 195-7.

CHAPTER 7

7-1.

Consider a sample of n observations $Y_1, \ldots, Y_n$. Let $\hat{\alpha}$ denote the BLUE of α. The condition of linearity requires

$$\hat{\alpha} = \Sigma a_i Y_i.$$

The condition of unbiasedness requires

$$E(\hat{\alpha}) = \alpha.$$

However,

$$E(\hat{\alpha}) = \Sigma a_i E(Y_i) = \Sigma a_i(\alpha + \beta X_i),$$

or

$$E(\hat{\alpha}) = \alpha\Sigma a_i + \beta\Sigma a_i X_i.$$

Thus for $\hat{\alpha}$ to be an unbiased estimator of α, Σa_i must be equal to one and $\Sigma a_i X_i$ must be equal to zero. The condition of being "best" requires

$$\text{Var}(\hat{\alpha}) = \Sigma a_i^2 \text{Var}(Y_i) = \sigma^2 \Sigma a_i^2,$$

to be the smallest among all linear unbiased estimators of α. Thus the problem reduces to minimizing variance of $\hat{\alpha}$ subject to the two constraints required by the condition of unbiasedness. Using the *Lagrange multiplier method*, we should minimize

$$H = \sigma^2\Sigma a_i^2 - \lambda_1 \Sigma a_i X_i - \lambda_2(\Sigma a_i - 1).$$

Setting the first partial derivatives equal to zero, we obtain

$$\partial H/\partial a_i \equiv 2\sigma^2 a_i - \lambda_1 X_i - \lambda_2 = 1,$$

$$\partial H/\partial \lambda_1 \equiv -\Sigma a_i X_i = 0,$$

and

$$\partial H/\partial \lambda_2 \equiv -(\Sigma a_i - 1) = 0.$$

Summing the first equation over all observations, we get

$$2\sigma^2 \Sigma a_i - n\bar{X}\lambda_1 - n\lambda_2 = 0.$$

Substituting one for Σa_i, we obtain

$$n\bar{X}\lambda_1 + n\lambda_2 = 2\sigma^2.$$

Multiplying the first equation by X_i and summing it over all observations, we get

$$2\sigma^2 \Sigma a_i X_i - \lambda_1 \Sigma X_i^2 - n\bar{X}\lambda_2 = 0.$$

Substituting zero for $\Sigma a_i X_i$, we obtain

$$\lambda_1 \Sigma X_i^2 + n\bar{X}\lambda_2 = 0.$$

Solving for λ_1 and λ_2, we get

$$\lambda_1 = \frac{-2\bar{X}\sigma^2}{\Sigma X_i^2 - n\bar{X}^2},$$

and

$$\lambda_2 = \frac{2\sigma^2 \Sigma X_i^2}{n(\Sigma X_i^2 - n\bar{X}^2)}.$$

Substituting for λ_1 and λ_2 in the first equation, we obtain

$$a_i = \frac{\Sigma X_i^2 - n\bar{X}X_i}{n(\Sigma X_i^2 - n\bar{X}^2)}.$$

Now consider

$$\hat{\alpha} = \Sigma a_i Y_i$$

$$= \Sigma[\frac{\Sigma X_i^2 - n\bar{X}X_i}{n(\Sigma X_i^2 - n\bar{X}^2)}]Y_i$$

$$= \frac{n\bar{Y}\Sigma X_i^2 - n\bar{X}\Sigma X_i Y_i}{n(\Sigma X_i^2 - n\bar{X}^2)}$$

$$= \frac{n\bar{Y}\Sigma X_i^2 - n^2\bar{Y}\bar{X}^2 + n^2\bar{Y}\bar{X}^2 - n\bar{X}\Sigma X_i Y_i}{n(\Sigma X_i^2 - n\bar{X}^2)}$$

$$= \bar{Y} - \hat{\beta}\bar{X},$$

where $\hat{\beta}$ is the LSE of β. Further,

$$\text{Var}(\hat{\alpha}) = \sigma^2 \Sigma a_i a_i$$

$$= \sigma^2 \Sigma a_i [\frac{\Sigma X_i^2 - n\bar{X}X_i}{n(\Sigma X_i^2 - n\bar{X}^2)}]$$

$$= \sigma^2 [\frac{\Sigma a_i \Sigma X_i^2 - n\bar{X}\Sigma a_i X_i}{n(\Sigma X_i^2 - n\bar{X}^2)}]$$

$$= \sigma^2 [\frac{\Sigma X_i^2}{n(\Sigma X_i^2 - n\bar{X}^2)}]$$

$$= \sigma^2 [\frac{\Sigma X_i^2 - n\bar{X}^2 + n\bar{X}^2}{n(\Sigma X_i^2 - n\bar{X}^2)}]$$

$$= \sigma^2 [\frac{1}{n} + \frac{\bar{X}^2}{\Sigma(X_i - \bar{X})^2}].$$

7-2.

$$\begin{aligned}
\mathrm{Var}(e_t) &= E(e_t^2) \\
&= E(Y_t - \hat{a} - \hat{\beta}X_t)^2 \\
&= E[a + \beta X_t + \epsilon_t - (\bar{Y} - \hat{\beta}\bar{X}) - \hat{\beta}X_t]^2 \\
&= E[\bar{Y} - \beta\bar{X} - \bar{\epsilon} + \beta X_t + \epsilon_t - (\bar{Y} - \hat{\beta}\bar{X}) - \hat{\beta}X_t]^2 \\
&= E[-(X_t - \bar{X})(\hat{\beta} - \beta) + \epsilon_t - \bar{\epsilon}]^2 \\
&= E[-x_t'(\hat{\beta} - \beta) + \epsilon_t']^2 \\
&= E[x_t'^2(\hat{\beta} - \beta)^2 - 2x_t'\epsilon_t'(\hat{\beta} - \beta) + \epsilon_t'^2] \\
&= x_t'^2E(\hat{\beta} - \beta)^2 - 2x_t'E[\epsilon_t'(\hat{\beta} - \beta)] + E(\epsilon_t'^2).
\end{aligned}$$

Consider

$$x_t'^2E(\hat{\beta} - \beta)^2 = x_t'^2\mathrm{Var}(\hat{\beta}) = x_t'^2\sigma^2/\Sigma x_i'^2,$$

and

$$x_t'E[\epsilon_t'(\hat{\beta} - \beta)] = x_t'E(\epsilon_t'\Sigma x_i'\epsilon_i'/\Sigma x_i'^2) = x_t'E(\epsilon_t'\Sigma x_i'\epsilon_i)/\Sigma x_i'^2,$$

where

$$\begin{aligned}
E(\epsilon_t'\Sigma x_i'\epsilon_i) &= E[\epsilon_t(x_1'\epsilon_1 + \cdots + x_n'\epsilon_n) - \bar{\epsilon}(x_1'\epsilon_1 + \cdots + x_n'\epsilon_n)] \\
&= \sigma^2 x_t' - \sigma^2\Sigma x_i'/n \\
&= \sigma^2 x_t',
\end{aligned}$$

and thus

$$x_t'E[\epsilon_t'(\hat{\beta} - \beta)] = x_t'E(\epsilon_t'\Sigma x_i'\epsilon_i)/\Sigma x_i'^2 = \sigma^2 x_t'^2/\Sigma x_i'^2.$$

Further,

$$E(\epsilon_t'^2) = E(\epsilon_t - \bar{\epsilon})^2 = E(\epsilon_t^2) - 2E(\epsilon_t\bar{\epsilon}) + E(\bar{\epsilon}^2) = \sigma^2 - \sigma^2/n.$$

Therefore

$$\begin{aligned}\text{Var}(e_t) &= \sigma^2 x_t'^2/\Sigma x_i'^2 - 2\sigma^2 x_t'^2/\Sigma x_2'^2 + \sigma^2 - \sigma^2/n \\ &= \sigma^2(1 - 1/n - x_t'^2/\Sigma x_i'^2),\end{aligned}$$

thus $\text{Var}(e_t) \neq \text{Var}(e_s)$. As for covariance of e_t and e_s, consider

$$\begin{aligned}&\text{Cov}(e_t, e_s) \\ &= E(e_t e_s) \\ &= E[-x_t'(\hat{\beta} - \beta) + \epsilon_t'][-x_s'(\hat{\beta} - \beta) + \epsilon_s'] \\ &= E[x_t'x_s'(\hat{\beta} - \beta)^2 - x_t'\epsilon_s'(\hat{\beta} - \beta) - x_s'\epsilon_t'(\hat{\beta} - \beta) + \epsilon_t'\epsilon_s'] \\ &= x_t'x_s'E(\hat{\beta} - \beta)^2 - x_t'E\epsilon_s'(\hat{\beta} - \beta) - x_s'E\epsilon_t'(\hat{\beta} - \beta) + E(\epsilon_t'\epsilon_s').\end{aligned}$$

Further,

$$\begin{aligned}E(\epsilon_t'\epsilon_s') &= E(\epsilon_t - \bar{\epsilon})(\epsilon_s - \bar{\epsilon}) \\ &= E(\epsilon_t\epsilon_s) - E(\epsilon_t\bar{\epsilon}) - E(\epsilon_s\bar{\epsilon}) + E(\bar{\epsilon}^2) \\ &= 0 - \sigma^2/n - \sigma^2/n + \sigma^2/n \\ &= -\sigma^2/n.\end{aligned}$$

Therefore

$$\begin{aligned}\text{Cov}(e_t, e_s) &= \frac{x_t'x_s'\sigma^2}{\Sigma x_i'^2} - \frac{x_t'x_s'\sigma^2}{\Sigma x_i'^2} - \frac{x_s'x_t'\sigma^2}{\Sigma x_i'^2} - \frac{\sigma^2}{n} \\ &= -\sigma^2(1/n + x_t'x_s'/\Sigma x_i'^2),\end{aligned}$$

i.e., e_t and e_s are not mutually independent because their covariance is not equal to zero.

7-3-a.

Solving for a and b, we get

$$b = (\bar{Y}_A - \bar{Y}_B)/(\bar{X}_A - \bar{X}_B),$$

and

$$a = \bar{Y}_A - b\bar{X}_A.$$

Checking for the condition of unbiasedness, we obtain

$$\begin{aligned} E(b) &= E(\bar{Y}_A - \bar{Y}_B)/(\bar{X}_A - \bar{X}_B) \\ &= E(\alpha + \beta\bar{X}_A + \bar{\epsilon}_A - \alpha - \beta\bar{X}_B - \bar{\epsilon}_B)/(\bar{X}_A - \bar{X}_B) \\ &= E[\beta(\bar{X}_A - \bar{X}_B) + \bar{\epsilon}_A - \bar{\epsilon}_B]/(\bar{X}_A - \bar{X}_B) \\ &= [\beta(\bar{X}_A - \bar{X}_B) + E(\bar{\epsilon}_A) - E(\bar{\epsilon}_B)]/(\bar{X}_A - \bar{X}_B) \\ &= \beta, \\ E(a) &= E(\bar{Y}_A - b\bar{X}_A) \\ &= E(\alpha + \beta\bar{X}_A + \bar{\epsilon}_A - b\bar{X}_A) \\ &= \alpha + \beta\bar{X}_A + E(\bar{\epsilon}_A) - \bar{X}_A E(b) \\ &= \alpha, \end{aligned}$$

i.e., both estimators are unbiased.

7-3-b.

$$\begin{aligned} \text{Var}(b) &= \text{Var}(\bar{Y}_A - \bar{Y}_B)/(\bar{X}_A - \bar{X}_B)^2 \\ &= [\text{Var}(\bar{Y}_A) + \text{Var}(\bar{Y}_B) - 2\text{Cov}(\bar{Y}_A, \bar{Y}_B)]/(\bar{X}_A - \bar{X}_B)^2 \\ &= [2\sigma^2/n + 2\sigma^2/n - 2(0)]/(\bar{X}_A - \bar{X}_B)^2 \\ &= 4\sigma^2/n(\bar{X}_A - \bar{X}_B)^2, \end{aligned}$$

and

$$\text{Var}(\hat{\beta}) = \sigma^2/\sum_i(X_i - \bar{X})^2,$$

where $(i = 1, \ldots, n)$, and $\bar{X} = \sum_i X_i/n$. Now let subscripts $(j = 1, \ldots, \frac{n}{2})$, and $(k = \frac{n}{2}+1, \ldots, n)$. Consider

$$\bar{X}_A = 2\sum_j X_j/n, \qquad \bar{X}_B = 2\sum_k X_k/n,$$

and
$$\bar{X} = \sum_i X_i/n = (\sum_j X_j + \sum_k X_k)/n = \bar{X}_A/2 + \bar{X}_B/2.$$

Then

$$\begin{aligned}\sum_i (X_i - \bar{X})^2 &= \sum_i (X_i - \bar{X}_A/2 - \bar{X}_B/2)^2 \\ &= \sum_j (X_j - \bar{X}_A/2 - \bar{X}_B/2)^2 + \sum_k (X_k - \bar{X}_A/2 - \bar{X}_B/2)^2 \\ &= \sum_j (X_j - \bar{X}_A + \frac{\bar{X}_A - \bar{X}_B}{2})^2 + \sum_k (X_k - \bar{X}_B - \frac{\bar{X}_A - \bar{X}_B}{2})^2 \\ &= \sum_j (X_j - \bar{X}_A)^2 + \sum_k (X_k - \bar{X}_B)^2 + n(\bar{X}_A - \bar{X}_B)^2/4.\end{aligned}$$

Thus

$$\sum_i (X_i - \bar{X})^2 \geq n(\bar{X}_A - \bar{X}_B)^2/4,$$

and, therefore

$$\mathrm{Var}(b) \geq \mathrm{Var}(\hat{\beta}) \qquad \text{Q.E.D.}$$

7-3-c.

There are 12 observations which can be divided into two groups of six. The sample values are

$$\bar{X}_A = 60, \qquad \bar{X}_B = 80.$$

Hence,

$$\frac{\mathrm{Var}(b)}{\mathrm{Var}(\hat{\beta})} = \frac{4\sum(X_i - \bar{X})^2}{n(\bar{X}_A - \bar{X}_B)^2} = \frac{4(2250)}{12(60 - 80)^2} = 1.8750.$$

7-4-a.

The condition of linearity requires

$$\tilde{\beta} = \Sigma a_i Y_i .$$

The condition of unbiasedness requires

$$E(\tilde{\beta}) = \beta .$$

However,

$$E(\tilde{\beta}) = \Sigma a_i E(Y_i) = \Sigma a_i (\beta X_i) = \beta \Sigma a_i X_i .$$

Therefore for $\tilde{\beta}$ to be an unbiased estimator of β, we require that

$$\Sigma a_i X_i = 1.$$

The condition of being "best" requires

$$\mathrm{Var}(\tilde{\beta}) = \Sigma a_i^2 \mathrm{Var}(Y_i) = \Sigma a_i^2 \sigma^2 ,$$

to be smallest among all linear unbiased estimators of β. Thus the problem is to find a_i such that $\mathrm{Var}(\tilde{\beta})$ is minimized subject to the unbiasedness condition. Using the *Lagrange multiplier method*, we should minimize

$$H = \Sigma a_i^2 \sigma^2 - \lambda(\Sigma a_i X_i - 1).$$

Setting the first partial derivatives equal to zero, we obtain

$$\partial H/\partial a_i \equiv 2a_i\sigma^2 - \lambda X_i = 0,$$

$$\partial H/\partial \lambda \equiv -\Sigma a_i X_i + 1 = 0.$$

Multiplying the first equation by X_i, summing over all i, and substituting the second equation into the resulting equality, we get

$$\lambda = 2\sigma^2/\Sigma X_i^2 .$$

Substituting this result into the first equation, we obtain

$$a_i = X_i/\Sigma X_i^2.$$

Therefore $$\tilde{\beta} = \Sigma X_i Y_i/\Sigma X_i^2,$$

and $$\mathrm{Var}(\tilde{\beta}) = \sigma^2/\Sigma X_i^2.$$

7-4-b.

A predictor of Y_o^2 could be $\tilde{Y}_o^2 = \tilde{\beta}^2 X_o^2$. Take the mathematical expectation. If the predictor is unbiased, i.e., if

$$E(Y_o^2) = E(\beta X_o + \epsilon_o)^2 = \beta^2 X_o^2 + \sigma^2,$$

it will be the solution, otherwise adjust for bias. Now

$$\begin{aligned} E(\tilde{Y}_o^2) &= X_o^2 E(\tilde{\beta}^2) \\ &= X_o^2 E(\tilde{\beta} - \beta + \beta)^2 \\ &= X_o^2[E(\tilde{\beta} - \beta)^2 + 2\beta E(\tilde{\beta} - \beta) + \beta^2] \\ &= \sigma^2 X_o^2/\Sigma X_i^2 + \beta^2 X_o^2. \end{aligned}$$

This means that $\tilde{Y}_o^2$ is biased. However, the value of bias is known but it involves unknown parameter σ^2. But s^2 is an unbiased estimator of σ^2. Thus an unbiased predictor of Y_o^2 is

$$\hat{Y}_o^2 = \tilde{Y}_o^2 - s^2 X_o^2/\Sigma X_i^2 + s^2 = \tilde{\beta}^2 X_o^2 - s^2 X_o^2/\Sigma X_i^2 + s^2,$$

where

$$\begin{aligned} E(\hat{Y}_o^2) &= E(\tilde{Y}_o^2) - E(s^2)X_o^2/\Sigma X_i^2 + E(s^2) \\ &= \sigma^2 X_o^2/\Sigma X_i^2 + \beta^2 X_o^2 - \sigma^2 X_o^2/\Sigma X_i^2 + \sigma^2 \\ &= \beta^2 X_o^2 + \sigma^2 \qquad \text{Q.E.D.} \end{aligned}$$

7-5.

Consider

$$F_{1,n-2} = (t_{n-2})^2,$$

$$(n - 2)R_A^2/(1 - R_A^2) = (\hat{\beta}/s_{\hat{\beta}})^2,$$

$$(52 - 2)R_A^2/(1 - R_A^2) = (1.00/0.10)^2,$$

and therefore

$$R_A^2 = 2/3.$$

7-6.

The value of the estimator proposed by the researcher I is

$$\tilde{\beta} = (\hat{\beta}_I + \hat{\beta}_{II})/2 = (2 + 2.50)/2 = 2.25.$$

and the value of its variance is

$$\mathrm{Var}(\tilde{\beta}) = \frac{\mathrm{Var}(\hat{\beta}_I) + \mathrm{Var}(\hat{\beta}_{II})}{4} = \frac{\frac{\sigma^2}{100} + \frac{\sigma^2}{400}}{4} = \frac{\sigma^2}{320},$$

where

$$\mathrm{Var}(\hat{\beta}_I) = \frac{\sigma^2}{(\Sigma X_i^2)_I - n_I\bar{X}_I^2} = \frac{\sigma^2}{600 - 20(5^2)} = \frac{\sigma^2}{100},$$

and similarly

$$\mathrm{Var}(\hat{\beta}_{II}) = \frac{\sigma^2}{400}.$$

However, researcher II proposed the least squares estimator of β based on all (or pooled) observations. Consider the pooled values

$$n = n_I + n_{II} = 40,$$

$$\bar{X} = [(\Sigma X_i)_I + (\Sigma X_i)_{II}]/40 = 7.50,$$

$$\bar{Y} = [(\Sigma Y_i)_I + (\Sigma Y_i)_{II}]/40 = 30.00,$$

$$\Sigma X_i^2 = (\Sigma X_i^2)_I + (\Sigma X_i^2)_{II} = 600 + 2,400 = 3,000,$$

and

$$\Sigma X_i Y_i = (\Sigma X_i Y_i)_I + (\Sigma X_i Y_i)_{II} = 2,700 + 8,000 = 10,700,$$

where

$$(\Sigma X_i Y_i)_I = \hat{\beta}_I[(\Sigma X_i^2)_I - n_I \bar{X}_I^2] + n_I \bar{X}_I \bar{Y}_I$$

$$= 2[600 - 20(25)] + 20(5)(25) = 2,700,$$

and similarly

$$(\Sigma X_i Y_i)_{II} = 8,000.$$

Therefore, the value of the best estimator of β, say $\hat{\beta}$, proposed by the researcher II is

$$\hat{\beta} = \frac{\Sigma X_i Y_i - n\bar{X}\bar{Y}}{\Sigma X_i^2 - n\bar{X}^2} = \frac{10,700 - 40(7.50)(30)}{3,000 - 40(7.50)^2},$$

or

$$\hat{\beta} = 2.2667,$$

and the value of its variance is

$$\mathrm{Var}(\hat{\beta}) = \sigma^2/(\Sigma X_i^2 - n\bar{X}^2) = \sigma^2/750.$$

Thus

$$\frac{\mathrm{Var}(\tilde{\beta}) - \mathrm{Var}(\hat{\beta})}{\mathrm{Var}(\tilde{\beta})} = \frac{\sigma^2/320 - \sigma^2/750}{\sigma^2/320},$$

or

$$\frac{\mathrm{Var}(\tilde{\beta}) - \mathrm{Var}(\hat{\beta})}{\mathrm{Var}(\tilde{\beta})} = 0.5733,$$

i.e., by using $\hat{\beta}$ the variance will be reduced by 57.33%.

7-7.

Letting $n = (n_1 + n_2)$, the sample values are calculated as

$$\bar{X} = n_2/n, \qquad \bar{Y} = (n_1\bar{Y}_1 + n_2\bar{Y}_2)/n,$$

and
$$\Sigma X_i^2 = n_2, \qquad \Sigma X_i Y_i = n_2\bar{Y}_2.$$

Substituting the above into the formulas for $\hat{\beta}$, $\hat{\alpha}$, $\text{Var}(\hat{\beta})$, and $\text{Var}(\hat{\alpha})$, we get

$$\hat{\beta} = (\Sigma X_i Y_i - n\bar{X}\bar{Y})/(\Sigma X_i^2 - n\bar{X}^2) = \bar{Y}_2 - \bar{Y}_1,$$

$$\text{Var}(\hat{\beta}) = \sigma^2/(\Sigma X_i^2 - n\bar{X}^2) = n\sigma^2/n_1 n_2,$$

$$\hat{\alpha} = \bar{Y} - \hat{\beta}\bar{X} = \bar{Y}_1,$$

and

$$\text{Var}(\hat{\alpha}) = \sigma^2[1/n + \bar{X}^2/(\Sigma X_i^2 - n\bar{X}^2)] = \sigma^2/n_1.$$

7-8-a.

Consider

$$Y_i = \beta X_i + \epsilon_i,$$

where

$$E(Y_i) = \beta X_i, \qquad \text{and} \qquad \text{Var}(Y_i) = \sigma^2.$$

Summing over all i and dividing by n, we get

$$\bar{Y} = \beta\bar{X} + \bar{\epsilon},$$

where

$$E(\bar{Y}) = \beta\bar{X}, \qquad \text{and} \qquad \text{Var}(\bar{Y}) = \sigma^2/n.$$

Further, note that

$$\hat{\beta}_3 = \frac{\Sigma(X_i - \bar{X})(Y_i - \bar{Y})}{\Sigma(X_i - \bar{X})^2} = \frac{\Sigma(X_i - \bar{X})Y_i}{\Sigma(X_i - \bar{X})X_i}.$$

Now

$$E(\hat{\beta}_1) = E(\bar{Y})/\bar{X} = \beta,$$

$$E(\hat{\beta}_2) = \Sigma X_i E(Y_i)/\Sigma X_i^2 = \quad ,$$

$$E(\hat{\beta}_3) = \Sigma(X_i - \bar{X})E(Y_i)/\Sigma(X_i - \bar{X})X_i = \beta,$$

i.e., all three estimators are unbiased.

7-8-b.

Consider

$$\mathrm{Var}(\hat{\beta}_1) = \mathrm{Var}(\bar{Y})/\bar{X}^2 = \sigma^2/n\bar{X}^2.$$

$$\mathrm{Var}(\hat{\beta}_2) = \Sigma X_i^2 \mathrm{Var}(Y_i)/(\Sigma X_i^2)^2 = \sigma^2/\Sigma X_i^2.$$

and

$$\mathrm{Var}(\hat{\beta}_3) = \frac{\Sigma(X_i - \bar{X})^2 \mathrm{Var}(Y_i)}{[\Sigma(X_i - \bar{X})X_i]^2} = \frac{\Sigma(X_i - \bar{X})^2 \mathrm{Var}(Y_i)}{[\Sigma(X_i - \bar{X})^2]^2} = \frac{\sigma^2}{\Sigma(X_i - \bar{X})^2}.$$

Assuming $X_i \neq \bar{X}$ for at least some i, and noting that $\bar{X} \neq 0$ since otherwise $\hat{\beta}_2 = \hat{\beta}_3$, we have

$$\Sigma(X_i - \bar{X})^2 = \Sigma X_i^2 - n\bar{X}^2 > 0,$$

or

$$\Sigma X_i^2 > n\bar{X}^2,$$

and further,

$$\Sigma X_i^2 > \Sigma X_i^2 - n\bar{X}^2 = \Sigma(X_i - \bar{X})^2.$$

Now since the denominator of $\mathrm{Var}(\hat{\beta}_2)$ is larger than those of $\mathrm{Var}(\hat{\beta}_1)$ and $\mathrm{Var}(\hat{\beta}_3)$, it follows that $\hat{\beta}_2$ has the smallest variance among these three estimators. It can be shown that the variance of $\hat{\beta}_2$ is equal to the Cramer-Rao lower bound (not shown here).

7-9-a.

Step 1: The null and the alternative hypotheses are

$$H_o: \beta = 0,$$

$$H_a: \beta \neq 0.$$

Steps 2 & 3: The test statistic and its distribution are

$$t = \sqrt{(n - 2)R^2/(1 - R^2)} \sim t_{n-2}.$$

Step 4: Do not reject the null hypothesis if

$$|t| < t_{\alpha/2,n-2} = t_{0.0250,20} = 2.0860,$$

otherwise reject it.

Step 5: The value of the test statistic is

$$t = \sqrt{(22 - 2)(0.80)/(1 - 0.80)} = 8.9443.$$

Step 6: Since the value of the test statistic falls in the rejection region, reject the null hypothesis. There is evidence that X and Y are linearly related.

7-9-b.

Step 1: The null and the alternative hypotheses are

$$H_o: \beta = 0,$$

$$H_a: \beta \neq 0.$$

Steps 2 & 3: The test statistic and its distribution are

$$F = (n - 2)R^2/(1 - R^2) \sim F_{1,n-2}.$$

Step 4: Do not reject the null hypothesis if

$$F < F_{\alpha,1,n-2} = F_{0.05,1,20} = 4.35,$$

which is square of $t_{0.0250,20} = 2.0860$ in part (a), otherwise reject it.

Step 5: The value of the test statistic is

$$F = (22 - 2)(0.80)/(1 - 0.80) = 80,$$

which is square of $t = 8.9443$ in part (a).

Step 6: Since the value of the test statistic falls in the rejection region, reject the null hypothesis. There is evidence that X and Y are linearly related.

7-10-a.

(1) Let X_B and Y_B denote the values of the two variables in metric tons as measured by researcher B. Therefore

$$X_A = 1{,}000X_B,$$

and

$$Y_A = 1{,}000Y_B,$$

denote the values of the two in kilograms as measured by researcher A. This means that

$$\bar{X}_A = 1{,}000\bar{X}_B,$$

$$\bar{Y}_A = 1{,}000\bar{Y}_B,$$

$$\Sigma x_A' y_A' = 1{,}000{,}000\Sigma x_B' y_B',$$

and

$$\Sigma x_A'^2 = 1{,}000{,}000\Sigma x_B'^2.$$

Now since

$$\frac{\Sigma x_A' y_A'}{\Sigma x_A'^2} = \frac{\Sigma x_B' y_B'}{\Sigma x_B'^2},$$

it follows that

$$\hat{\beta}_A = \hat{\beta}_B.$$

(2) Consider

$$\Sigma y_A'^2 = 1,000,000 \Sigma y_B'^2,$$

or

$$SST_A = 1,000,000 SST_B,$$

and

$$\hat{\beta}_A^2 \Sigma x_A'^2 = 1,000,000 \hat{\beta}_B^2 \Sigma x_B'^2,$$

or

$$SSR_A = 1,000,000 SSR_B,$$

which imply

$$SSE_A = 1,000,000 SSE_B,$$

and $$s_A^2 = 1,000,000 s_B^2.$$

Now since

$$s_A^2/\Sigma x_A'^2 = s_B^2/\Sigma x_B'^2,$$

then

$$(s_{\hat{\beta}}^2)_A = (s_{\hat{\beta}}^2)_B,$$

and since

$$\hat{\beta}_A/(s_{\hat{\beta}})_A = \hat{\beta}_B/(s_{\hat{\beta}})_B,$$

it follows that

$$t_A = t_B.$$

(3) From part (2), we have

$$SSR_A/SST_A = SSR_B/SST_B,$$

which implies

$$R_A^2 = R_B^2.$$

7-10-b.

(1) Let X_B and Y_B denote the values of the two variables in kilograms and metric tons, respectively, as measured by researcher B. Therefore

$$X_A = X_B, \qquad \text{and} \qquad Y_A = 1{,}000Y_B,$$

denote the values of the two in kilograms as measured by researcher A. This means that

$$\bar{X}_A = \bar{X}_B,$$

$$\bar{Y}_A = 1{,}000\bar{Y}_B,$$

$$\Sigma x_A' y_A' = 1{,}000\Sigma x_B' y_B',$$

and

$$\Sigma x_A'^2 = \Sigma x_B'^2.$$

Now since

$$\frac{\Sigma x_A' y_A'}{\Sigma x_A'^2} = \frac{1{,}000\Sigma x_B' y_B'}{\Sigma x_B'^2},$$

it follows that

$$\hat{\beta}_A = 1{,}000\hat{\beta}_B.$$

(2) Consider

$$\Sigma y_A'^2 = 1{,}000{,}000\Sigma y_B'^2,$$

or

$$SST_A = 1{,}000{,}000SST_B,$$

$$\hat{\beta}_A^2\Sigma x_A'^2 = 1{,}000{,}000\hat{\beta}_B^2\Sigma x_B'^2,$$

or

$$SSR_A = 1{,}000{,}000SSR_B,$$

which imply

$$SSE_A = 1{,}000{,}000SSE_B,$$

and

$$s_A^2 = 1{,}000{,}000s_B^2.$$

Now since

$$s_A^2/\Sigma x_A'^2 = 1,000,000 s_B^2/\Sigma x_B'^2,$$

then

$$(s_{\hat{\beta}}^2)_A = 1,000,000(s_{\hat{\beta}}^2)_B,$$

or

$$(s_{\hat{\beta}})_A = 1,000(s_{\hat{\beta}})_B,$$

and since

$$\hat{\beta}_A/(s_{\hat{\beta}})_A = \hat{\beta}_B/(s_{\hat{\beta}})_B,$$

it follows that

$$t_A = t_B.$$

(3) From part (2), we have

$$SSR_A/SST_A = SSR_B/SST_B,$$

which implies

$$R_A^2 = R_B^2.$$

7-11.

Consider

$$\begin{aligned}
\hat{\beta}^2/s_{\hat{\beta}}^2 &= \hat{\beta}^2\Sigma(X_i - \bar{X})^2/s^2 \\
&= SSR/[SSE/(n - 2)] \\
&= (n - 2)SSR/SSE \\
&= (n - 2)SSR/(SST - SSR) \\
&= [(n - 2)SSR/SST]/(1 - SSR/SST) \\
&= (n - 2)R^2/(1 - R^2),
\end{aligned}$$

or

$$\hat{\beta}/s_{\hat{\beta}} = [R^2(n - 2)/(1 - R^2)]^{1/2}.$$

7-12-a.

The observed values of X and Y are presented in table 7-1.

TABLE 7-1

Observed Values of X and Y	
X	Y
1.0000	5.4640
2.0000	8.1370
3.0000	13.4550
4.0000	13.6770
5.0000	16.9320
6.0000	20.2960
7.0000	22.7120
8.0000	27.2980
9.0000	29.2410
10.0000	31.0430

7-12-b.

The sample values are

$$\bar{X} = 5.5000, \qquad \bar{Y} = 18.8255,$$

$$\Sigma x_i' y_i' = 238.8115, \qquad \Sigma x_i'^2 = 82.5000,$$

$$SST = 698.5088, \qquad SSR = 691.2840,$$

and

$$SSE = 7.2248, \qquad s^2 = 0.9031.$$

The estimated regression equation is

$$\underset{}{Y_i} = \underset{(0.6492)}{2.9047} + \underset{(0.1046)}{2.8947}X_i + e_i, \qquad R^2 = 0.9897.$$

7-12-c.

Step 1: The null and the alternative hypotheses are

$$H_o: \beta = 0,$$

$$H_a: \beta \neq 0.$$

Steps 2 & 3: The test statistic and its distribution are

$$t = \hat{\beta}/s_{\hat{\beta}} \sim t_{n-2}.$$

Step 4: Do not reject the null hypothesis if

$$|t| < t_{\alpha/2,n-2} = t_{0.0250,8} = 2.3060,$$

otherwise reject it.

Step 5: The value of the test statistic is

$$t = 2.8947/0.1046 = 27.6670.$$

Step 6: Since the value of the test statistic falls in the rejection region, reject the null hypothesis. There is evidence that X and Y are linearly related.

7-12-d.

The predicted value of Y for X = 12 is

$$\hat{Y}_{12} = 2.9047 + 2.8947(12) = 37.6410,$$

and the values of its variance and standard error are

$$s_F^2 = 0.9031[1 + \frac{1}{10} + \frac{(12 - 5.50)^2}{82.50}] = 1.4559,$$

and

$$s_F = 1.2066.$$

Thus the 95% prediction interval of Y given X = 12 is

$$\hat{Y}_{12} \pm 2.3060(1.2066),$$

or

$$P\{34.8585 \leq Y_{12} \leq 40.4234\} = 0.95.$$

7-13-a.

Consider the prior distribution of β

$$g(\beta) \propto \text{constant},$$

and the likelihood function for the sample data on Y

$$l = (2\pi\sigma^2)^{-n/2}\exp[-\Sigma(Y_i - \beta X_i)^2/2\sigma^2].$$

Combining the two distributions, we obtain the posterior distribution of β as

$$\begin{aligned} f(\beta|\text{data}) &\propto \exp[-\Sigma(Y_i - \beta X_i)^2/2\sigma^2] \\ &\propto \exp\{-\Sigma[Y_i - \hat{\beta}X_i - (\beta - \hat{\beta})X_i]^2/2\sigma^2\} \\ &\propto \exp[-(\beta - \hat{\beta})^2\Sigma X_i^2/2\sigma^2], \end{aligned}$$

where $\hat{\beta}$ is the least squares estimate of β, the term

$$\exp\{-\Sigma(Y_i - \hat{\beta}X_i)^2/2\sigma^2\},$$

is absorbed in the factor of proportionality since it does not contain β, and the term

$$\exp[(\beta - \hat{\beta})\Sigma(Y_i - \hat{\beta}X_i)X_i/\sigma^2],$$

is zero because the part inside the bracket is one of the normal equations. Therefore, the posterior distribution of β is a univariate normal distribution with mean of $\hat{\beta}$ and variance of

$$\sigma^2/\Sigma X_i^2,$$

or

$$\beta \sim N(\hat{\beta}, \sigma^2/\Sigma X_i^2).$$

7-13-b.

Consider the prior distribution of β

$$g(\beta) \propto \exp[-(\beta - \beta_o)^2/2\sigma_o^2],$$

and the likelihood function for the sample data on Y

$$l = (2\pi\sigma^2)^{-n/2}\exp[-\Sigma(Y_i - \beta X_i)^2/2\sigma^2].$$

Combining the two distributions we identify the posterior distribution of β as a univariate normal distribution. The posterior distribution of β with its mean as a weighted average of $\hat{\beta}$ and β_o and its variance as a function of σ^2 and σ_o^2 is presented as

$$\beta \sim N\left(\frac{\hat{\beta}\sigma_o^2\Sigma X_i^2 + \beta_o\sigma^2}{\sigma_o^2\Sigma X_i^2 + \sigma^2}, \frac{\sigma^2\sigma_o^2}{\sigma_o^2\Sigma X_i^2 + \sigma^2}\right),$$

or

$$\beta \sim N\left[\frac{\hat{\beta}/(\sigma^2/\Sigma X_i^2) + \beta_o/(1/\sigma_o^2)}{1/(\sigma^2/\Sigma X_i^2) + 1/(1/\sigma_o^2)}, \frac{1}{1/(\sigma^2/\Sigma X_i^2) + 1/(1/\sigma_o^2)}\right].$$

Note that when σ_o^2 approaches infinity (∞), the mean and the variance of the posterior distribution of β will approach $\hat{\beta}$ and $\sigma^2/\Sigma X_i^2$, and when $\sigma_o^2 = 0$, they will be equal to β_o and zero, respectively.

CHAPTER 8

8-1-a.

Consider minimizing the sum of absolute vertical deviations

$$\Sigma|\tilde{e}_i| = \Sigma|Y_i - \tilde{Y}_i| = \Sigma|Y_i - \tilde{\alpha} - \tilde{\beta}X_i|,$$

where $\tilde{\alpha}$ and $\tilde{\beta}$ are the MAD estimators of α and β, and $\tilde{Y}_i$ is the fitted value of Y_i. Since it is not known, *a priori*, that the i-th observed value of Y_i is greater than, equal to, or less than the fitted value $\tilde{Y}_i$, the i-th deviation $\tilde{e}_i$ may be represented by the sum of two non-negative variables U_i and V_i such that

$$\text{if } Y_i > \tilde{Y}_i, \text{ then } U_i > 0 \text{ and } V_i = 0, \text{ or } Y_i = \tilde{Y}_i + U_i,$$

$$\text{if } Y_i < \tilde{Y}_i, \text{ then } U_i = 0 \text{ and } V_i > 0, \text{ or } Y_i = \tilde{Y}_i - V_i,$$

or

$$\text{if } Y_i = \tilde{Y}_i, \text{ then } U_i = 0 \text{ and } V_i = 0.$$

The MAD estimation, thus, is reduced to the following linear programming problem

Minimize $\qquad \Sigma U_i + \Sigma V_i,$

Subject to $\qquad \tilde{\alpha} + \tilde{\beta}X_i + U_i - V_i = Y_i,$

where U_i and V_i are non-negative, $\tilde{\alpha}$ and $\tilde{\beta}$ are free in sign, and $(i = 1, \ldots, n)$. Transforming the above model into a dual problem employing dual variable Z_i, and further using a linear transformation $W_i = (Z_i + 1)$, the MAD estimation reduces to the following linear programming problem

Maximize $$\Sigma Y_i W_i - \Sigma Y_i,$$

subject to

$$\Sigma W_i = n,$$

$$\Sigma X_i W_i = \Sigma X_i,$$

$$W_i \le 2,$$

where W_i is non-negative. The solution will yield the values of $\tilde{\alpha}$ and $\tilde{\beta}$ as the dual prices. Using the above procedure the MAD estimates are

$$Y_i = -280.5741 + 0.1413X_i + \tilde{e}_i,$$

and the LS estimates are

$$Y_i = \underset{(1976.20)}{-6837.00} + \underset{(0.1887)}{1.0170}X_i + e_i, \qquad R^2 = 0.6173.$$

8-1-b.

Step 1: The null and the alternative hypotheses are

H_o: ϵ's are normally distributed,

H_a: H_o is not true and the distribution belongs to Pearson family.

Under H_o, the standard measure of symmetry

$$\sqrt{\beta_1} = \mu_3/\mu_2^{3/2},$$

will be equal to zero, and the standard of peakedness or kurtosis

$$\beta_2 = \mu_4/\mu_2^2,$$

will be equal to three, where μ_r is the r-th moment about the mean and is defined as

$$\mu_r = E(\epsilon_i^r).$$

Steps 2 & 3: The test statistic and its distribution are

$$\chi^2 = n[\frac{b_1}{6} + \frac{(b_2 - 3)^2}{24}] \sim \chi^2_2,$$

where b_1 and b_2 are the estimators of β_1 and β_2, respectively, where μ's are replaced by

$$\hat{\mu}_r = \Sigma e_i^r/n.$$

Step 4: Do not reject the null hypothesis if

$$\chi^2 < \chi^2_{\alpha,2} = \chi^2_{0.05,2} = 5.9910,$$

otherwise reject it.

Step 5: The sample values are

$$\hat{\mu}_2 = 17,590,210,$$

$$\hat{\mu}_3 = 61,841,730(10)^3,$$

$$\hat{\mu}_4 = 1,295,757(10)^9,$$

$$b_1 = 0.7027,$$

and

$$b_2 = 4.1878.$$

Thus the value of the test statistic is

$$\chi^2 = 20[\frac{0.7027}{6} + \frac{(4.1878 - 3)^2}{24}] = 3.5180.$$

Step 6: Since the value of the test statistic falls in the acceptance region, do not reject the null hypothesis. There is no evidence to indicate that the regression disturbances are not normally distributed.

8-2.

Consider the LSE of a

$$\hat{a} = \bar{Y} - \hat{\beta}\bar{X}$$

$$= a + \beta\bar{X} + \bar{\epsilon} - \hat{\beta}\bar{X}$$

$$= a - \bar{X}(\hat{\beta} - \beta) + \bar{\epsilon}$$

$$= a - \bar{X}\Sigma x_i'\epsilon_i'/\Sigma x_i'^2 + \bar{\epsilon}.$$

Now

$$E(\hat{a}) = a - \bar{X}\Sigma x_i'E(\epsilon_i')/\Sigma x_i'^2 + E(\bar{\epsilon})$$

$$= a - \gamma\bar{X}\Sigma x_i'z_i'/\Sigma x_i'^2 + \gamma\bar{Z}$$

$$= a + \gamma\bar{Z}.$$

Thus the bias is $\gamma\bar{Z}$.

8-3.

Consider dividing both sides of the model by $\sqrt{X_i}$

$$Y_i/\sqrt{X_i} = a/\sqrt{X_i} + \epsilon_i/\sqrt{X_i},$$

where the disturbance has mean of zero, is non-autocorrelated, and has a constant variance of σ^2. In the transformed regression there is one non-stochastic explanatory variable and there is no intercept term. Thus the BLUE of a is

$$\hat{a} = \Sigma(Y_i/X_i)/\Sigma(1/X_i),$$

and its variance is

$$\text{Var}(\hat{a}) = \sigma^2/\Sigma(1/X_i).$$

8-4-a.

Consider

$$Y_i/X_i = \alpha/X_i + \beta + \epsilon_i/X_i.$$

Applying the LS estimation to the above model

$$Y_i/X_i = \underset{(1.1500)}{0.8751}/X_i + \underset{(0.0549)}{0.8054} + e_i/X_i, \qquad R^2 = 0.0032,$$

or

$$Y_i = \underset{(1.1500)}{0.8751} + \underset{(0.0549)}{0.8054}X_i + e_i, \qquad R^2 = 0.5860,$$

where

$$R^2 = 1 - \frac{\Sigma(Y_i - 0.8751 - 0.8054X_i)^2}{\Sigma y_i'^2}$$

$$= 1 - \frac{2,509.9980}{6,062.1000}$$

$$= 0.5860.$$

8-4-b.

Consider

$$Y_i/\hat{Y}_i = \alpha/\hat{Y}_i + \beta X_i/\hat{Y}_i + \epsilon_i/\hat{Y}_i,$$

where $\hat{Y}_i$ represents the i-th fitted value of Y using the LS estimation. Applying the LS estimation to the above model

$$Y_i/\hat{Y}_i = \underset{(1.1452)}{0.8972}/\hat{Y}_i + \underset{(0.0544)}{0.8043}X_i/\hat{Y}_i + e_i/\hat{Y}_i, \qquad R^2 = 0.0006.$$

or

$$Y_i = \underset{(1.1452)}{0.8972} + \underset{(0.0544)}{0.8043}X_i + e_i, \qquad R^2 = 0.5860,$$

where

$$R^2 = 1 - \frac{\Sigma(Y_i - 0.8972 - 0.8043X_i)^2}{\Sigma y_i'^2}$$

$$= 1 - \frac{2,509.7880}{6,062.1000}$$

$$= 0.5860.$$

8-4-c.

Consider

$$Y_{ij}/s_i = \alpha/s_i + \beta X_i/s_i + \epsilon_{ij}/s_i,$$

where s_i is the standard deviation of Y_{ij} for the i-th value of X, where

$$s_i^2 = \sum_j (Y_{ij} - \bar{Y}_i)^2/(n_i - 1).$$

Applying the LS estimation to the above model

$$Y_{ij}/s_i = \underset{(1.1058)}{0.5563}/s_i + \underset{(0.0542)}{0.8212}X_i/s_i + e_{ij}/s_i, \qquad R^2 = 0.4126.$$

or

$$Y_{ij} = \underset{(1.1058)}{0.5563} + \underset{(0.0542)}{0.8212}X_i + e_{ij}, \qquad R^2 = 0.5851,$$

where

$$R^2 = 1 - \frac{\Sigma(Y_i - 0.5563 - 0.8212X_i)^2}{\Sigma y_i'^2}$$

$$= 1 - \frac{2,515.0750}{6,062.1000}$$

$$= 0.5851.$$

8-5-a.

Step 1: The null and the alternative hypotheses are

$$H_o: \sigma_2^2/\sigma_1^2 = 1,$$

$$H_a: \sigma_2^2/\sigma_1^2 > 1.$$

Steps 2 & 3: The test statistic and its distribution are

$$F = s_2^2/s_1^2 \sim F_{n_2-2,n_1-1}.$$

The reason that the degree of freedom of the denominator is $(n_1 - 1)$ is given in step 5.

Step 4: Do not reject the null hypothesis if

$$F < F_{\alpha,n_2-2,n_1-1} = F_{0.01,73,74} = 1.77,$$

otherwise reject it.

Step 5: Consider dropping about one-sixth or (p = 31) of the middle observations and calculating s_1^2 and s_2^2 based on the first and the last 75 observations. Note that for the first 75 observations X = 18. Then

$$s_1^2 = \sum_1^{75}(Y_i - \bar{Y})^2/(75 - 1) = 1/3,$$

and

$$s_2^2 = \sum_{i=107}^{181} e_{i2}^2/(75 - 2) = 22.2740.$$

Thus the value of the test statistic is

$$F = 22.2740/(1/3) = 66.8220.$$

Step 6: Since the value of the test statistic falls in the rejection region, reject the null hypothesis. There is a strong evidence to doubt the existence of homoskedasticity.

8-5-b.

Step 1: The null and the alternative hypotheses are

$$H_0: \sigma_i^2 = \sigma^2,$$

$$H_a: \sigma_i^2 = g(\gamma_0 + \gamma_1 X_i),$$

where (i = 1, ..., 181).

Steps 2 & 3: The test statistic and its distribution are

$$\chi^2 = SSR_{BP}/2 \sim \chi_1^2,$$

where SSR_{BP} is regression sum of squares from regression model

$$e_i^2/\hat{\sigma}^2 = \gamma_0 + \gamma_1 X_i + v_i,$$

where

$$\hat{\sigma}^2 = \Sigma e_i^2/n.$$

Step 4: Do not reject the null hypothesis if

$$\chi^2 < \chi^2_{\alpha,1} = \chi^2_{0.01,1} = 6.6350,$$

otherwise reject it.

Step 5: The sample values are

$$\hat{\sigma}^2 = 13.8571,$$

$$e_i^2/\hat{\sigma}^2 = \underset{(0.4375)}{-1.5909} + \underset{(0.0188)}{0.1146}X_i + \hat{v}_i, \qquad R^2 = 0.1723,$$

and

$$SSR_{BP} = 75.2690.$$

Thus the value of the test statistic is

$$\chi^2 = 75.2690/2 = 37.6345.$$

Step 6: Since the value of the test statistic falls in the rejection region, reject the null hypothesis. There is a strong evidence to doubt the existence of homoskedasticity.

8-5-c.

Step 1: The null and the alternative hypotheses are

$$H_o: \sigma_i^2 = \sigma^2,$$

$$H_a: \sigma_i^2 = g(\delta_0 + \delta_1 X_i + \delta_2 X_i^2),$$

where (i = 1, ..., 181).

Steps 2 & 3: The test statistic and its distribution are

$$\chi^2 = nR_W^2 \sim \chi_2^2.$$

where R_W^2 is the coefficient of determination from the regression model

$$e_i^2 = \delta_0 + \delta_1 X_i + \delta_2 X_i^2 + u_i.$$

Step 4: Do not reject the null hypothesis if

$$\chi^2 < \chi^2_{\alpha,2} = \chi^2_{0.01,2} = 9.2100,$$

otherwise reject it.

Step 5: The sample values are

$$\underset{}{e_i^2} = \underset{(31.4520)}{-50.4950} + \underset{(2.6318)}{4.0022}X_i - \underset{(0.0522)}{0.0481}X_i^2 + \hat{u}_i, \qquad R_W^2 = 0.1762,$$

Thus the value of the test statistic is

$$nR_W^2 = 181(0.1762) = 31.8922.$$

Step 6: Since the value of the test statistic falls in the rejection region, reject the null hypothesis. There is a strong evidence to doubt the existence of homoskedasticity.

8-5-d.

Step 1: The null and the alternative hypotheses are

$$H_o: \sigma_i^2 = \sigma^2,$$

$$H_a: H_o \text{ is not true,}$$

where (i = 1, ..., m), and m = 9.

Steps 2 & 3: The test statistic and its distribution are

$$\chi^2 = (-4.605170)\log(M)/(1 + N) \sim \chi^2_{m-1},$$

where

$$\log(M) = [\frac{\Sigma(n_i - 1)}{2}]\log(s_i^2) - (\frac{n - m}{2})\log[\frac{\Sigma(n_i - 1)s_i^2}{n - m}],$$

$$N = [\Sigma(1/n_i) - 1/n]/3(m - 1),$$

and

$$s_i^2 = \sum_j (Y_{ij} - \bar{Y}_i)^2/(n_i - 1),$$

where (i = 1, ..., 9), and (j = 1, ..., n_i).

Step 4: Do not reject the null hypothesis if

$$\chi^2 < \chi^2_{\alpha,m-1} = \chi^2_{0.01,8} = 20.0900,$$

otherwise reject it.

Step 5: The sample values are

$$\log(M) = -9.6368,$$

$$N = 0.0431.$$

Thus the value of the test statistic is

$$\chi^2 = -4.605170(-9.6368)/(1 + 0.0431) = 42.5454.$$

Step 6: Since the value of the test statistic falls in the rejection region, reject the null hypothesis. There is a strong evidence to doubt the existence of homoskedasticity.

8-6.

Consider dividing both sides of the model by X_i

$$Y_i/X_i = \beta + \epsilon_i/X_i,$$

where the disturbance has mean of zero, is non-autocorrelated, and has a constant variance of σ^2. In the transformed regression there is no non-stochastic explanatory variable, however, there is an intercept term. Thus the BLUE of β is

$$\tilde{\beta} = \Sigma(Y_i/X_i)/n,$$

and its variance is

$$\text{Var}(\tilde{\beta}) = \sigma^2/n.$$

8-7-a.

Consider the first sample disturbance given as

$$\epsilon_1 = u_1/\sqrt{1 - \rho^2}$$

while the rest of them are

$$\epsilon_t = \rho\epsilon_{t-1} + u_t,$$

where $(0 \leq \rho^2 < 1)$, and $(t = 2, \ldots, n)$. Using the Prais-Winsten transformation, we have

$$Y_1\sqrt{1 - \rho^2} = \alpha\sqrt{1 - \rho^2} + u_1,$$

and

$$Y_t - \rho Y_{t-1} = \alpha(1 - \rho) + u_t.$$

This model can be equally written as

$$Z_t = \alpha W_t + u_t,$$

where

$$Z_1 = Y_1\sqrt{1 - \rho^2},$$

$$W_1 = \sqrt{1 - \rho^2},$$

$$Z_t = Y_t - \rho Y_{t-1},$$

and

$$W_t = (1 - \rho),$$

where $(t = 2, \ldots, n)$. Since the transformed disturbances u's are normally and independently distributed with mean of zero, constant variance of σ_u^2, and are non-correlated, and since the transformed model has one non-stochastic variable and no intercept, the LSE (which is the same as MLE and BLUE) is the best estimation procedure. The LSE of a, which has all desirable properties, is

$$\hat{a} = \Sigma W_t Z_t / \Sigma W_t^2,$$

or

$$\hat{a} = \frac{(1 + \rho)Y_1 + \Sigma(Y_t - \rho Y_{t-1})}{1 + \rho + (n - 1)(1 - \rho)}.$$

8-7-b.

For $t = 1$, we have

$$\epsilon_1 = u_1/\sqrt{1 - \rho^2},$$

and

$$\text{Var}(\epsilon_1) = \text{Var}(u_1)/(1 - \rho^2),$$

or

$$\text{Var}(u_1) = (1 - \rho^2)\sigma^2 X_1^2.$$

Further, for (t = 2, ..., n), we have

$$\epsilon_t = \rho\epsilon_{t-1} + u_t,$$

and

$$\mathrm{Var}(\epsilon_t) = \rho^2\mathrm{Var}(\epsilon_{t-1}) + \mathrm{Var}(u_t),$$

$$\sigma^2X_t^2 = \rho^2\sigma^2X_{t-1}^2 + \mathrm{Var}(u_t),$$

or

$$\mathrm{Var}(u_t) = \sigma^2(X_t^2 - \rho^2X_{t-1}^2).$$

This means that the transformed model is both heteroskedastic and autoregressive. To remove them, we use the Prais-Winsten transformation corrected for heteroskedasticity as follows

$$\frac{Y_1}{X_1} = \frac{a}{X_1} + \frac{u_1}{X_1\sqrt{1 - \rho^2}},$$

and

$$\frac{Y_t - \rho Y_{t-1}}{\sqrt{X_t^2 - \rho^2X_{t-1}^2}} = \frac{a(1 - \rho)}{\sqrt{X_t^2 - \rho^2X_{t-1}^2}} + \frac{u_t}{\sqrt{X_t^2 - \rho^2X_{t-1}^2}},$$

where (t = 2, ..., n). Now the disturbances are normally and independently distributed with mean of zero and constant variance of σ^2. Therefore, the best estimation procedure would be the LS estimation. Since the model has one non-stochastic explanatory variable and no intercept term and since ρ is known, the LSE of a, which has all desirable properties, would be

$$\hat{a} = \frac{Y_1/X_1^2 + \Sigma[(Y_t - \rho Y_{t-1})/(X_t^2 - \rho^2X_{t-1}^2)]}{1/X_1^2 + (1 - \rho)\Sigma[1/(X_t^2 - \rho^2X_{t-1}^2)]}.$$

8-8.

Consider the Cochrane-Orcutt transformation,

$$Y_t = \gamma + \rho Y_{t-1} + u_t,$$

where (t = 2, ..., 5), $\gamma = a(1 - \rho)$, and the u's are normally and independently distributed with mean of zero and a constant variance. Applying the LS estimation to the above model, we get

$$\underset{}{Y_t} = \underset{(2.7042)}{4.0000} + \underset{(0.6124)}{0.5000}Y_{t-1} + \hat{u}_t, \qquad R^2 = 0.2500.$$

Now since $\hat{\gamma} = 4$ and $\hat{\rho} = 0.50$, and since $a = \gamma/(1 - \rho)$, the best estimate of a would be $\tilde{a} = 8$. For this model the above method is exactly the same as the Durbin two-step method, and leads to the same estimate of a as the Cochrane-Orcutt iterative method. This estimator of a has all desirable asymptotic properties.

8-9.

Using the Prais-Winsten transformation, we obtain

$$Y_1\sqrt{1 - \rho^2} = \beta X_1\sqrt{1 - \rho^2} + u_1,$$

and
$$Y_t - \rho Y_{t-1} = \beta(X_t - \rho X_{t-1}) + u_t,$$

where (t = 2, ..., n), and u's are normally and independently distributed with mean of zero and variance of $\sigma^2(1 - \rho^2)$. In the above regression model there is one non-stochastic explanatory variable and there is no intercept term. Thus, the BLUE of β is

$$\hat{\beta} = \frac{X_1Y_1(1 - \rho^2) + \Sigma(Y_t - \rho Y_{t-1})(X_t - \rho X_{t-1})}{X_1^2(1 - \rho^2) + \Sigma(X_t - \rho X_{t-1})^2},$$

and its variance is

$$\mathrm{Var}(\hat{\beta}) = \sigma^2(1 - \rho^2)/[X_1^2(1 - \rho^2) + \Sigma(X_t - \rho X_{t-1})^2].$$

8-10-a.

Consider

$$\log(P_t/L_t) = \alpha + \beta\log(W_t) + \epsilon_t,$$

where the variables are measured in *natural* logarithms. Applying the LS estimation to the above model

$$\log(P_t/L_t) = \underset{(0.1281)}{-8.3243} + \underset{(0.0268)}{(0.6201)}\log(W_t) + e_t, \qquad R^2 = 0.9402.$$

8-10-b.

Step 1: The null and the alternative hypotheses are

$$H_o\colon \rho = 0,$$

$$H_a\colon \rho \neq 0.$$

Steps 2 & 3: The test statistic is

$$d = \sum_{t=2}^{n} (e_t - e_{t-1})^2 / \sum_{t=1}^{n} e_t^2.$$

Step 4: Do not reject the null hypothesis if

$$d_{u,\alpha,k',n} = d_{u,0.01,1,36} = 1.32 < d < 4 - d_{u,\alpha,k',n} = 2.68,$$

reject it if

$$d < d_{l,\alpha,k',n} = d_{l,0.01,1,36} = 1.21,$$

or

$$d > 4 - d_{l,\alpha,k',n} = 4 - 1.21 = 2.79,$$

otherwise the test is inconclusive.

Step 5: The value of the test statistic is

$$d = 0.1092.$$

Step 6: Since the value of the test statistic falls in the rejection region, reject the null hypothesis. There is a strong evidence to doubt the absence of autocorrelation.

8-10-c.

Here we conduct three tests corresponding to the first-, the second-, and the third-order autoregressive process. Consider the first-order autoregressive process.

Step 1: The null and the alternative hypotheses are

$$H_o: \rho_1 = 0,$$

$$H_a: \rho_1 \neq 0.$$

Steps 2 & 3: The test statistic and its distribution are

$$Q = \frac{n(\sum_{t=2}^{n} e_t e_{t-1})^2}{(\sum_{t=1}^{n} e_t^2)^2} \sim \chi_1^2.$$

Step 4: Do not reject the null hypothesis if

$$\chi^2_{1-\frac{\alpha}{2},1} = \chi^2_{0.9950,1} \cong 0 < Q < \chi^2_{\frac{\alpha}{2},1} = \chi^2_{0.0050,1} = 7.8790$$

otherwise reject it.

Step 5: The value of the test statistic is

$$\chi^2 = 36(0.1863/0.2493)^2 = 20.1024.$$

Step 6: Since the value of the test statistic falls in the rejection region, reject the null hypothesis. There is a strong evidence to doubt the absence of first-order autoregressive process.

Consider the second-order autoregressive process.

Step 1: The null and the alternative hypotheses are

$$H_o: \rho_2 = 0,$$

$$H_a: \rho_2 \neq 0.$$

Steps 2 & 3: The test statistic and its distribution are

$$Q = \frac{n[(\sum_{t=2}^{n} e_t e_{t-1})^2 + (\sum_{t=3}^{n} e_t e_{t-2})^2]}{(\sum_{t=1}^{n} e_t^2)^2} \sim \chi_2^2.$$

Step 4: Do not reject the null hypothesis if

$$\chi^2_{1-\frac{\alpha}{2},2} = \chi^2_{0.9950,2} = 0.0100 < Q < \chi^2_{\frac{\alpha}{2},2} = \chi^2_{0.0050,2} = 10.5970,$$

otherwise reject it.

Step 5: The value of the test statistic is

$$\chi^2 = 36(0.1863^2 + 0.1474^2)/0.2493^2 = 36.6880.$$

Step 6: Since the value of the test statistic falls in the rejection region, reject the null hypothesis. There is a strong evidence to doubt the absence of second-order autoregressive process.

Consider the third-order autoregressive process.

Step 1: The null and the alternative hypotheses are

$$H_o: \rho_3 = 0,$$

$$H_a: \rho_3 \neq 0.$$

Steps 2 & 3: The test statistic and its distribution are

$$Q = \frac{n[(\sum_{t=2}^{n} e_t e_{t-1})^2 + (\sum_{t=3}^{n} e_t e_{t-2})^2 + (\sum_{t=4}^{n} e_t e_{t-3})^2]}{(\sum_{t=1}^{n} e_t^2)^2} \sim \chi_3^2.$$

Step 4: Do not reject the null hypothesis if

$$\chi^2_{1-\frac{\alpha}{2},3} = \chi^2_{0.9950,3} = 0.0717 < Q < \chi^2_{\frac{\alpha}{2},3} = \chi^2_{0.0050,3} = 12.8380,$$

otherwise reject it.

Step 5: The value of the test statistic is

$$\chi^2 = 36(0.1863^2 + 0.1474^2 + 0.1266^2)/0.2493^2 = 41.9698.$$

Step 6: Since the value of the test statistic falls in the rejection region, reject the null hypothesis. There is a strong evidence to doubt the absence of third-order autoregressive process.

8-11.

Continuing with (7-a), $\hat{\alpha}$ was found to be BLUE of α in the Cochrane-Orcutt transformed model. The variance of $\hat{\alpha}$, which is the same as the Cramer-Rao lower bound is

$$\text{Var}(\hat{\alpha}) = \frac{\sigma_u^2}{1 - \rho^2 + (n-1)(1-\rho)^2} = \frac{\sigma^2(1-\rho^2)}{1 - \rho^2 + (n-1)(1-\rho)^2},$$

since $\sigma_u^2 = \sigma^2(1-\rho^2)$. Consider asymptotic variance of $\hat{\alpha}$

$$\text{Asympt. Var}(\hat{\alpha}) = (1/n)\lim_{n\to\infty}[(n)\text{Var}(\hat{\alpha})]$$

$$= (1/n)\lim_{n\to\infty}\left[\frac{\sigma^2(1-\rho^2)}{(1-\rho^2)/n + (1-1/n)(1-\rho)^2}\right]$$

$$= \frac{\sigma^2(1-\rho^2)}{n(1-\rho)^2}.$$

Consider the LSE of α, say $\tilde{\alpha}$, in the original model

$$\tilde{\alpha} = \bar{Y} = \Sigma Y_t/n = \Sigma(\alpha + \epsilon_t)/n = \alpha + \Sigma\epsilon_t/n.$$

Now

$$\begin{aligned}
\mathrm{Var}(\tilde{a}) &= E[\tilde{a} - E(\tilde{a})]^2 \\
&= E(\Sigma\epsilon_t/n)^2 \\
&= E(\Sigma\epsilon_t^2 + 2\sum_{s<t}\epsilon_t\epsilon_s)/n^2 \\
&= [\Sigma E(\epsilon_t^2) + 2\Sigma E(\epsilon_t\epsilon_s)]/n^2 \\
&= [n\sigma^2 + 2\sigma^2\sum_{t=1}^{n-1}(n - t)\rho^t]/n^2.
\end{aligned}$$

Consider the summation term above

$$\Sigma(n - t)\rho^t = (n - 1)\rho + (n - 2)\rho^2 + \cdots + \rho^{n-1}.$$

Multiplying the above equality by $(1 - \rho)^2$, we get

$$(1 - \rho)^2\Sigma(n - t)\rho^t = (n - 1)\rho - n\rho^2 + \rho^{n+1},$$

and dividing it by $(1 - \rho)^2$, we obtain

$$\Sigma(n - t)\rho^t = [(n - 1)\rho - n\rho^2 + \rho^{n+1}]/(1 - \rho)^2.$$

Substituting the above equality in the variance of $\tilde{a}$, we get

$$\begin{aligned}
\mathrm{Var}(\tilde{a}) &= \{n\sigma^2 + 2\sigma^2[(n - 1)\rho - n\rho^2 + \rho^{n+1}]/(1 - \rho)^2\}/n^2 \\
&= \sigma^2[n(1 - \rho^2) - 2\rho(1 - \rho^n)]/n^2(1 - \rho)^2.
\end{aligned}$$

Consider asymptotic variance of $\tilde{a}$

$$\begin{aligned}
\text{Asympt. Var}(\tilde{a}) &= (1/n)\lim_{n\to\infty}[(n)\mathrm{Var}(\tilde{a})] \\
&= (1/n)\lim_{n\to\infty}\{\frac{\sigma^2[(1 - \rho^2) - 2\rho(1 - \rho^n)/n]}{(1 - \rho)^2}\} \\
&= \frac{\sigma^2(1 - \rho^2)}{n(1 - \rho)^2},
\end{aligned}$$

which is equal to the asymptotic variance of $\hat{a}$ in the Cochrane-Orcutt transformed model. Thus, $\tilde{a}$ is asymptotically efficient.

8-12.

Consider

$$Y_t^* = \alpha W_t^* + \beta X_t^* + u_t, \qquad (t = 1, \ldots, n),$$

where ρ is known, u's are normally and independently distributed with mean of zero and variance of σ_u^2, and where for t = 1

$$Y_1^* = Y_1\sqrt{1 - \rho^2}, \qquad W_1^* = \sqrt{1 - \rho^2}, \qquad X_1^* = X_1\sqrt{1 - \rho^2},$$

and for (t = 2, ..., n)

$$Y_t^* = Y_t - \rho Y_{t-1}, \qquad W_t^* = 1 - \rho, \qquad X_t^* = X_t - \rho X_{t-1}.$$

Consider the log-likelihood function of the regression model

$$\begin{aligned} L &= \log[f(Y_1^*, \ldots, Y_n^*)] \\ &= \log[|\partial u/\partial Y| f(u_1, \ldots, u_n)] \\ &= \log[\sqrt{1 - \rho^2} f(u_1)\cdots f(u_n)] \\ &= (\tfrac{1}{2})\log(1 - \rho^2) - (\tfrac{n}{2})\log(2\pi\sigma_u^2) - \Sigma(Y_t^* - \alpha W_t^* - \beta X_t^*)^2/2\sigma_u^2. \end{aligned}$$

Differentiating L with respect to parameters α, β, and σ_u^2, we obtain

$$\partial L/\partial\alpha = \Sigma(Y_t^*W_t^* - \alpha W_t^{*2} - \beta X_t^*W_t^*)/\sigma_u^2,$$

$$\partial L/\partial\beta = \Sigma(Y_t^*X_t^* - \alpha W_t^*X_t^* - \beta X_t^{*2})/\sigma_u^2,$$

and

$$\partial L/\partial\sigma_u^2 = -n/2\sigma_u^2 + \Sigma(Y_t^* - \alpha W_t^* - \beta X_t^*)^2/2\sigma_u^4.$$

Equating these to zero and putting a "~" on the parameters to denote their estimated values, we obtain the MLE's of α, β, and σ_u^2, which are the same as the BLUE's (not shown here).

Differentiating the first-order derivatives with respect to α, β, and σ_u^2, we get

$$\partial L/\partial \alpha^2 = -\Sigma W_t^{*2}/\sigma_u^2,$$

$$\partial L/\partial \beta^2 = -\Sigma X_t^{*2}/\sigma_u^2,$$

$$\partial^2 L/\partial(\sigma_u^2)^2 = n/2\sigma_u^4 - \Sigma u_t^2/\sigma_u^6,$$

$$\partial^2 L/\partial\alpha\partial\beta = \partial^2 L/\partial\beta\partial\alpha = -\Sigma W_t^* X_t^*/\sigma_u^2,$$

$$\partial^2 L/\partial\alpha\partial\sigma_u^2 = \partial^2 L/\partial\sigma_u^2\partial\alpha = -\Sigma W_t^* u_t/\sigma_u^4,$$

and

$$\partial^2 L/\partial\beta\partial\sigma_u^2 = \partial^2 L/\partial\sigma_u^2\partial\beta = -\Sigma X_t^* u_t/\sigma_u^4.$$

Forming the variance-covariance matrix which we denote by Σ, we obtain

$$\Sigma = \begin{bmatrix} \mathrm{Var}(\tilde{\alpha}) & \mathrm{Cov}(\tilde{\alpha},\tilde{\beta}) & \mathrm{Cov}(\tilde{\alpha},\tilde{\sigma}_u^2) \\ \mathrm{Cov}(\tilde{\beta},\tilde{\alpha}) & \mathrm{Var}(\tilde{\beta}) & \mathrm{Cov}(\tilde{\beta},\tilde{\sigma}_u^2) \\ \mathrm{Cov}(\tilde{\sigma}_u^2,\tilde{\alpha}) & \mathrm{Cov}(\tilde{\sigma}_u^2,\tilde{\beta}) & \mathrm{Var}(\tilde{\sigma}_u^2) \end{bmatrix}$$

$$= \begin{bmatrix} -E(\partial^2 L/\partial\alpha^2) & -E(\partial^2 L/\partial\alpha\partial\beta) & -E(\partial^2 L/\partial\alpha\partial\sigma_u^2) \\ -E(\partial^2 L/\partial\beta\partial\alpha) & -E(\partial^2 L/\partial\beta^2) & -E(\partial^2 L/\partial\beta\partial\sigma_u^2) \\ -E(\partial^2 L/\partial\sigma_u^2\partial\alpha) & -E(\partial^2 L/\partial\sigma_u^2\partial\beta) & -E[\partial^2 L/\partial(\sigma_u^2)^2] \end{bmatrix}^{-1}$$

$$= \begin{bmatrix} \Sigma W_t^{*2}/\sigma_u^2 & \Sigma W_t^* X_t^*/\sigma_u^2 & 0 \\ \Sigma X_t^* W_t^*/\sigma_u^2 & \Sigma X_t^{*2}/\sigma_u^2 & 0 \\ 0 & 0 & n/2\sigma_u^4 \end{bmatrix}^{-1}$$

$$= \begin{bmatrix} \sigma_u^2 \Sigma X_t^{*2}/\Delta & -\sigma_u^2 \Sigma W_t^* X_t^*/\Delta & 0 \\ -\sigma_u^2 \Sigma X_t^* W_t^*/\Delta & \sigma_u^2 \Sigma W_t^{*2}/\Delta & 0 \\ 0 & 0 & 2\sigma_u^4/n \end{bmatrix},$$

where

$$\Delta = \Sigma W_t^{*2} \Sigma X_t^{*2} - (\Sigma W_t^* X_t^*)^2.$$

Now consider the prediction error

$$Y_{n+1}^* - \tilde{Y}_{n+1}^* = (\alpha - \tilde{\alpha})W_{n+1}^* + (\beta - \tilde{\beta})X_{n+1}^* + u_{n+1},$$

and its variance

$$\sigma_F^{*2} = \text{Var}(Y_{n+1}^* - \tilde{Y}_{n+1}^*),$$

or

$$\sigma_F^{*2} = W_{n+1}^{*2}\text{Var}(\tilde{\alpha}) + X_{n+1}^{*2}\text{Var}(\tilde{\beta}) + 2W_{n+1}^* X_{n+1}^* \text{Cov}(\tilde{\alpha},\tilde{\beta}) + \text{Var}(u_{n+1}).$$

Note that u_{n+1} is uncorrelated with $\tilde{\alpha}$ and $\tilde{\beta}$ because the last two are functions of u_1 through u_n. Substituting for variances and covariance in the above equation from the above matrix

$$\sigma_F^{*2} = (W_{n+1}^{*2}\sigma_u^2 \Sigma X_t^{*2} + X_{n+1}^{*2}\sigma_u^2 \Sigma W_t^{*2} - 2W_{n+1}^* X_{n+1}^* \sigma_u^2 \Sigma W_t^* X_t^*)/\Delta + \sigma_u^2$$

$$= \sigma_u^2[1 + (W_{n+1}^{*2}\Sigma X_t^{*2} + X_{n+1}^{*2}\Sigma W_t^{*2} - 2W_{n+1}^* X_{n+1}^* \Sigma W_t^* X_t^*)/\Delta].$$

8-13.

Consider the LSE of δ, say $\hat{\delta}$,

$$\hat{\delta} = \Sigma X_i Y_i / \Sigma Y_i^2.$$

Using $1/\hat{\delta}$ as an estimator of β we have

$$\begin{aligned}
\tilde{\beta} &= 1/\hat{\delta} \\
&= \Sigma Y_i^2 / \Sigma X_i Y_i \\
&= \Sigma(\beta X_i + \epsilon_i)^2 / \Sigma X_i(\beta X_i + \epsilon_i) \\
&= \beta + \frac{\beta \Sigma X_i \epsilon_i + \Sigma \epsilon_i^{\,2}}{\beta \Sigma (X_i - \bar{X})^2 + n\beta \bar{X}^2 + \Sigma X_i \epsilon_i} \\
&= \beta + \frac{\beta \Sigma X_i \epsilon_i / n + \Sigma \epsilon_i^2 / n}{\beta \Sigma x_i'^{\,2}/n + \beta \bar{X}^2 + \Sigma X_i \epsilon_i / n}.
\end{aligned}$$

$$\begin{aligned}
\text{plim}(\tilde{\beta}) &= \beta + \text{plim}\left(\frac{\beta \Sigma X_i \epsilon_i / n + \Sigma \epsilon_i^2 / n}{\beta \Sigma x_i'^{\,2}/n + \beta \bar{X}^2 + \Sigma X_i \epsilon_i / n}\right) \\
&= \beta + \frac{\beta \text{plim}(\Sigma X_i \epsilon_i / n) + \text{plim}(\Sigma \epsilon_i^2 / n)}{\beta \text{plim}(\Sigma x_i'^{\,2}/n) + \beta \text{plim}(\bar{X}^2) + \text{plim}(\Sigma X_i \epsilon_i / n)} \\
&= \beta + \frac{\sigma^2}{\beta(\sigma_X^2 + \mu_X^2)},
\end{aligned}$$

since

$$\text{plim}(\Sigma X_i \epsilon_i / n) = \text{plim}(\Sigma x_i' \epsilon_i / n) = 0,$$

because $\Sigma x_i' \epsilon_i / n$ is a consistent estimator of the population covariance of X_i and ϵ_i, which is zero (because they are independent),

$$\text{plim}(\Sigma \epsilon_i^2 / n) = \text{plim}(\Sigma \epsilon_i'^{\,2} / n),$$

and $\Sigma\epsilon_i'^2/n$, $\Sigma x_i'^2/n$, and $\bar{X}$ are consistent estimators of the variance of ϵ_i (or σ^2), the variance of X_i (or σ_X^2), and the mean of X_i (or μ_X), respectively, which are finite numbers different from zero. Thus, $\tilde{\beta}$ is not a consistent estimator of β.

8-14.

Lagging the demand function by one period and substituting the result into the supply function, we get

$$Q_t = \gamma + a\delta + \beta\delta Q_{t-1} + \delta u_{t-1} + v_t.$$

Successive substitution for Q_{t-1}, Q_{t-2}, ... leads to

$$Q_t = (\gamma + a\delta)/(1 + \beta\delta) + \sum_{i=0}^{\infty} (\beta\delta)^i(\delta u_{t-1-i} + v_{t-i}),$$

Now

$$E(Q_t) = (\gamma + a\delta)/(1 + \beta\delta),$$

and

$$\begin{aligned} \text{Cov}(Q_t, u_t) &= E[Q_t - E(Q_t)][u_t - E(u_t)] \\ &= E[\Sigma(\beta\delta)^i(\delta u_{t-1-i} + v_{t-i})u_t] \\ &= 0. \end{aligned}$$

Consider the LSE of β, say $\hat{\beta}$,

$$\hat{\beta} = \beta + (\Sigma q_t' u_t'/n)/(\Sigma q_t'^2/n).$$

Then

$$\text{plim } \hat{\beta} = \beta + \text{plim}(\Sigma q_t' u_t'/n)/\text{plim}(\Sigma q_t'^2/n) = \beta,$$

since $\Sigma q_t' u_t'/n$ is a consistent estimator of the population covariance of Q_t and u_t, which is equal to zero, and $\Sigma q_t'^2/n$ is a consistent estimator of the variance of Q_t, which is a finite value different from zero. So, $\hat{\beta}$ is a consistent estimator of β.

CHAPTER 9

9-1.

Since m^*_{xy} is positive, the weighted regression estimate of β is the positive root of the following quadratic equation

$$2(0.1401)\tilde{\beta}^2 + [0.1669 - 2(0.1194)]\tilde{\beta} - 0.1401 = 0,$$

or

$$\tilde{\beta} = 0.8470.$$

Now the weighted regression estimate of α is

$$\tilde{\alpha} = \bar{Y}^* - \tilde{\beta}\bar{X}^* = 0.2136 - 0.8470(2.9773) = -2.3081.$$

Thus

$$Y_i^* = -2.3081 + 0.8470X_i^* + e_i.$$

9-2.

The number of observations and the values of $\bar{X}_g$ and $\bar{Y}_g$ for different income classes are presented in table 9-1.

TABLE 9-1

Values of n, $\bar{X}$, and $\bar{Y}$		
n	$\bar{X}$	$\bar{Y}$
51	15.5000	13.9000
44	20.0000	16.7430
36	23.7222	20.4221
26	28.0769	23.6423
16	31.8750	26.3627
8	36.0000	28.2500

The estimated regression equation based on the above information is

$$\bar{Y}_g = \underset{(0.7593)}{2.1120} + \underset{(0.0328)}{0.7553}\bar{X}_g + e_g, \qquad R^2 = 0.9925,$$

whereas that of based on the information as originally given in the table (9-2), section (9-2) of the text,[1] is

$$\bar{Y}_g = \underset{(0.9858)}{1.9253} + \underset{(0.0425)}{0.7637}\bar{X}_g + e_g, \qquad R^2 = 0.9729.$$

9-3.

Consider the log-likelihood function for $(Y_1, \ldots, Y_n)$

$$L = (\frac{-n}{2})\log(2\pi\sigma^2) - \sum_x (Y_i - \alpha - \beta X_i)^2/2\sigma^2 - \sum_o (Y_i - \alpha - \beta\xi_i)^2/2\sigma^2,$$

where $\sum_x$ and $\sum_o$ represent the summation over complete and incomplete pairs. Differentiating L with respect to each of the ξ_i's, α, and β, setting each of them equal to zero, and putting a "^" on the unknown parameters to denote their MLE's, we have

(1) $$Y_i - \hat{\alpha} - \hat{\beta}\hat{\xi}_i = 0,$$

(2) $$\sum_x (Y_i - \hat{\alpha} - \hat{\beta}X_i) + \sum_o (Y_i - \hat{\alpha} - \hat{\beta}\hat{\xi}_i) = 0,$$

and

(3) $$\sum_x (Y_i - \hat{\alpha} - \hat{\beta}X_i)X_i + \sum_o (Y_i - \hat{\alpha} - \hat{\beta}\hat{\xi}_i)\hat{\xi}_i = 0,$$

noting that (1) represents m_x (or the number of incomplete pairs) equations. Substituting (1) into (2) and (3), we get

$$\sum_x (Y_i - \hat{\alpha} - \hat{\beta}X_i) = 0,$$

and

---

[1] P. 372. In the earlier print of the second edition of the text, the first entry under $\bar{X}$ is incorrectly printed as 15.10.

$$\sum_x (Y_i - \hat{a} - \hat{\beta}X_i)X_i = 0,$$

which yield

$$\hat{\beta}_c = \sum_x (X_i - \bar{X})(Y_i - \bar{Y})/\sum_x (X_i - \bar{X})^2,$$

and

$$\hat{a}_c = \bar{Y} - \hat{\beta}\bar{X},$$

since $\bar{X} = \sum_x X_i/n_x$, and $\bar{Y} = \sum_x Y_i/n_x$, where n_x is the number of complete pairs. Solving for $\hat{\xi}_i$'s from (1), we obtain

$$\hat{\xi}_i = (Y_i - \hat{a}_c)/\hat{\beta}_c.$$

9-4.

Consider the least squares estimation based on the first twelve observations

$$Y_i = 210.4600 - 1.5780X_i + e_i.$$

Now

$$\tilde{\xi}_{13} = \frac{130 - 210.4600}{-1.5780} = 50.9886,$$

$$\tilde{\xi}_{14} = \frac{140 - 210.4600}{-1.5780} = 44.6515,$$

and

$$\bar{\xi} = (\tilde{\xi}_{13} + \tilde{\xi}_{14})/2 = 47.8201.$$

Using the formula (9.64), section (9-3) of the text,[1] we get

$$\text{Est. }\left[\frac{\text{Var}(\hat{\beta}_c)}{\text{Var}(\hat{\beta}_y)}\right] = 1 + \frac{20.0796 + \frac{12(2)(70 - 47.8201)^2}{14}}{2250} = 1.3837,$$

meaning that the loss of efficiency is estimated to be 38.37%.

---

[1]P. 382.

9-5.

Values of $\hat{\beta}$ for selected values of λ are presented in table 9-2.

TABLE 9-2

Values of λ and $\hat{\beta}$	
λ	$\hat{\beta}$
0	0.8402
1	0.8452
2	0.8470
5	0.8493
10	0.8504
20	0.8511
∞	0.8519

The relation between $\hat{\beta}$ and λ is depicted in figure 9-1.

FIGURE 9-1

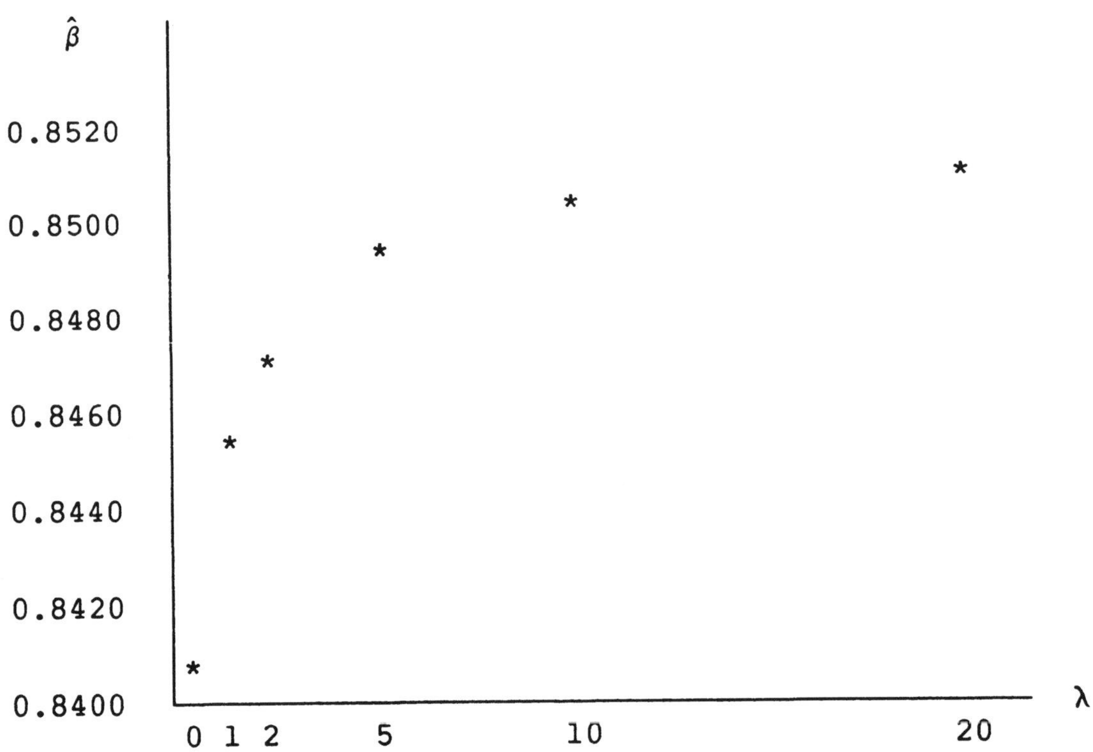

9-6.

Consider the regression model

$$Y_i = \alpha + \beta X_i + \epsilon_i,$$

where X contains error, so that instead of X_i we observe X_i^*, which is given as

$$X_i^* = X_i + w_i,$$

where w_i represents the error in measuring the i-th value of X,

$$\epsilon_i \sim N(0, \sigma^2), \qquad \text{and} \qquad w_i \sim N(0, \sigma_w^2),$$

and $$E(\epsilon_i \epsilon_j) = E(\epsilon_i w_i) = E(w_i w_j) = 0 \qquad (i \neq j).$$

Thus $$Y_i = \alpha + \beta X_i^* + \epsilon_i^*,$$

where $$\epsilon_i^* = \epsilon_i - \beta w_i.$$

Consider the instrumental variable Z such that

$$X_i^* = \gamma + \delta Z_i + u_i \qquad (\delta \neq 0),$$

where Z is correlated with X but asymptotically uncorrelated with ϵ and w, the disturbance u is uncorrelated with Z, and

$$E(u_i u_j) = E(u_i \epsilon_i) = E(u_i w_i) = 0 \qquad (i \neq j).$$

Consider the three common terms in the asymptotic variances of $\beta\dagger$ and $\alpha\dagger$, or the formulas (9.25a) and (9.25b), section (9-1) of the text.[1] The first term which appears in both numerators is

$$\sigma_{\epsilon^*}^2 = \text{Var}(\epsilon_i^*) = \text{Var}(\epsilon_i - \beta w_i) = \sigma^2 + \beta^2 \sigma_w^2.$$

The second term which also appears in both numerators is

$$\text{plim}(\Sigma z_i'^2/n) = \sigma_z^2.$$

---

[1] P. 360.

The last common term which appears in both denominators is

$$\text{plim}(\Sigma x_i^{*\prime} z_i^{\prime}/n)^2 = [\text{plim}(\Sigma x_i^{*\prime} z_i^{\prime}/n)]^2$$

$$= \{\text{plim}[\Sigma(\delta z_i^{\prime} + u_i^{\prime})z_i^{\prime}/n]\}^2$$

$$= \{\text{plim}[\Sigma(\delta z_i^{\prime 2} + u_i^{\prime} z_i^{\prime})/n]\}^2$$

$$= [\text{plim}(\Sigma\delta z_i^{\prime 2}/n) + \text{plim}(u_i^{\prime} z_i^{\prime}/n)]^2$$

$$= \delta^2(\sigma_z^2)^2.$$

Substituting the above results into the asymptotic variances of $\beta\dagger$ and $\alpha\dagger$, we obtain

$$\text{Asympt. Var}\sqrt{n}(\beta\dagger - \beta) = \frac{\sigma^2 + \beta^2\sigma_w^2}{\delta^2\sigma_z^2},$$

and

$$\text{Asympt. Var}\sqrt{n}(\alpha\dagger - \alpha) = (\sigma^2 + \beta^2\sigma_w^2)[1 + \frac{\text{plim}(\bar{X}^{*2})}{\delta^2\sigma_z^2}].$$

Consider

$$X_i^* = X_i + w_i = \gamma + \delta Z_i + u_i,$$

and

$$\text{Var}(X_i^*) = \text{Var}(X_i + w_i) = \text{Var}(\gamma + \delta Z_i + u_i),$$

or

$$\sigma_x^2 + \sigma_w^2 = \delta^2\sigma_z^2 + \sigma_u^2,$$

because X and Z are uncorrelated with w and u, respectively. Now the stronger the relation between X* and Z, *ceteris paribus*,[1] the smaller the σ_u^2. However, since variance of X* remains

---

[1]If all other relevant things, factors, or elements remain constant.

constant, because it is the sum of variances of X and w which are not changed, the smaller the variance of u, the larger the variance of δZ. Thus the stronger the relation between X* and Z, the smaller σ_u^2, the larger $\delta^2\sigma_z^2$, and the smaller the asymptotic variances of the instrumental variables estimators of α and β.

Alternatively we may present the asymptotic variances of $\beta\dagger$ and $\alpha\dagger$ in terms of the probability limit of the coefficient of determination between X* and Z, defined as

$$\text{plim}(R^2) = \frac{\text{plim}(\Sigma x_i^{*\prime} z_i^{\prime}/n)^2}{\text{plim}(\Sigma x_i^{*\prime 2}/n)\text{plim}(\Sigma z_i^{\prime 2}/n)},$$

which may be written as

$$\frac{\text{plim}(\Sigma z_i^{\prime 2}/n)}{\text{plim}(\Sigma x_i^{*\prime} z_i^{\prime}/n)^2} = \frac{1}{\text{plim}(R^2)\text{plim}(\Sigma x_i^{*\prime 2}/n)}.$$

Substituting the above result into the asymptotic variances of $\beta\dagger$ and $\alpha\dagger$, we obtain

$$\text{Asympt. Var}\sqrt{n}(\beta\dagger - \beta) = \frac{\sigma^2 + \beta^2\sigma_w^2}{\text{plim}(R^2)\text{plim}(\Sigma x_i^{*\prime 2}/n)},$$

and

$$\text{Asympt. Var}\sqrt{n}(\alpha\dagger - \alpha) = (\sigma^2 + \beta^2\sigma_w^2)[1 + \frac{\text{plim}(\bar{X}^{*2})}{\text{plim}(R^2)\text{plim}(\Sigma x_i^{*\prime 2}/n)}].$$

Now the stronger the relation between X* and Z, *ceteris paribus*, the larger the $\text{plim}(R^2)$. However, $\text{plim}(\Sigma x_i^{*\prime 2}/n)$ remains constant because X* is the sum of X and w which are not changed. Thus the stronger the relation between the two, the smaller the asymptotic variances of the instrumental variables estimators of α and β.

9-7.

Consider

$$m^*_{xx} = \Sigma x_i^{*\prime 2}/n$$

$$= \Sigma(x_i' + w_i')^2/n$$

$$= \Sigma x_i'^2/n + 2\Sigma x_i' w_i'/n + \Sigma w_i'^2/n.$$

Thus

$$\text{plim}(m^*_{xx}) = \sigma_x^2 + \sigma_w^2.$$

Now

$$m^*_{xy} = \Sigma x_i^{*\prime} y_i^{*\prime}/n$$

$$= \Sigma x_i^{*\prime}(\beta x_i^{*\prime} + \epsilon_i^{*\prime})/n$$

$$= \beta\Sigma x_i^{*\prime 2}/n + \Sigma x_i^{*\prime}\epsilon_i^{*\prime}/n$$

$$= \beta\Sigma x_i^{*\prime 2}/n + \Sigma(x_i' + w_i')(\epsilon_i' - \beta w_i')/n$$

$$= \beta\Sigma x_i^{*\prime 2}/n + (\Sigma x_i'\epsilon_i' + \Sigma w_i'\epsilon_i' - \beta\Sigma x_i' w_i' - \beta\Sigma w_i'^2)/n.$$

Thus

$$\text{plim}(m^*_{xy}) = \beta(\sigma_x^2 + \sigma_w^2) - \beta\sigma_w^2 = \beta\sigma_x^2.$$

Further,

$$m^*_{yy} = \Sigma y_i^{*\prime 2}/n$$

$$= \Sigma(\beta x_i^{*\prime} + \epsilon_i^{*\prime})^2/n$$

$$= \Sigma[\beta(x_i' + w_i') + \epsilon_i' - \beta w_i']^2/n$$

$$= \beta^2\Sigma x_i'^2/n + 2\beta\Sigma x_i'\epsilon_i'/n + \Sigma\epsilon_i'/n.$$

Thus

$$\text{plim}(m^*_{yy}) = \beta^2\sigma^2_x + \sigma^2.$$

Taking probability limit of the quadratic equation, we have

$$\lambda\text{plim}(\tilde{\beta}^2)\text{plim}(m^*_{xy})$$

$$+ \text{plim}(\tilde{\beta})[\text{plim}(m^*_{xx}) - \lambda\text{plim}(m^*_{yy})] - \text{plim}(m^*_{xy}) = 0.$$

Substituting for probability limits of m^*_{xx}, m^*_{xy}, and m^*_{yy} in the above equation, we have

$$\lambda\beta\sigma^2_x\text{plim}(\tilde{\beta}^2) + [\sigma^2_x + \sigma^2_w - \lambda(\beta^2\sigma^2_x + \sigma^2)]\text{plim}(\tilde{\beta}) - \beta\sigma^2_x = 0.$$

Simplifying the above equation noting that $\sigma^2_w = \lambda\sigma^2$ and that σ^2_x is a finite number different from zero

$$\lambda\beta\text{plim}(\tilde{\beta}^2) + (1 - \lambda\beta^2)\text{plim}(\tilde{\beta}) - \beta = 0.$$

To show that $\tilde{\beta}$ is a consistent estimator of β, it is sufficient to show that the above equation has a solution at the point where $\text{plim}(\tilde{\beta}) = \beta$. Note that the latter condition implies $\text{plim}(\tilde{\beta}^2) = \beta^2$. Substituting these two conditions into the above equation, we obtain

$$\lambda\beta\beta^2 + (1 - \lambda\beta^2)\beta - \beta = 0 \qquad \text{Q.E.D.}$$

Thus, $\tilde{\beta}$ is in fact a consistent estimator of β.

Now maximizing the log-likelihood function (9.14), section (9-1) of the text,[1] with respect to α, β, and the X's (which are treated as unknown parameters) is equivalent to minimizing

$$S = \lambda\Sigma(Y^*_i - \alpha - \beta X_i)^2 + \Sigma(X^*_i - X_i)^2,$$

noting that $\sigma^2_w = \lambda\sigma^2$. Differentiating S with respect to the

[1] P. 352.

unknown parameters, equating them to zero, and putting a "~" on the parameters to denote their MLE's, we obtain

(1) $$\Sigma(Y_i^* - \tilde{\alpha} - \tilde{\beta}\tilde{X}_i) = 0,$$

(2) $$\Sigma(Y_i^* - \tilde{\alpha} - \tilde{\beta}\tilde{X}_i)\tilde{X}_i = 0,$$

and

(3) $$\lambda\tilde{\beta}(Y_i^* - \tilde{\alpha} - \tilde{\beta}\tilde{X}_i) + X_i^* - \tilde{X}_i = 0,$$

where (3) represents n equations. Finding $\tilde{\alpha}$ from (1), we get

(4) $$\tilde{\alpha} = \bar{Y}^* - \tilde{\beta}\bar{X},$$

where $\bar{X} = \Sigma\tilde{X}_i/n$. Substituting (4) into (2), we obtain

(5) $$\tilde{\beta} = \Sigma\tilde{x}_i'y_i^{*\prime}/\Sigma\tilde{x}_i'^2.$$

Consider (3). Summing over all i's and dividing by n, we get

(6) $$\lambda\tilde{\beta}(\bar{Y}^* - \tilde{\alpha} - \tilde{\beta}\bar{X}) + \bar{X}^* - \bar{X} = 0,$$

where $\bar{X}^* = \Sigma X_i^*/n$. Subtracting (6) from (3) and rearranging, we obtain

(7) $$\tilde{x}_i' = (\lambda\tilde{\beta}y_i^{*\prime} + x_i^{*\prime})/(1 + \lambda\tilde{\beta}^2).$$

Multiplying (7) by $y_i^{*\prime}$ and summing over all i's, we get

(8) $$\Sigma\tilde{x}_i'y_i^{*\prime} = n(\lambda\tilde{\beta}m_{yy}^* + m_{xy}^*)/(1 + \lambda\tilde{\beta}^2).$$

Squaring (7) and summing over all i's, we obtain

(9) $$\Sigma\tilde{x}_i'^2 = n(\lambda^2\tilde{\beta}^2m_{yy}^* + 2\lambda\tilde{\beta}m_{xy}^* + m_{xx}^*)/(1 + \lambda\tilde{\beta}^2)^2.$$

Substituting (7) and (8) into (5) and simplifying, we obtain the weighted regression estimator of β

$$\tilde{\beta}^2\lambda m_{xy}^* + \tilde{\beta}(m_{xx}^* - \lambda m_{yy}^*) - m_{xy}^* = 0.$$

9-8.

Consider the regression model

$$Y_i = \alpha + \beta X_i + \epsilon_i,$$

where instead of X_i we observe X_i^*, given as

$$X_i^* = X_i + w_i,$$

where w_i represents the error in measuring the i-th value of X^*,

$$\epsilon_i \sim N(0, \sigma^2), \qquad \text{and} \qquad w_i \sim N(0, \sigma_i^{*2} = X_i^2/10^1),$$

and

$$E(\epsilon_i w_i) = E(\epsilon_i \epsilon_j) = E(w_i w_j) = 0 \qquad (i \neq j).$$

Thus

$$Y_i = \alpha + \beta X_i^* + \epsilon_i^*,$$

where

$$\epsilon_i^* = \epsilon_i - \beta w_i.$$

We start from the LSE of β, say $\hat{\beta}$

$$\begin{aligned}
\hat{\beta} &= \Sigma x_i^{*\prime} y_i^{\prime} / \Sigma x_i^{*\prime 2} \\
&= \Sigma x_i^{*\prime}(\beta x_i^{*\prime} + \epsilon_i^{\prime} - \beta w_i^{\prime}) / \Sigma x_i^{*\prime 2} \\
&= \beta + \Sigma x_i^{*\prime}(\epsilon_i^{\prime} - \beta w_i^{\prime}) / \Sigma x_i^{*\prime 2} \\
&= \beta + \frac{\Sigma(x_i^{\prime} + w_i^{\prime})(\epsilon_i^{\prime} - \beta w_i^{\prime})/n}{\Sigma(x_i^{\prime} + w_i^{\prime})^2/n} \\
&= \beta + \frac{\Sigma x_i^{\prime}\epsilon_i^{\prime}/n - \beta\Sigma x_i^{\prime}w_i^{\prime}/n + \Sigma w_i^{\prime}\epsilon_i^{\prime}/n - \beta\Sigma w_i^{\prime 2}/n}{\Sigma x_i^{\prime 2}/n + 2\Sigma x_i^{\prime}w_i^{\prime}/n + \Sigma w_i^{\prime 2}/n}.
\end{aligned}$$

---

[1] In the earlier print of the second edition of the text, this is incorrectly printed as $\bar{X}_i^2/10$.

Now

$$\text{plim}(\hat{\beta}) = \beta - \frac{\beta\,\text{plim}(\Sigma w_i'^2/n)}{\lim\limits_{n\to\infty}(\Sigma x_i'^2/n) + \text{plim}(\Sigma w_i'^2/n)}$$

$$= \beta - \frac{\beta \lim\limits_{n\to\infty}(\Sigma X_i^2/10n)}{\sigma_x^2 + \lim\limits_{n\to\infty}(\Sigma X_i^2/10n)}$$

$$= \beta - \frac{0.10\beta(\sigma_x^2 + \mu_x^2)}{\sigma_x^2 + 0.10(\sigma_x^2 + \mu_x^2)}$$

$$= \left(\frac{\sigma_x^2}{1.10\sigma_x^2 + 0.10\mu_x^2}\right)\beta.$$

Thus a consistent estimator of β is

$$\left(\frac{1.10\hat{\sigma}_x^2 + 0.10\hat{\mu}_x^2}{\hat{\sigma}_x^2}\right)\hat{\beta},$$

where $\hat{\mu}_x^2$ and $\hat{\sigma}_x^2$ are consistent estimators of μ_x^2 and σ_x^2. In order to find $\hat{\mu}_x^2$ consider

$$\text{plim}(\bar{X}^{*2}) = [\text{plim}(\bar{X}^*)]^2$$

$$= [\text{plim}(\bar{X} + \bar{w})]^2$$

$$= [\text{plim}(\bar{X}) + \text{plim}(\bar{w})]^2$$

$$= [\text{plim}(\bar{X})]^2$$

$$= \mu_x^2,$$

which implies that $\hat{\mu}_x^2 = \bar{X}^{*2}$ is a consistent estimator of μ_x^2.

Now in order to find $\hat{\sigma}_x^2$ consider

$$\begin{aligned}
\text{plim}[\Sigma(X_i^* - \bar{X}^*)^2/n] &= \text{plim}(\Sigma x_i^{*\prime 2}/n) \\
&= \text{plim}[\Sigma(x_i' + w_i')^2/n] \\
&= \text{plim}[\Sigma(x_i'^2 + 2x_i'w_i' + w_i'^2)/n] \\
&= \lim_{n\to\infty}(\Sigma x_i'^2/n) + \text{plim}(\Sigma w_i'^2/n) \\
&= \sigma_x^2 + \lim_{n\to\infty}(\Sigma X_i^2/10n) \\
&= \sigma_x^2 + 0.10(\sigma_x^2 + \mu_x^2) \\
&= 1.10\sigma_x^2 + 0.10\mu_x^2,
\end{aligned}$$

which means that

$$1.10\hat{\sigma}_x^2 + 0.10\hat{\mu}_x^2 = \Sigma(X_i^* - \bar{X}^*)^2/n$$

is a consistent estimator of

$$1.10\sigma_x^2 + 0.10\mu_x^2,$$

and hence

$$\hat{\sigma}_x^2 = [\Sigma(X_i^* - \bar{X}^*)^2/n - 0.10\bar{X}^{*2}]/1.10,$$

is a consistent estimator of σ_x^2. Therefore, a consistent estimator of β is

$$\left[\frac{1.10\Sigma(X_i^* - \bar{X}^*)^2/n}{\Sigma(X_i^* - \bar{X}^*)^2/n - 0.10\bar{X}^{*2}}\right]\hat{\beta}.$$

9-9-a.

The LSE of the regression equation (9.49), section (9-2) of the text,[1] is

$$M_g = \underset{(268.9800)}{139.2800} + \underset{(0.0257)}{0.0867}X_{ig} + e_{ig}, \qquad R^2 = 0.3874,$$

where M_g is the midpoint of the g-th group of saving, and where $M_1 = -250$ and $M_6 = 2,250$.

9-9-b.

The LSE of the regression equation (9.52), section (9-2) of the text,[2] is

$$Y_{ig} = \underset{(1895.8000)}{-6590.7000} + \underset{(0.1758)}{0.9702}M^*_g + e_{ig}, \qquad R^2 = 0.6285,$$

where M^*_g is the midpoint of the g-th group of income.

9-9-c.

Step 1: The null and the alternative hypotheses are

$$H_o: \beta = 0,$$

$$H_a: \beta \neq 0.$$

Steps 2 & 3: The test statistic and its distribution are

$$F = \frac{\sum_g n_g(\bar{Y}_g - \bar{Y})^2/(G - 1)}{\sum_i\sum_g(Y_{ig} - \bar{Y}_g)^2/(n - G)} \sim F_{G-1,n-G},$$

where $(g = 1, \ldots, G)$, $G = 5$, $(i = 1, \ldots, n_g)$, and

$$\sum_g n_g = n = 20.$$

---

[1]P. 374.

[2]P. 375.

Step 4: Do not reject the null hypothesis if

$$F < F_{\alpha,G-1,n-G} = F_{0.01,4,15} = 4.89,$$

otherwise reject it.

Step 5: The value of test statistic is

$$F = [903{,}338{,}000/(5 - 1)]/[15{,}926{,}000/(20 - 5)] = 212.72.$$

Step 6: Since the value of the test statistic falls in the rejection region, reject the null hypothesis. There is a strong evidence that the mean value of Y is affected by moving from one category of the values of X into another.

9-10.

Let $\hat{\beta}_i$, (i = 1, 2, 3), denote the estimator of β using the i-th way. Consider the first estimator

$$\hat{\beta}_1 = \sum_c (X_i - \bar{X}_c)(Y_i - \bar{Y}_c)/\sum_c (X_i - \bar{X}_c)^2,$$

where $\bar{X}_c$ and $\bar{Y}_c$ are the sample means of X and Y calculated from the complete pairs, and summations are over all such pairs. Since $\hat{\beta}_1$ is LSE of β in the class of all estimators that use the same information, it is unbiased and consistent.

For the second way of estimating β consider

$$Y_i = \alpha + \beta X_i + \epsilon_i,$$

and

$$X_i = \gamma + \delta Z_i + u_i,$$

where X is stochastic but independent of ϵ, Z is non-stochastic,

$$\epsilon_i \sim N(0, \sigma^2), \qquad \text{and} \qquad u_i \sim N(0, \sigma_u^2),$$

and

$$E(\epsilon_i \epsilon_j) = E(\epsilon_i u_i) = E(\epsilon_i u_j) = E(u_i u_j) = 0 \qquad (i \neq j).$$

Consider the following notation for triplets Y_i, X_i, and Z_i, $(i = 1, \ldots, n)$

$\sum_y$ the summation over all triplets for which Y is observed,

$\sum_x$ the summation over all triplets for which X is observed,

$\sum_o$ the summation over all triplets for which $\hat{X}$ is calculated,

n the number triplets for which Y is observed,

n_x the number triplets for which X is observed,

and

m_x the number triplets for which $\hat{X}$ is calculated.

Further,

$$\bar{Y}_y = \sum_y Y_i/n, \qquad \bar{\epsilon}_y = \sum_y \epsilon_i/n,$$

$$\bar{X}_y = (\sum_x X_i + \sum_o \hat{X}_i)/n, \qquad \bar{X}_x = \sum_x X_i/n_x,$$

$$\bar{Z}_y = \sum_y Z_i/n, \qquad \bar{Z}_x = \sum_x Z_i/n_x,$$

$$n_x + m_x = n, \qquad \hat{X}_i = \hat{\gamma} + \hat{\delta} Z_i,$$

where

$$\hat{\delta} = \sum_x (Z_i - \bar{Z}_x)(X_i - \bar{X}_x)/\sum_x (Z_i - \bar{Z}_x)^2,$$

and

$$\hat{\gamma} = \bar{X}_x - \hat{\delta}\bar{Z}_x.$$

The second estimator of β is defined as

$$\hat{\beta}_2 = \frac{\sum_x (X_i - \bar{X}_y)(Y_i - \bar{Y}_y) + \sum_o (\hat{X}_i - \bar{X}_y)(Y_i - \bar{Y}_y)}{\sum_x (X_i - \bar{X}_y)^2 + \sum_o (\hat{X}_i - \bar{X}_y)^2} = \frac{A}{B}.$$

Now

$$\bar{Y}_y = \sum_y Y_i/n = \sum_y(a + \beta X_i + \epsilon_i)/n = a + \beta\sum_y X_i/n + \bar{\epsilon}_y.$$

But

$$\sum_y X_i/n = \sum_x X_i/n + \sum_o(\hat{X}_i + \hat{u}_i)/n = \bar{X}_y + \sum_o \hat{u}_i/n = \bar{X}_y + \hat{u}_o,$$

where

$$\hat{u}_o = \sum_o \hat{u}_i/n.$$

Then

$$\bar{Y}_y = a + \beta\bar{X}_y + \bar{\epsilon}_y + \beta\hat{u}_o,$$

and

$$Y_i - \bar{Y}_y = \beta(X_i - \bar{X}_y) + \epsilon_i - \bar{\epsilon}_y - \beta\hat{u}_o.$$

Thus we can write

$$\begin{aligned} A = &\sum_x(X_i - \bar{X}_y)[\beta(X_i - \bar{X}_y) + \epsilon_i - \bar{\epsilon}_y - \beta\hat{u}_o] \\ &+ \sum_o(\hat{X}_i - \bar{X}_y)[\beta(X_i - \bar{X}_y) + \epsilon_i - \bar{\epsilon}_y - \beta\hat{u}_o] \\ = &\ \beta[\sum_x(X_i - \bar{X}_y)^2 + \sum_o(\hat{X}_i - \bar{X}_y)(X_i - \bar{X}_y)] \\ &+ \sum_x(X_i - \bar{X}_y)(\epsilon_i - \bar{\epsilon}_y) + \sum_o(\hat{X}_i - \bar{X}_y)(\epsilon_i - \bar{\epsilon}_y), \end{aligned}$$

since

$$\sum_x(X_i - \bar{X}_y)\hat{u}_o + \sum_o(\hat{X}_i - \bar{X}_y)\hat{u}_o = 0.$$

Further,

$$\begin{aligned} \sum_o(\hat{X}_i - \bar{X}_y)(X_i - \bar{X}_y) &= \sum_o(\hat{X}_i - \bar{X}_y)(\hat{X}_i + \hat{u}_i - \bar{X}_y) \\ &= \sum_o(\hat{X}_i - \bar{X}_y)^2 + \sum_o(\hat{X}_i - \bar{X}_y)\hat{u}_i. \end{aligned}$$

Therefore,

$$A = \beta[\sum_x(X_i - \bar{X}_y)^2 + \sum_o(\hat{X}_i - \bar{X}_y)^2] + \sum_x(X_i - \bar{X}_y)(\epsilon_i - \bar{\epsilon}_y)$$

$$+ \sum_o(\hat{X}_i - \bar{X}_y)(\epsilon_i - \bar{\epsilon}_y + \beta\hat{u}_i),$$

so that

$$\hat{\beta}_2 = \beta + \frac{\sum_x(X_i - \bar{X}_y)(\epsilon_i - \bar{\epsilon}_y) + \sum_o(\hat{X}_i - \bar{X}_y)(\epsilon_i - \bar{\epsilon}_y + \beta\hat{u}_i)}{\sum_x(X_i - \bar{X}_y)^2 + \sum_o(\hat{X}_i - \bar{X}_y)^2}.$$

Now

$$E(\hat{\beta}_2) \neq \beta,$$

since disturbance u is present in both the numerator and the denominator of $\hat{\beta}_2$ through X's, and hence we cannot separate out u's when we take mathematical expectation of $\hat{\beta}_2$. However, dividing all the terms by n and taking probability limit, we get

$$\text{plim}(\hat{\beta}_2) = \beta,$$

since

$$\text{plim}[\sum_x(X_i - \bar{X}_y)(\epsilon_i - \bar{\epsilon}_y)/n] = 0,$$

$$\text{plim}[\sum_o(\hat{X}_i - \bar{X}_y)(\epsilon_i - \bar{\epsilon}_y)/n] = 0,$$

$$\text{plim}[\sum_o(\hat{X}_i - \bar{X}_y)\hat{u}_i/n] = \text{plim}[\sum_o(\hat{\gamma} + \hat{\delta}Z_i - \bar{X}_y)\hat{u}_i/n] = 0,$$

$$\text{plim}[\sum_x(X_i - \bar{X}_y)^2/n] \neq 0,$$

and

$$\text{plim}[\sum_o(\hat{X}_i - \bar{X}_y)^2/n] \neq 0,$$

since Z and u, Z and ϵ, and X and ϵ are uncorrelated, and the variances of X and Z are finite numbers different from zero. Thus $\hat{\beta}_2$ is a consistent estimator of β.

Consider the third estimator of β

$$\hat{\beta}_3 = \hat{\mu}/\hat{\delta}$$

$$= \frac{\sum_y (Z_i - \bar{Z}_y)(Y_i - \bar{Y}_y)/\sum_y (Z_i - \bar{Z}_y)^2}{\sum_x (Z_i - \bar{Z}_x)(X_i - \bar{X}_x)/\sum_x (Z_i - \bar{Z}_x)^2}$$

$$= \frac{\mu + \sum_y (Z_i - \bar{Z}_y)\epsilon_i^*/\sum_y (Z_i - \bar{Z}_y)^2}{\delta + \sum_x (Z_i - \bar{Z}_x)u_i/\sum_x (Z_i - \bar{Z}_x)^2}$$

$$= \frac{\beta\delta + \sum_y (Z_i - \bar{Z}_y)(\beta u_i + \epsilon_i)/\sum_y (Z_i - \bar{Z}_y)^2}{\delta + \sum_x (Z_i - \bar{Z}_x)u_i/\sum_x (Z_i - \bar{Z}_x)^2}.$$

Now

$$E(\hat{\beta}_3) \neq \beta,$$

since the second term in the numerator is not independent of the second term in the denominator. Thus $\hat{\beta}_3$ is not unbiased. However,

$$\text{plim}(\hat{\beta}_3) = \text{plim}(\hat{\mu}/\hat{\delta}) = \mu/\delta = \beta,$$

since $\hat{\mu}$ and $\hat{\delta}$ are consistent estimators of μ and δ, respectively. Therefore, $\hat{\beta}_3$ is consistent.

CHAPTER 10

10-1-a.

Consider the complete model $y = \mathbf{X}_Q\beta_Q + \epsilon$ and the reduced model $y = \mathbf{X}_K\beta_K + \epsilon$, where $y \rightarrow nx1$, $\mathbf{X}_Q \rightarrow nxQ$, $\mathbf{X}_K \rightarrow nxK$, $\beta_Q \rightarrow Qx1$, $\beta_K \rightarrow Kx1$, and $\epsilon \rightarrow nx1$. Let the column vectors $\hat{\beta}_Q \rightarrow Qx1$ and $\hat{\beta}_K \rightarrow Kx1$ denote the ordinary least squares estimators of β_Q and β_K, respectively. Since the former minimizes SSE of the complete model at the value of SSE_Q, any other column vector, say $\tilde{\beta}$, provides a value of SSE which is equal to or greater than SSE_Q. For instance, consider $\tilde{\beta}' = \begin{bmatrix} \hat{\beta}'_K & 0' \end{bmatrix}$ which is a vector consisting of the ordinary least squares of the reduced model as the first K elements and zeros as the next (Q - K) elements. Since vector $\tilde{\beta}$ minimizes SSE of the reduced model at the value of SSE_K, it follows that

$$SSE_Q \le SSE_K,$$

and since

$$SST = SSR_Q + SSE_Q = SSR_K + SSE_K,$$

it follows that

$$SSR_Q \ge SSR_K.$$

10-1-b.

Dividing both sides of the inequality by SST

$$SSR_Q/SST \ge SSR_K/SST,$$

or

$$R_Q^2 \ge R_K^2.$$

10-2-a.

Consider

$$m_{kY} = \sum_i (X_{ik} - \bar{X}_k)(Y_i - \bar{Y}) = \Sigma X_{ik}Y_i - n\bar{X}_k\bar{Y},$$

and

$$m_{gk} = \sum_i (X_{ig} - \bar{X}_g)(X_{ik} - \bar{X}_k) = \Sigma X_{ig}X_{ik} - n\bar{X}_g\bar{X}_k,$$

where $(i = 1, \ldots, n)$, and $(g, k = 2, \ldots, K)$. Further, consider the least squares normal equations

$$\Sigma Y_i = n\hat{\beta}_1 + \hat{\beta}_2\Sigma X_{i2} + \cdots + \hat{\beta}_K\Sigma X_{iK},$$

$$\Sigma X_{i2}Y_i = n\bar{X}_2\hat{\beta}_1 + \hat{\beta}_2\Sigma X_{i2}^2 + \cdots + \hat{\beta}_K\Sigma X_{i2}X_{iK},$$

$$\vdots$$

$$\Sigma X_{iK}Y_i = n\bar{X}_K\hat{\beta}_1 + \hat{\beta}_2\Sigma X_{i2}X_{iK} + \cdots + \hat{\beta}_K\Sigma X_{iK}^2.$$

Dividing both sides of the first normal equation by n and rearranging the equation, we get

$$\hat{\beta}_1 = \bar{Y} - \hat{\beta}_2\bar{X}_2 - \cdots - \hat{\beta}_K\bar{X}_K.$$

Substituting this equation into the remaining normal equations one by one, we get

$$\Sigma X_{i2}Y_i - n\bar{X}_2\bar{Y} = \hat{\beta}_2(\Sigma X_{i2}^2 - n\bar{X}_2^2) + \cdots + \hat{\beta}_K(\Sigma X_{i2}X_{iK} - n\bar{X}_2\bar{X}_K),$$

$$\Sigma X_{i3}Y_i - n\bar{X}_3\bar{Y} = \hat{\beta}_2(\Sigma X_{i2}X_{i3} - n\bar{X}_2\bar{X}_3) + \cdots + \hat{\beta}_K(\Sigma X_{i3}X_{iK} - n\bar{X}_3\bar{X}_K),$$

$$\vdots$$

$$\Sigma X_{iK}Y_i - n\bar{X}_K\bar{Y} = \hat{\beta}_2(\Sigma X_{i2}X_{iK} - n\bar{X}_2\bar{X}_K) + \cdots + \hat{\beta}_K(\Sigma X_{iK}^2 - n\bar{X}_K^2),$$

or equivalently

$$m_{2Y} = \hat{\beta}_2 m_{22} + \cdots + \hat{\beta}_K m_{2K},$$

$$m_{3Y} = \hat{\beta}_2 m_{32} + \cdots + \hat{\beta}_K m_{3K},$$

$$\vdots$$

$$m_{KY} = \hat{\beta}_2 m_{K2} + \cdots + \hat{\beta}_K m_{KK},$$

or in matrix notation

$$\underline{X}'\underline{y} = (\underline{X}'\underline{X})\hat{\underline{\beta}}.$$

Pre-multiplying by $(\underline{X}'\underline{X})^{-1}$, we obtain

$$\hat{\underline{\beta}} = (\underline{X}'\underline{X})^{-1}\underline{X}'\underline{y} \qquad \text{Q.E.D.}$$

10-2-b.

Consider

$$Y_i = \beta_1 + \beta_2 X_{i2} + \cdots + \beta_K X_{iK} + \epsilon_i.$$

Summing over all i's and dividing by n, we get

$$\bar{Y} = \beta_1 + \beta_2 \bar{X}_2 + \cdots + \beta_K \bar{X}_K + \bar{\epsilon}.$$

Subtracting the latter from the former, we obtain

$$Y_i - \bar{Y} = \beta_2(X_{i2} - \bar{X}_2) + \cdots + \beta_K(X_{iK} - \bar{X}_K) + \epsilon_i - \bar{\epsilon},$$

or in matrix notation

$$\underline{y} = \underline{X}\underline{\beta} + \underline{\epsilon}.$$

Now from part (a), we have

$$\hat{\underline{\beta}} = (\underline{X}'\underline{X})^{-1}\underline{X}'\underline{y} = (\underline{X}'\underline{X})^{-1}\underline{X}'(\underline{X}\underline{\beta} + \underline{\epsilon}) = \underline{\beta} + (\underline{X}'\underline{X})^{-1}\underline{X}'\underline{\epsilon},$$

or

$$\hat{\underline{\beta}} - \underline{\beta} = (\underline{X}'\underline{X})^{-1}\underline{X}'\underline{\epsilon},$$

and

$$(\hat{\underline{\beta}} - \underline{\beta})' = \underline{\epsilon}'\underline{X}(\underline{X}'\underline{X})^{-1}.$$

Further,

$$\underline{\mathbf{X}}'\underline{\epsilon} = \begin{bmatrix} \Sigma(X_{i1}-\bar{X}_1)(\epsilon_i-\bar{\epsilon}) \\ \Sigma(X_{i2}-\bar{X}_2)(\epsilon_i-\bar{\epsilon}) \\ \cdot \\ \cdot \\ \cdot \\ \Sigma(X_{iK}-\bar{X}_K)(\epsilon_i-\bar{\epsilon}) \end{bmatrix} = \begin{bmatrix} \Sigma(X_{i1}-\bar{X}_1)\epsilon_i \\ \Sigma(X_{i2}-\bar{X}_2)\epsilon_i \\ \cdot \\ \cdot \\ \cdot \\ \Sigma(X_{iK}-\bar{X}_K)\epsilon_i \end{bmatrix} = \underline{\mathbf{X}}'\epsilon,$$

and similarly $\underline{\epsilon}'\underline{\mathbf{X}} = \epsilon'\underline{\mathbf{X}}$.

Therefore

$$\begin{aligned} \mathrm{Var}(\hat{\underline{\beta}}) &= \mathbf{E}(\hat{\underline{\beta}} - \underline{\beta})(\hat{\underline{\beta}} - \underline{\beta})' \\ &= \mathbf{E}[(\underline{\mathbf{X}}'\underline{\mathbf{X}})^{-1}\underline{\mathbf{X}}'\epsilon\epsilon'\underline{\mathbf{X}}(\underline{\mathbf{X}}'\underline{\mathbf{X}})^{-1}] \\ &= (\underline{\mathbf{X}}'\underline{\mathbf{X}})^{-1}\underline{\mathbf{X}}'\mathbf{E}(\epsilon\epsilon')\underline{\mathbf{X}}(\underline{\mathbf{X}}'\underline{\mathbf{X}})^{-1} \\ &= (\underline{\mathbf{X}}'\underline{\mathbf{X}})^{-1}\underline{\mathbf{X}}'\sigma^2\mathbf{I}\underline{\mathbf{X}}(\underline{\mathbf{X}}'\underline{\mathbf{X}})^{-1} \\ &= \sigma^2(\underline{\mathbf{X}}'\underline{\mathbf{X}})^{-1} \qquad \text{Q.E.D.} \end{aligned}$$

10-2-c.

Consider the following two row vectors

$$\underline{y}' = \begin{bmatrix} Y_1-\bar{Y} & Y_2-\bar{Y} & \cdot\cdot\cdot & Y_n-\bar{Y} \end{bmatrix},$$

$$\mathbf{y}' = \begin{bmatrix} Y_1 & Y_2 & \cdot\cdot\cdot & Y_n \end{bmatrix}.$$

Then

$$\underline{y}'\underline{y} = \Sigma(Y_t - \bar{Y})^2 = \Sigma Y_t^2 - (\Sigma Y_t)^2/n = \mathbf{y}'\mathbf{y} - (\Sigma Y_t)^2/n \qquad \text{Q.E.D.}$$

10-3.

Consider $n = 100$, $r_{23} = 0.50$, $r_{23}^2 = 0.25$, $(1 - r_{23}^2) = 0.75$, $\hat{\beta}_2 = 3$, $\hat{\beta}_3 = 10$, $s_{\hat{\beta}_2} = 1$, $s_{\hat{\beta}_2}^2 = 1$, $s_{\hat{\beta}_3} = 2$, and $s_{\hat{\beta}_3}^2 = 4$. Now

$$s_{\hat{\beta}_2}^2 = s^2/m_{22}(1 - r_{23}^2),$$

$$1 = s^2/0.75m_{22},$$

or

$$s^2 = 0.75m_{22}.$$

Further,

$$s_{\hat{\beta}_3}^2 = s^2/m_{33}(1 - r_{23}^2),$$

$$4 = s^2/0.75m_{33},$$

or

$$s^2 = 3m_{33}.$$

Thus

$$m_{22} = 4m_{33}.$$

Now

$$r_{23} = m_{23}/\sqrt{m_{22}m_{33}},$$

$$0.50 = m_{23}/\sqrt{4m_{33}m_{33}},$$

or

$$m_{23} = m_{33}.$$

Substituting the above results into the formulas for SSE and SSR, we obtain

$$SSE = (n - 3)s^2 = 291m_{33},$$

and

$$SSR = \hat{\beta}_2^2 m_{22} + 2\hat{\beta}_2\hat{\beta}_3 m_{23} + \hat{\beta}_3^2 m_{33} = 196m_{33}.$$

Therefore

$$R^2 = \frac{SSR}{SSR + SSE} = \frac{196m_{33}}{196m_{33} + 291m_{33}} = 0.4025.$$

10-4.

Consider

$$\mathbf{y} = \mathbf{X}\beta + \epsilon,$$

or

$$\begin{bmatrix} Y_1 \\ Y_2 \\ \cdot \\ \cdot \\ \cdot \\ Y_n \end{bmatrix} = \begin{bmatrix} 1 & X_1 \\ 1 & X_2 \\ \cdot & \cdot \\ \cdot & \cdot \\ \cdot & \cdot \\ 1 & X_n \end{bmatrix} \begin{bmatrix} \beta_1 \\ \beta_2 \end{bmatrix} + \begin{bmatrix} \epsilon_1 \\ \epsilon_2 \\ \cdot \\ \cdot \\ \cdot \\ \epsilon_n \end{bmatrix},$$

and

$$\mathbf{X'X} = \begin{bmatrix} n & n\bar{X} \\ n\bar{X} & \Sigma X_i^2 \end{bmatrix}, \qquad (\mathbf{X'X})^{-1} = \frac{1}{\Delta}\begin{bmatrix} \Sigma X_i^2 & -n\bar{X} \\ -n\bar{X} & n \end{bmatrix},$$

where

$$\Delta = n\Sigma X_i^2 - n^2\bar{X}^2 = n\Sigma(X_i - \bar{X})^2,$$

and

$$\mathbf{X'y} = \begin{bmatrix} n\bar{Y} \\ \Sigma X_i Y_i \end{bmatrix}.$$

Now

$$\hat{\beta} = (\mathbf{X'X})^{-1}\mathbf{X'y},$$

or

$$\begin{bmatrix} \hat{\beta}_1 \\ \hat{\beta}_2 \end{bmatrix} = \frac{1}{\Delta}\begin{bmatrix} \Sigma X_i^2 & -n\bar{X} \\ -n\bar{X} & n \end{bmatrix}\begin{bmatrix} n\bar{Y} \\ \Sigma X_i Y_i \end{bmatrix} = \frac{1}{\Delta}\begin{bmatrix} n\bar{Y}\Sigma X_i^2 - n\bar{X}\Sigma X_i Y_i \\ n\Sigma X_i Y_i - n^2\bar{X}\bar{Y} \end{bmatrix}.$$

Thus

$$\hat{\beta}_2 = (n\Sigma X_i Y_i - n^2\bar{X}\bar{Y})/\Delta.$$

$$= \Sigma(X_i - \bar{X})(Y_i - \bar{Y})/\Sigma(X_i - \bar{X})^2 \qquad \text{Q.E.D.},$$

and

$$\hat{\beta}_1 = (n\bar{Y}\Sigma X_i^2 - n\bar{X}\Sigma X_i Y_i)/\Delta$$

$$= (n\bar{Y}\Sigma X_i^2 - n^2\bar{X}^2\bar{Y} + n^2\bar{X}^2\bar{Y} - n\bar{X}\Sigma X_i Y_i)/\Delta$$

$$= [\Delta\bar{Y} - (n\Sigma X_i Y_i - n^2\bar{X}\bar{Y})\bar{X}]/\Delta$$

$$= \bar{Y} - \hat{\beta}_2\bar{X} \qquad \text{Q.E.D.}$$

Further,

$$\text{Var-Cov}(\hat{\beta}) = \sigma^2(\mathbf{X'X})^{-1},$$

or

$$\begin{bmatrix} \text{Var}(\hat{\beta}_1) & \text{Cov}(\hat{\beta}_1,\hat{\beta}_2) \\ \text{Cov}(\hat{\beta}_1,\hat{\beta}_2) & \text{Var}(\hat{\beta}_2) \end{bmatrix} = \frac{\sigma^2}{\Delta}\begin{bmatrix} \Sigma X_i^2 & -n\bar{X} \\ -n\bar{X} & n \end{bmatrix}.$$

Thus

$$\text{Var}(\hat{\beta}_1) = \sigma^2\Sigma X_i^2/\Delta$$

$$= \sigma^2(\Sigma X_i^2 - n\bar{X}^2 + n\bar{X}^2)/\Delta$$

$$= \sigma^2[1/n + \bar{X}^2/\Sigma(X_i - \bar{X})^2] \qquad \text{Q.E.D.},$$

$$\text{Var}(\hat{\beta}_2) = n\sigma^2/\Delta$$

$$= \sigma^2/\Sigma(X_i - \bar{X})^2 \qquad \text{Q.E.D.},$$

and

$$\text{Cov}(\hat{\beta}_1,\hat{\beta}_2) = -n\bar{X}\sigma^2/\Delta = -\bar{X}\sigma^2/\Sigma(X_i - \bar{X})^2 \qquad \text{Q.E.D.}$$

10-5-a.

$$I_t = \underset{(97.4360)}{-109.8000} + \underset{(0.0235)}{0.1142}F_{t-1} + \underset{(0.0394)}{0.3261}K_{t-1} + e_t, \qquad R^2 = 0.8907.$$

10-5-b.

$$R^2 = 0.8907.$$

Step 1: The null and the alternative hypotheses are

$$H_o: \beta_2 = \beta_3 = 0,$$

$$H_a: H_o \text{ is not true.}$$

Steps 2 & 3: The test statistic and its distribution are

$$F = (SSR/2)/[SSE/(n - 3)] \sim F_{2,n-3}.$$

Step 4: Do not reject the null hypothesis if

$$F < F_{\alpha,2,n-3} = F_{0.01,2,16} = 6.23,$$

otherwise reject it.

Step 5: The value of the test statistic is

$$F = (897,970/2)/(110,210/16) = 65.1840.$$

Step 6: Since the value of the test statistic falls in the rejection region, reject the null hypothesis. There is strong evidence for the existence of relationship.

10-5-c.

Consider

$$\hat{I}_{1954} = -109.80 + 0.1142(5,593.60) + 0.3261(2,226.30)$$

$$= 1,254.9856,$$

$$s_F = 105.9274.$$

Now a 95% forecast interval for I_{1954} is

$$\hat{I}_{1954} \pm t_{0.0250,16}s_F = 1,254.9856 \pm 2.12(105.9274)$$

or

$$P\{1,030.4195 \leq I_{1954} \leq 1,479.5517\} = 0.95.$$

10-6-a.

A sufficient condition is that E_i and N_i be uncorrelated in the sample. To look for other conditions, sum the model over all g's

$$\Sigma X_{ig} = \Sigma a_g + E_i \Sigma \beta_g + N_i \Sigma \gamma_g + \Sigma u_{ig}.$$

Consider

$$E_i = \Sigma X_{ig} + v_i = \Sigma X_{ig} - \Sigma u_{ig} = \Sigma a_g + E_i \Sigma \beta_g + N_i \Sigma \gamma_g.$$

Solving for N_i, we get

$$N_i \Sigma \gamma_g = -\Sigma a_g + (1 - \Sigma \beta_g) E_i,$$

or

$$N_i = -\Sigma a_g / \Sigma \gamma_g + [(1 - \Sigma \beta_g)/\Sigma \gamma_g] E_i.$$

Multiplying the above equation by γ_g and substituting the result in the model, we obtain

$$\begin{aligned} X_{ig} &= a_g + \beta_g E_i + \gamma_g N_i + u_{ig} \\ &= a_g + \beta_g E_i - \frac{\gamma_g \Sigma a_g}{\Sigma \gamma_g} + [\frac{\gamma_g (1 - \Sigma \beta_g)}{\Sigma \gamma_g}] E_i + u_{ig} \\ &= \gamma_g - \frac{\gamma_g \Sigma a_g}{\Sigma \gamma_g} + [\beta_g + \frac{\gamma_g (1 - \Sigma \beta_g)}{\Sigma \gamma_g}] E_i + u_{ig}. \end{aligned}$$

The only plausible condition under which the above equation reduces to a form

$$X_{ig} = \delta_g + \beta_g E_i + u_{ig},$$

is when $\Sigma \beta_g = 1$. Note that if $\gamma_g = 0$ for all g then $\Sigma \gamma_g = 0$ which makes the coefficient of E_i undefined. Also note that $\Sigma \gamma_g = \infty$ implies either N_i being zero or Σa_g, $(1 - \Sigma \beta_g)$, or E_i being infinity. Thus, b_g will be an unbiased estimator of β_g if

$$\Sigma \beta_g = 1.$$

10-6-b.

The only plausible condition under which the above equation reduces to a form

$$X_{ig} = \alpha_g + \eta_g E_i + u_{ig},$$

is when $\Sigma\alpha_g = 0$. The above two notes also apply here. Thus, a_g will be an unbiased estimator of α_g if

$$\Sigma\alpha_g = 0.$$

10-7.

In order to conduct the RESET test consider

$$I_t = \beta_1 + \beta_2 F_{t-1} + \beta_3 K_{t-1} + \beta_4 F_{t-1}^2 + \beta_5 K_{t-1}^2$$
$$+ \beta_6 F_{t-1}^3 + \beta_7 K_{t-1}^3 + \beta_8 F_{t-1}^4 + \beta_9 K_{t-1}^4 + \epsilon_t.$$

Step 1: The null and the alternative hypotheses are

$$H_o\colon E(I_t) = \beta_1 + \beta_2 F_{t-1} + \beta_3 K_{t-1},$$
$$H_a\colon H_o \text{ is not true.}$$

Steps 2 & 3: The test statistic and its distribution are

$$F = \frac{(SSR_Q - SSR_K)/(Q - K)}{SSE_Q/(n - Q)} \sim F_{Q-K,n-Q},$$

where Q = 9 and K = 3.

Step 4: Do not reject the null hypothesis if

$$F < F_{\alpha,Q-K,n-Q} = F_{0.05,6,10} = 3.22,$$

otherwise reject it.

Step 5: The value of the test statistic is

$$F = \frac{(964{,}180 - 897{,}970)/(9 - 3)}{43{,}996/(19 - 9)} = 2.5082.$$

Step 6: Since the value of the test statistic falls in the acceptance region, do not reject the null hypothesis. There is no evidence that any relevant explanatory variables have been omitted.

In order to conduct the "rainbow" test consider

Step 1: The null and the alternative hypotheses are

$$H_o: E(I_t) = \beta_1 + \beta_2 F_{t-1} + \beta_3 K_{t-1},$$

$$H_a: H_o \text{ is not true.}$$

Steps 2 & 3: The test statistic and its distribution are

$$F = \frac{(SSE - SSE_D)/(n - m)}{SSE_D/(m - K)} \sim F_{n-m,m-K},$$

where m = 9 is the number of approximately one half middle observations (fifth to thirteenth) whose h_{ii}'s are smaller than those of the rest of the observations, and K = 3.

Step 4: Do not reject the null hypothesis if

$$F < F_{\alpha,n-m,m-K} = F_{0.05,10,6} = 4.06,$$

otherwise reject it.

Step 5: The value of the test statistic is

$$F = \frac{(110,210 - 37,782)/(19 - 9)}{37,782/(9 - 3)} = 1.1502.$$

Step 6: Since the value of the test statistic falls in the acceptance region, do not reject the null hypothesis. There is no evidence that any relevant explanatory variables have been omitted.

10-8.

Consider the production functions of industries A and B under the hypothesis that they differ, i.e.,

$$Y_{ia} = \alpha_a + \beta_a X_{ia} + \epsilon_{ia},$$

and

$$Y_{ib} = \alpha_b + \beta_b X_{ib} + \epsilon_{ib},$$

and under the hypothesis that they are the same, i.e.,

$$Y_j = \alpha + \beta X_j + \epsilon_j,$$

where subscripts a and b stand for industries A and B, respectively, the terms without them denote the pooled values of the two industries, (i = 1, ..., 20), and (j = 1, ..., 40).

Step 1: The null and the alternative hypotheses are

$$H_o: \alpha_a = \alpha_b, \quad \text{and} \quad \beta_a = \beta_b,$$

$$H_a: H_o \text{ is not true.}$$

Steps 2 & 3: The test statistic and its distribution are

$$F = \frac{(SSE - SSE_a - SSE_b)/K}{(SSE_a + SSE_b)/(n_a + n_b - 2K)} \sim F_{K,n_a+n_b-2K},$$

where K = 2 is the number of restrictions imposed by the null hypothesis.

Step 4: Do not reject the null hypothesis if

$$F < F_{\alpha,K,n_a+n_b-2K} = F_{0.05,2,36} = 4.1160,$$

otherwise reject it.

Step 5: The sample values are

$$\bar{X}_a = 1, \quad \bar{X}_b = 1, \quad \bar{X} = 1,$$

and

$$\bar{Y}_a = 8, \quad \bar{Y}_b = 9, \quad \bar{Y} = 8.50.$$

Further,

$$\sum_j (X_j - \bar{X})^2 = \sum_i (X_{ia} - \bar{X})^2 + \sum_i (X_{ib} - \bar{X})^2$$

$$= \sum_i (X_{ia} - \bar{X}_a)^2 + \sum_i (X_{ib} - \bar{X}_b)^2$$

$$= 12 + 10$$

$$= 22,$$

and

$$\sum_j (X_j - \bar{X})(Y_j - \bar{Y}) = \sum_j (X_j - \bar{X})Y_j$$

$$= \sum_i (X_{ia} - \bar{X})Y_{ia} + \sum_i (X_{ib} - \bar{X})Y_{ib}$$

$$= \sum_i (X_{ia} - \bar{X}_a)(Y_{ia} - \bar{Y}_a) + \sum_i (X_{ib} - \bar{X}_b)(Y_{ib} - \bar{Y}_b)$$

$$= 10 + 12$$

$$= 22.$$

Using the general formula

$$\sum_t Y_t^2 = \sum_t (Y_t - \bar{Y})^2 + T\bar{Y}^2,$$

where $(t = 1, \ldots, T)$, the following sums are calculated

$$\sum_i Y_{ia}^2 = 1{,}290,$$

and

$$\sum_i Y_{ib}^2 = 1{,}638.$$

Now

$$\sum_j Y_j^2 = \sum_i Y_{ia}^2 + \sum_i Y_{ib}^2 = 1{,}290 + 1{,}638 = 2{,}928,$$

and

$$\sum_j (Y_j - \bar{Y})^2 = 2{,}928 - 40(8.50)^2 = 38.$$

Using the general formula

$$SSE = SST - [\sum_t (X_t - \bar{X})(Y_t - \bar{Y})]^2/\sum_t (X_t - \bar{X})^2,$$

the following sums are calculated

$$SSE_a = 10 - 100/12 = 5/3,$$

$$SSE_b = 18 - 144/10 = 3.60,$$

and

$$SSE = 38 - 484/22 = 16.$$

Thus the value of the test statistic is

$$F = \frac{(16 - 5/3 - 3.60)/2}{(5/3 + 3.60)/36} = 36.6835.$$

Step 6: Since the value of the test statistic falls in the rejection region, reject the null hypothesis. There is evidence to indicate that the two production functions differ.

10-9.

Consider regressing X and Y on t, (t = 1, ..., T), i.e.,

$$X_t = \alpha + \beta t + u_t,$$

and

$$Y_t = \gamma + \delta t + v_t.$$

Let a, b, c, and d be LSE's of α, β, γ and δ, respectively, where

$$a = \bar{X} - b\bar{t}, \qquad b = m_{tX}/m_{tt},$$

and

$$c = \bar{Y} - d\bar{t}, \qquad d = m_{tY}/m_{tt}.$$

Consider

$$X_t^* = X_t - a - bt.$$

Summing over all t's and dividing by T, we get

$$\bar{X}^* = \bar{X} - a - b\bar{t}.$$

Subtracting the latter from the former, we obtain

$$X_t^* - \bar{X}^* = X_t - \bar{X} - b(t - \bar{t}).$$

similarly

$$Y_t^* - \bar{Y}^* = Y_t - \bar{Y} - d(t - \bar{t}).$$

Multiplying $(X_t^* - \bar{X}^*)$ by $(Y_t^* - \bar{Y}^*)$, we get

$$(X_t^* - \bar{X}^*)(Y_t^* - \bar{Y}^*) = [X_t - \bar{X} - b(t - \bar{t})][Y_t - \bar{Y} - d(t - \bar{t})],$$

summing over all t's, we obtain

$$\Sigma(X_t^* - \bar{X}^*)(Y_t^* - \bar{Y}^*) = m_{XY} - bm_{tY} - dm_{tX} + bdm_{tt},$$

substituting for b and d and simplifying, we get

$$\Sigma(X_t^* - \bar{X}^*)(Y_t^* - \bar{Y}^*) = m_{XY} - m_{tX}m_{tY}/m_{tt}.$$

Now squaring $(X_t^* - \bar{X}^*)$, summing over all t's, substituting for b, and simplifying, we obtain

$$\Sigma(X_t^* - \bar{X}^*)^2 = m_{XX} - m_{tX}^2/m_{tt}.$$

Consider

$$Y_t^* = \beta_1 + \beta_2 X_t^* + \epsilon_t^*,$$

and LSE of β_2

$$\hat{\beta}_2 = \Sigma(X_t^* - \bar{X}^*)(Y_t^* - \bar{Y}^*)/\Sigma(X_t^* - \bar{X}^*)^2$$

$$= (m_{XY} - m_{tX}m_{tY}/m_{tt})/(m_{XX} - m_{tX}^2/m_{tt})$$

$$= (m_{XY}m_{tt} - m_{tX}m_{tY})/(m_{XX}m_{tt} - m_{tX}^2),$$

which is the same as the LSE of β_2 in the model

$$Y_t = \beta_1 + \beta_2 X_t + \beta_3 t + \epsilon_t.$$

10-10.

Writing the model in matrix notation, we have

$$\hat{\beta} = (\mathbf{X}'\mathbf{X})^{-1}\mathbf{X}'\mathbf{y} = (\mathbf{X}'\mathbf{X})^{-1}\mathbf{X}'(\mathbf{X}\beta + \epsilon) = \beta + (\mathbf{X}'\mathbf{X})^{-1}\mathbf{X}'\epsilon.$$

Consider

$$E(\hat{\beta}) = \beta + (\mathbf{X}'\mathbf{X})^{-1}\mathbf{X}'E(\epsilon) = \beta + \gamma(\mathbf{X}'\mathbf{X})^{-1}\mathbf{X}'\mathbf{x}_2,$$

where $\mathbf{x}_2$ is a column vector of $(X_{i2} - \bar{X}_2)$, $(i = 1, \ldots, n)$, and

$$\mathbf{X}'\mathbf{X} = \begin{bmatrix} m_{22} & m_{23} \\ m_{23} & m_{33} \end{bmatrix}, \qquad \mathbf{X}'\mathbf{x}_2 = \begin{bmatrix} m_{22} \\ m_{23} \end{bmatrix}.$$

Now

$$E(\hat{\beta}) = \beta + \frac{\gamma}{m_{22}m_{33} - m_{23}^2}\begin{bmatrix} m_{33} & -m_{23} \\ -m_{23} & m_{22} \end{bmatrix}\begin{bmatrix} m_{22} \\ m_{23} \end{bmatrix} = \beta + \gamma\begin{bmatrix} 1 \\ 0 \end{bmatrix}.$$

Therefore

$$\begin{bmatrix} E(\hat{\beta}_2) \\ E(\hat{\beta}_3) \end{bmatrix} = \begin{bmatrix} \beta_2+\gamma \\ \beta_3 \end{bmatrix} \qquad \text{Q.E.D.}$$

10-11.

(1) The method is feasible. Consider the correct model

$$Y_i = \beta_1 + \beta_2 X_{i2} + \beta_3 X_{i3} + \epsilon_i,$$

or in partitioned matrix notation

$$\mathbf{y} = \beta_2\mathbf{x}_2 + \beta_3\mathbf{x}_3 + \epsilon,$$

and the suggested model

$$Y_i = \beta_1 + \beta_2 X_{i2} + \epsilon_i,$$

or in matrix notation

$$\mathbf{y} = \beta_2 \mathbf{x}_2 + \boldsymbol{\epsilon}.$$

The LSE of β_2 under the the suggested model, say $\hat{\beta}_2$, is

$$\hat{\beta}_2 = (\mathbf{x}_2'\mathbf{x}_2)^{-1}\mathbf{x}_2'\mathbf{y}.$$

Substituting the correct value of $\mathbf{y}$ in the above equation, we get

$$\hat{\beta}_2 = (\mathbf{x}_2'\mathbf{x}_2)^{-1}\mathbf{x}_2'(\mathbf{x}_2\beta_2 + \mathbf{x}_3\beta_3 + \boldsymbol{\epsilon}) = \beta_2 + (\mathbf{x}_2'\mathbf{x}_2)^{-1}\mathbf{x}_2'(\mathbf{x}_3\beta_3 + \boldsymbol{\epsilon}).$$

Now

$$E(\hat{\beta}_2) = \beta_2 + (\mathbf{x}_2'\mathbf{x}_2)^{-1}\mathbf{x}_2'\mathbf{x}_3\beta_3.$$

Therefore, $\hat{\beta}_2$ is a biased estimator of β_2 and the conventional t-tests are invalid.

(2) Since

$$X_{t3} = a + bX_{t2},$$

and

$$X_{t-1,3} = a + bX_{t-1,2},$$

it follows that

$$X_{t3} - X_{t-1,3} = b(X_{t2} - X_{t-1,2}),$$

which implies that the method is not feasible. The **X'X** matrix will be singular and the LSE's cannot be calculated.

(3) Searching over different values of β_3 is the same as minimizing

$$\mathbf{e}'\mathbf{e} = (\mathbf{y} - \beta_2\mathbf{x}_2 - \beta_3\mathbf{x}_3)'(\mathbf{y} - \beta_2\mathbf{x}_2 - \beta_3\mathbf{x}_3),$$

with respect tc β_2 and β_3, which is not feasible.

10-12-a.

$$\begin{bmatrix}\hat{\beta}_2\\ \hat{\beta}_3\end{bmatrix} = \frac{1}{80}\begin{bmatrix}12 & -8\\ -8 & 12\end{bmatrix}\begin{bmatrix}10\\ 8\end{bmatrix} = \begin{bmatrix}0.70\\ 0.20\end{bmatrix}.$$

$$SSR = \begin{bmatrix}0.70 & 0.20\end{bmatrix}\begin{bmatrix}10\\ 8\end{bmatrix} = 8.60.$$

$$R^2 = 8.60/10 = 0.86.$$

10-12-b.

Step 1: The null and the alternative hypotheses are

$$H_o\colon \beta_2 + \beta_3 - 1 = 0,$$

$$H_a\colon \beta_2 + \beta_3 - 1 \neq 0,$$

Steps 2 & 3: The test statistic and its distribution are

$$t = (\hat{\beta}_2 + \hat{\beta}_3 - 1)/s_{\hat{\beta}_2+\hat{\beta}_3-1} \sim t_{n-3}.$$

Step 4: Do not reject the null hypothesis if

$$|t| < t_{\alpha/2,n-3} = t_{0.0250,20} = 2.0860,$$

otherwise reject it.

Step 5: The sample values are

$$\hat{\beta}_2 + \hat{\beta}_3 - 1 = 0.70 + 0.20 - 1 = -0.10,$$

$$SSE = 10 - 8.60 = 1.40,$$

$$s^2 = 1.40/20 = 0.07,$$

$$s^2_{\hat{\beta}_2+\hat{\beta}_3-1} = \frac{0.07}{80}\begin{bmatrix}1 & 1\end{bmatrix}\begin{bmatrix}12 & -8\\ -8 & 12\end{bmatrix}\begin{bmatrix}1\\ 1\end{bmatrix} = 0.0070,$$

$$s_{\hat{\beta}_2+\hat{\beta}_3-1} = \sqrt{0.0070} = 0.0837.$$

Thus the value of the test statistic is

$$t = -0.10/0.0837 = -1.1952.$$

Step 6: Since the value of the test statistic falls in the acceptance region, do not reject the null hypothesis. There is evidence that the function exhibits constant returns to scale.

10-12-c.

Consider

$$Y_i = \beta_1 + \beta_2 X_{i2} + (1 - \beta_2)X_{i3} + \epsilon_i,$$

or
$$Y_i - X_{i3} = \beta_1 + \beta_2(X_{i2} - X_{i3}) + \epsilon_i.$$

Now

$$\begin{aligned} \tilde{\beta}_2 &= \Sigma(x'_{i2} - x'_{i3})(y'_i - x'_{i3})/\Sigma(x'_{i2} - x'_{i3})^2 \\ &= (m_{2Y} - m_{23} - m_{3Y} + m_{33})/(m_{22} - 2m_{23} + m_{33}) \\ &= (10 - 8 - 8 + 12)/(12 - 16 + 12) \\ &= 0.75. \end{aligned}$$

10-12-d.

(i) If the assumption of constant returns to scale is correct, the correct model to be used would be

$$Y_i = \beta_1 + \beta_2 X_{i2} + (1 - \beta_2)X_{i3} + \epsilon_i,$$

or in partitioned matrix notation

$$\underline{y} = \beta_2\underline{x}_2 + (1 - \beta_2)\underline{x}_3 + \underline{\epsilon},$$

but by ignoring the assumption we use the incorrect model

$$Y_i = \beta_1 + \beta_2 X_{i2} + \beta_3 X_{i3} + \epsilon_i,$$

or in partitioned matrix notation

$$\underline{y} = \beta_2\underline{x}_2 + \beta_3\underline{x}_3 + \underline{\epsilon},$$

Given the assumption is correct the LSE of β_2 under the correct model, say $\tilde{\beta}_2$, has all desirable properties and the conventional t-tests are valid. Consider the LSE of β_2 under the incorrect model, say $\hat{\beta}_2$,

$$\begin{aligned}\hat{\beta}_2 &= (\underline{x}_2'M_3\underline{x}_2)^{-1}\underline{x}_2'M_3\underline{y} \\ &= (\underline{x}_2'M_3\underline{x}_2)^{-1}\underline{x}_2'M_3[\beta_2\underline{x}_2 + (1 - \beta_2)\underline{x}_3 + \underline{\epsilon}] \\ &= \beta_2 + (1 - \beta_2)(\underline{x}_2'M_3\underline{x}_2)^{-1}\underline{x}_2'M_3\underline{x}_3 + (\underline{x}_2'M_3\underline{x}_2)^{-1}\underline{x}_2'M_3\underline{\epsilon} \\ &= \beta_2 + (\underline{x}_2'M_3\underline{x}_2)^{-1}\underline{x}_2'M_3\underline{\epsilon},\end{aligned}$$

where

$$M_3 = I - \underline{x}_3(\underline{x}_3'\underline{x}_3)^{-1}\underline{x}_3'.$$

Now

$$E(\hat{\beta}_2) = \beta_2 + (\underline{x}_2'M_3\underline{x}_2)^{-1}\underline{x}_2'M_3E(\underline{\epsilon}) = \beta_2.$$

Therefore, $\hat{\beta}_2$ is an unbiased estimator of β_2. Consider

$$\begin{aligned}\text{Var}(\hat{\beta}_2) &= \sigma^2(\underline{x}_2'M_3\underline{x}_2)^{-1} \\ &= \sigma^2\underline{x}_3'\underline{x}_3/[\underline{x}_2'\underline{x}_2\underline{x}_3'\underline{x}_3 - (\underline{x}_2'\underline{x}_3)^2] \\ &= \sigma^2 m_{33}/(m_{22}m_{33} - m_{23}^2),\end{aligned}$$

and

$$\begin{aligned}\text{Var}(\tilde{\beta}_2) &= \sigma^2[(\underline{x}_2 - \underline{x}_3)'(\underline{x}_2 - \underline{x}_3)]^{-1} \\ &= \sigma^2/(\underline{x}_2'\underline{x}_2 + \underline{x}_3'\underline{x}_3 - 2\underline{x}_2'\underline{x}_3) \\ &= \sigma^2/(m_{22} + m_{33} - 2m_{23}).\end{aligned}$$

However,

$$\mathrm{Var}(\hat{\beta}_2) \geq \mathrm{Var}(\tilde{\beta}_2),$$

because $$m_{33}(m_{22} + m_{33} - 2m_{23}) \geq m_{22}m_{33} - m_{23}^2,$$

or $$(m_{33} - m_{23})^2 \geq 0 \qquad \text{Q.E.D.}$$

Note that in this case since $m_{33} = 12$ and $m_{23} = 8$

$$\mathrm{Var}(\hat{\beta}_2) > \mathrm{Var}(\tilde{\beta}_2),$$

i.e., $\hat{\beta}_2$ is inefficient. As for estimation of σ^2, consider

$$s^2 = \mathbf{e}'\mathbf{e}/(n - 3),$$

where $\mathbf{e}$ is the residual vector of the incorrect model defined as

$$\mathbf{e} = \underline{\mathbf{y}} - \hat{\beta}_2\underline{\mathbf{x}}_2 - \hat{\beta}_3\underline{\mathbf{x}}_3.$$

Substituting the correct model for $\underline{\mathbf{y}}$, we have

$$\begin{aligned}\mathbf{e} &= -(\hat{\beta}_2 - \beta_2)\underline{\mathbf{x}}_2 - [\hat{\beta}_3 - (1 - \beta_2)]\underline{\mathbf{x}}_3 + \underline{\epsilon} \\ &= -(\hat{\beta}_2 - \beta_2)\underline{\mathbf{x}}_2 - [\hat{\beta}_3 - \beta_3 - (1 - \beta_2 - \beta_3)]\underline{\mathbf{x}}_3 + \underline{\epsilon} \\ &= -(\hat{\beta}_2 - \beta_2)\underline{\mathbf{x}}_2 - (\hat{\beta}_3 - \beta_3)\underline{\mathbf{x}}_3 + \underline{\epsilon},\end{aligned}$$

since

$$1 - \beta_2 - \beta_3 = 0.$$

Now by reference to the section **(10-4)** of the text, under the heading of "Inclusion of an Irrelevant Explanatory Variable,"[1] we have

$$E(s^2) = E[\mathbf{e}'\mathbf{e}/(n - 3)] = \sigma^2.$$

This means that ignoring the additional information of constant returns to scale does not lead to a bias in estimation of σ^2 and, therefore, does not invalidate the conventional t-tests.

---

[1]P. 448.

(ii) If the assumption of constant returns to scale is incorrect, the correct model to be used would be

$$Y_i = \beta_1 + \beta_2 X_{i2} + \beta_3 X_{i3} + \epsilon_i,$$

or in partitioned matrix notation

$$\underline{y} = \beta_2 \underline{x}_2 + \beta_3 \underline{x}_3 + \underline{\epsilon},$$

but by incorporating the assumption we use the incorrect model

$$Y_i = \beta_1 + \beta_2 X_{i2} + (1 - \beta_2) X_{i3} + \epsilon_i,$$

or in partitioned matrix notation

$$\underline{y} = \beta_2 \underline{x}_2 + (1 - \beta_2)\underline{x}_3 + \underline{\epsilon},$$

which can be written as

$$\underline{y} - \underline{x}_3 = \beta_2(\underline{x}_2 - \underline{x}_3) + \underline{\epsilon}.$$

Consider now the LSE of β_2 under the incorrect model, say $\hat{\beta}_2$,

$$\hat{\beta}_2 = [(\underline{x}_2 - \underline{x}_3)'(\underline{x}_2 - \underline{x}_3)]^{-1}(\underline{x}_2 - \underline{x}_3)'(\underline{y} - \underline{x}_3)$$

$$= (z'z)^{-1}z'(\beta_2\underline{x}_2 + \beta_3\underline{x}_3 + \underline{\epsilon} - \underline{x}_3),$$

where

$$z = \underline{x}_2 - \underline{x}_3.$$

Now

$$E(\hat{\beta}_2) = (z'z)^{-1}z'(\beta_2\underline{x}_2 + \beta_3\underline{x}_3 - \underline{x}_3)$$

$$= (z'z)^{-1}z'(\beta_2\underline{x}_2 - \beta_2\underline{x}_3 + \beta_2\underline{x}_3 + \beta_3\underline{x}_3 - \underline{x}_3)$$

$$= (z'z)^{-1}z'(z\beta_2 + \beta_2\underline{x}_3 + \beta_3\underline{x}_3 - \underline{x}_3)$$

$$= \beta_2 - (1 - \beta_2 - \beta_3)(z'z)^{-1}z'\underline{x}_3.$$

Thus, $\hat{\beta}_2$ is biased and the conventional t-tests are invalid.

10-13-a.

Consider

$$Y_i - X_{i2} = \beta_1 + (\beta_2 - 1)X_{i2} + \beta_3 X_{i3} + \epsilon_i,$$

or

$$Z_i = \beta_1 + (\beta_2 - 1)X_{i2} + \beta_3 X_{i3} + \epsilon_i.$$

Step 1: The null and the alternative hypotheses are

$$H_o\colon \beta_2 - 1 = \beta_3 = 0,$$

$$H_a\colon H_o \text{ is not true.}$$

Steps 2 & 3: The test statistic and its distribution are

$$F = (SSR/2)/[SSE/(n - 3)] \sim F_{2,n-3}.$$

Step 4: Do not reject the null hypothesis if

$$F < F_{\alpha,2,n-3} = F_{0.05,2,20} = 3.49,$$

otherwise reject it.

Step 5: In order to calculate sample values, consider

$$\hat{\underline{\beta}} = (\underline{X}'\underline{X})^{-1}\underline{X}'\underline{z} = (\underline{X}'\underline{X})^{-1}\underline{X}'(\underline{y} - \underline{x}_2),$$

or

$$\begin{bmatrix} \hat{\beta}_2 - 1 \\ \hat{\beta}_3 \end{bmatrix} = \begin{bmatrix} m_{22} & m_{23} \\ m_{23} & m_{33} \end{bmatrix}^{-1} \begin{bmatrix} m_{2Y} - m_{22} \\ m_{3Y} - m_{23} \end{bmatrix}$$

$$= \frac{1}{80}\begin{bmatrix} 12 & -8 \\ -8 & 12 \end{bmatrix}\begin{bmatrix} 10-12 \\ 8-8 \end{bmatrix}$$

$$= \begin{bmatrix} -0.30 \\ 0.20 \end{bmatrix}.$$

Further,

$$\begin{aligned} SST &= \Sigma(Z_i - \bar{Z})^2 \\ &= \Sigma[Y_i - \bar{Y} - (X_{i2} - \bar{X}_2)]^2 \\ &= \Sigma(Y_i - \bar{Y})^2 + \Sigma(X_{i2} - \bar{X}_2)^2 - 2\Sigma(Y_i - \bar{Y})(X_{i2} - \bar{X}_2) \\ &= 10 + 12 - 2(10) \\ &= 2, \end{aligned}$$

$$SSR = \begin{bmatrix} -0.30 & 0.20 \end{bmatrix} \begin{bmatrix} -2 \\ 0 \end{bmatrix} = 0.60,$$

and

$$SSE = 2 - 0.60 = 1.40.$$

Thus the value of the test statistic is

$$F = (0.60/2)/(1.40/20) = 4.2857.$$

Step 6: Since the value of the test statistic falls in the rejection region, reject the null hypothesis.

10-13-b.

Consider

$$Y_i = \beta_1 + \beta_2 X_{i2} + \beta_3 X_{i3} + \epsilon_i.$$

Step 1: The null and the alternative hypotheses are

$$H_o: 3\beta_2 - 5\beta_3 = 0,$$

$$H_a: H_o \text{ is not true.}$$

Steps 2 & 3: The test statistic and its distribution are

$$t = \frac{3\hat{\beta}_2 - 5\hat{\beta}_3}{s_{3\hat{\beta}_2 - 5\hat{\beta}_3}} \sim t_{n-3}.$$

Step 4: Do not reject the null hypothesis if

$$|t| < t_{\alpha/2,n-3} = t_{0.0250,20} = 2.0860,$$

otherwise reject it.

Step 5: Sample values are

$$\begin{bmatrix} \hat{\beta}_2 \\ \hat{\beta}_3 \end{bmatrix} = \frac{1}{80}\begin{bmatrix} 12 & -8 \\ -8 & 12 \end{bmatrix}\begin{bmatrix} 10 \\ 8 \end{bmatrix} = \begin{bmatrix} 0.70 \\ 0.20 \end{bmatrix},$$

$$SSR = \begin{bmatrix} 0.70 & 0.20 \end{bmatrix}\begin{bmatrix} 10 \\ 8 \end{bmatrix} = 8.60,$$

$$R^2 = 8.60/10 = 0.86,$$

$$SSE = 10 - 8.60 = 1.40,$$

$$s^2 = 1.40/20 = 0.07,$$

$$s^2_{3\hat{\beta}_2-5\hat{\beta}_3} = \frac{0.07}{80}\begin{bmatrix} 3 & -5 \end{bmatrix}\begin{bmatrix} 12 & -8 \\ -8 & 12 \end{bmatrix}\begin{bmatrix} 3 \\ -5 \end{bmatrix} = 0.5670,$$

and

$$s_{3\hat{\beta}_2-5\hat{\beta}_3} = 0.7530.$$

Thus the value of the test statistic is

$$t = \frac{3(0.70) - 5(0.20)}{0.7530} = 1.4608.$$

Step 6: Since the value of the test statistic falls in the acceptance region, do not reject the null hypothesis.

10-13-c.

Consider

$$\beta_3 = 0.60\beta_2,$$

and

$$Y_i = \beta_1 + \beta_2(X_{i2} + 0.60X_{i3}) + \epsilon_i.$$

Now

$$\begin{aligned}\hat{\beta}_2 &= \Sigma(x'_{i2} + 0.60x'_{i3})y'_i/\Sigma(x'_{i2} + 0.60x'_{i3})^2 \\ &= (m_{2Y} + 0.60m_{3Y})/(m_{22} + 1.20m_{23} + 0.36m_{33}) \\ &= [10 + 0.60(8)]/[12 + 1.20(8) + 0.36(12)] \\ &= 14.80/25.92 \\ &= 0.5710,\end{aligned}$$

and

$$\hat{\beta}_3 = 0.60(0.5710) = 0.3426.$$

10-13-d.

Consider

$$SSR = \hat{\beta}_2(m_{2Y} + 0.60m_{3Y}) = 0.5710(14.80) = 8.4506,$$

$$SSE = 10 - 8.4506 = 1.5494,$$

$$s^2 = 1.5494/20 = 0.0775,$$

$$s^2_{\hat{\beta}_2} = s^2/(m_{22} + 1.20m_{23} + 0.36m_{33}) = 0.0775/25.92 = 0.0030.$$

Then

$$s_{\hat{\beta}_2} = 0.0547,$$

and

$$s_{\hat{\beta}_3} = 0.60(0.0547) = 0.0328.$$

CHAPTER 11

11-1.

Consider the **X** matrix

$$\mathbf{X}' = \begin{bmatrix} 1 & 1 & 1 & 1 & 1 & 1 & 1 & 1 & 1 & 1 & 1 & 1 & 1 & 1 & 1 \\ 0 & 0 & 0 & 0 & 0 & 1 & 1 & 1 & 1 & 1 & 0 & 0 & 0 & 0 & 0 \\ 0 & 0 & 0 & 0 & 0 & 0 & 0 & 0 & 0 & 0 & 1 & 1 & 1 & 1 & 1 \end{bmatrix},$$

where $\bar{X}_2 = \bar{X}_3 = 1/3$, and the **y** vector

$$\mathbf{y}' = \begin{bmatrix} 185.60 & \cdots & 185.60 & 184.80 & \cdots & 184.80 & 158.60 & \cdots & 158.60 \end{bmatrix}$$

where $\bar{Y} = 529/3$. The sample values, then, are

$$\mathbf{X}'\mathbf{X} = \begin{bmatrix} 15 & 5 & 5 \\ 5 & 5 & 0 \\ 5 & 0 & 5 \end{bmatrix}, \qquad (\mathbf{X}'\mathbf{X})^{-1} = \begin{bmatrix} 0.20 & -0.20 & -0.20 \\ -0.20 & 0.40 & 0.20 \\ -0.20 & 0.20 & 0.40 \end{bmatrix},$$

$$\mathbf{X}'\mathbf{y} = \begin{bmatrix} 2,645 \\ 924 \\ 793 \end{bmatrix}, \qquad \text{and} \qquad \underline{\mathbf{X}}'\underline{\mathbf{y}} = \begin{bmatrix} 127/3 \\ -266/3 \end{bmatrix}.$$

Now

$$\hat{\beta} = (\mathbf{X}'\mathbf{X})^{-1}\mathbf{X}'\mathbf{y},$$

or

$$\begin{bmatrix}\hat{\beta}_1\\ \hat{\beta}_2\\ \hat{\beta}_3\end{bmatrix} = \begin{bmatrix}0.20 & -0.20 & -0.20\\ -0.20 & 0.40 & 0.20\\ -0.20 & 0.20 & 0.40\end{bmatrix}\begin{bmatrix}2,645\\ 924\\ 793\end{bmatrix} = \begin{bmatrix}185.60\\ -0.80\\ -27.00\end{bmatrix}$$

$$SSR = \hat{\underline{\beta}}'\underline{\underline{X}}'\underline{y} = \begin{bmatrix}-0.80 & -27.00\end{bmatrix}\begin{bmatrix}127/3\\ -266/3\end{bmatrix} = 7,080.40/3.$$

Now since $$F = SSR/s^2(K - 1),$$

or $$5 = (7,080.40/3)/s^2(3 - 1),$$

then $$s^2 = 708.04/3.$$

Further,

$$\textbf{Est. Var-Cov}(\hat{\beta}) = s^2(X'X)^{-1},$$

or $$\text{Est. Var-Cov}\begin{bmatrix}\hat{\beta}_1\\ \hat{\beta}_2\\ \hat{\beta}_3\end{bmatrix} = \begin{bmatrix}47.20 & -47.20 & -47.20\\ -47.20 & 94.41 & -47.20\\ -47.20 & -47.20 & 94.41\end{bmatrix}$$

and $$\text{Est. Standard Error}\begin{bmatrix}\hat{\beta}_1\\ \hat{\beta}_2\\ \hat{\beta}_3\end{bmatrix} = \begin{bmatrix}6.8704\\ 9.7162\\ 9.7162\end{bmatrix}$$

Also $$F = (n - K)R^2/(K - 1)(1 - R^2),$$

$$5 = (15 - 3)R^2/(3 - 1)(1 - R^2),$$

or $$R^2 = 0.4545.$$

11-2.

Consider $X_t = Z_t/2$, and hence $\bar{X} = \bar{Z}/2$ and $x_t' = z_t'/2$, where X_t and Z_t are the correct and the incorrect values of the explanatory variable. Let subscripts c and i stand for correct and incorrect, respectively. Thus

$$\hat{\beta}_c = \Sigma x_t' y_t' / \Sigma x_t'^2$$

$$= \Sigma(z_t'/2) y_t' / \Sigma(z_t'/2)^2$$

$$= 2\Sigma z_t' y_t' / \Sigma z_t'^2$$

$$= 2\hat{\beta}_i,$$

or

$$\hat{\beta}_c = 10,$$

and

$$\hat{\alpha}_c = \bar{Y} - \hat{\beta}_c \bar{X}$$

$$= \bar{Y} - 2\hat{\beta}_i(\bar{Z}/2)$$

$$= \bar{Y} - \hat{\beta}_i \bar{Z}$$

$$= \hat{\alpha}_i,$$

or

$$\hat{\alpha}_c = 10.$$

Further,

$$s_c^2 = \Sigma(Y_t - \hat{\alpha}_c - \hat{\beta}_c X_t)^2/(n - 2)$$

$$= \Sigma(Y_t - \hat{\alpha}_i - \hat{\beta}_i Z_t)^2/(n - 2)$$

$$= s_i^2,$$

$$s^2_{\hat{\beta}_c} = s^2_c/\Sigma x'^2_t$$

$$= s^2_i/\Sigma(z'_t/2)^2$$

$$= 4s^2_i/\Sigma z'^2_t$$

$$= 4s^2_{\hat{\beta}_i}$$

$$= 4(0.50)$$

$$= 2,$$

or

$$s_{\hat{\beta}_c} = 1.4142,$$

and

$$s^2_{\hat{a}_c} = s^2_c(\frac{1}{n} + \frac{\bar{X}^2}{\Sigma x'^2_t})$$

$$= s^2_i[\frac{1}{n} + \frac{(\bar{Z}/2)^2}{\Sigma(z'_t/2)^2}]$$

$$= s^2_i(\frac{1}{n} + \frac{\bar{Z}^2}{\Sigma z'^2_t})$$

$$= s^2_{\hat{a}_i}$$

$$= 1,$$

or

$$s_{\hat{a}_c} = 1.$$

Thus

$$Y_t = \underset{(1)}{10} + \underset{(1.4142)}{10.0000}X_t + e_t.$$

11-3-a.

The estimated regression equation containing four seasonal dummies and no constant term is

$$Y_t = -25D_{t1} + 10D_{t2} + 15D_{t3} - 40D_{t4} + 0.05X_t + e_t.^1$$

11-3-b.

First we calculate the value of k as follows

$$k = -(\gamma_2 + \gamma_3 + \gamma_4)/4 = -(35 + 40 - 15)/4 = -15.$$

Next we estimate the coefficients of the regression equation using the above result to obtain

$$\alpha^* = \alpha - k = -25 + 15 = -10,$$

$$\beta^* = \beta = 0.05,$$

$$\gamma_1^* = k = -15,$$

$$\gamma_2^* = \gamma_2 + k = 35 - 15 = 20,$$

$$\gamma_3^* = \gamma_3 + k = 40 - 15 = 25,$$

and

$$\gamma_4^* = \gamma_4 + k = -15 - 15 = -30.$$

Thus the estimated regression equation containing four seasonal dummies *and* the constant term, where the coefficients of the seasonal dummies represent deviations from the annual averages, is

$$Y_t = -10 - 15D_{t1} + 20D_{t2} + 25D_{t3} - 30D_{t4} + 0.05X_t + e_t.$$

---

[1]In the earlier print of the second edition of the text the reader is asked to determine the estimated standard errors of the estimated coefficients which is not feasible.

11-4-a.

Consider

$$\hat{\underline{\beta}} = (\underline{X}'\underline{X})^{-1}\underline{X}'\underline{Y},$$

or

$$\begin{bmatrix} \hat{\beta}_2 \\ \hat{\beta}_3 \end{bmatrix} = \frac{1}{80}\begin{bmatrix} 12 & -8 \\ -8 & 12 \end{bmatrix}\begin{bmatrix} 10 \\ 8 \end{bmatrix} = \begin{bmatrix} 0.70 \\ 0.20 \end{bmatrix},$$

$$SSR = \begin{bmatrix} 0.70 & 0.20 \end{bmatrix}\begin{bmatrix} 10 \\ 8 \end{bmatrix} = 8.60,$$

$$SSE = 10 - 8.60 = 1.40,$$

and

$$s^2 = 1.40/20 = 0.07.$$

Now

$$\text{Est. Var-Cov}(\hat{\underline{\beta}}) = s^2(\underline{X}'\underline{X})^{-1},$$

or

$$\text{Est. Var-Cov}\begin{bmatrix} \hat{\beta}_2 \\ \hat{\beta}_3 \end{bmatrix} = 0.07\begin{bmatrix} 12 & 8 \\ 8 & 12 \end{bmatrix}^{-1} = \begin{bmatrix} 0.0105 & -0.0070 \\ -0.0070 & 0.0105 \end{bmatrix}.$$

Thus

$$\text{Est. Standard Error}\begin{bmatrix} \hat{\beta}_2 \\ \hat{\beta}_3 \end{bmatrix} = \begin{bmatrix} 0.1025 \\ 0.1025 \end{bmatrix},$$

and

$$R^2 = 8.60/10 = 0.86.$$

11-4-b.

(i) Using the t-test

Step 1: The null and the alternative hypotheses are

$$H_o: \beta_2 + \beta_3 - 1 = 0,$$

$$H_a: \beta_2 + \beta_3 - 1 \neq 0.$$

Steps 2 & 3: The test statistic and its distribution are

$$t = (\hat{\beta}_2 + \hat{\beta}_3 - 1)/s_{\hat{\beta}_2+\hat{\beta}_3-1} \sim t_{n-3}.$$

Step 4: Do not reject the null hypothesis if

$$|t| < t_{a/2,n-3} = t_{0.0250,20} = 2.0860,$$

otherwise reject it.

Step 5: The sample values are

$$\hat{\beta}_2 + \hat{\beta}_3 - 1 = 0.70 + 0.20 - 1 = -0.10,$$

$$s^2_{\hat{\beta}_2+\hat{\beta}_3-1} = \frac{0.07}{80}\begin{bmatrix}1 & 1\end{bmatrix}\begin{bmatrix}12 & -8\\ -8 & 12\end{bmatrix}\begin{bmatrix}1\\ 1\end{bmatrix} = 0.0070,$$

and

$$s_{\hat{\beta}_2+\hat{\beta}_3-1} = 0.0837.$$

Thus the value of the test statistic is

$$t = -0.10/0.0837 = -1.1952.$$

Step 6: Since the value of the test statistic falls in the acceptance region, do not reject the null hypothesis. There is evidence that the function exhibits constant returns to scale.

(ii) Using the F-test

Step 1: The null and the alternative hypotheses are

$$H_o: \beta_2 + \beta_3 - 1 = 0,$$

$$H_a: \beta_2 + \beta_3 - 1 > 0.$$

Steps 2 & 3: The test statistic and its distribution are

$$F = [(SSE_R - SSE)/r]/[SSE/(n - K)] \sim F_{r,n-K},$$

where r = 1 and K = 3.

Step 4: Do not reject the null hypothesis if

$$F < F_{\alpha,r,n-K} = F_{0.05,1,20} = 4.35,$$

otherwise reject it.

Step 5: Consider

$$Y_i = \beta_1 + \beta_2 X_{i2} + (1 - \beta_2)X_{i3} + \epsilon_i,$$

or

$$Y_i - X_{i3} = \beta_1 + \beta_2(X_{i2} - X_{i3}) + \epsilon_i.$$

Then the sample values are

$$\begin{aligned}\tilde{\beta}_2 &= \Sigma(x'_{i2} - x'_{i3})(y'_i - x'_{i3})/\Sigma(x'_{i2} - x'_{i3})^2 \\ &= (m_{2Y} - m_{23} - m_{3Y} + m_{33})/(m_{22} - 2m_{23} + m_{33}) \\ &= (10 - 8 - 8 + 12)/(12 - 16 + 12) \\ &= 0.75,\end{aligned}$$

and

$$\begin{aligned}SSE_R &= \Sigma[y'_i - \tilde{\beta}_2 x'_{i2} - (1 - \tilde{\beta}_2)x'_{i3}]^2 \\ &= m_{YY} + \tilde{\beta}_2^2 m_{22} + (1 - \tilde{\beta}_2)^2 m_{33} - 2\tilde{\beta}_2 m_{2Y} - 2(1 - \tilde{\beta}_2)m_{3Y} \\ &\quad + 2\tilde{\beta}_2(1 - \tilde{\beta}_2)m_{23} \\ &= 1.50.\end{aligned}$$

Thus the value of the test statistic is

$$F = [(1.50 - 1.40)/1]/[1.40/(23 - 3)] = 1.4286.$$

Step 6: Since the value of the test statistic falls in the acceptance region, do not reject the null hypothesis. There is evidence that the function exhibits constant returns to scale.

(iii) Using the likelihood ratio test

Step 1: The null and the alternative hypotheses are

$$H_o: \beta_2 + \beta_3 - 1 = 0,$$

$$H_a: \beta_2 + \beta_3 - 1 \neq 0.$$

Steps 2 & 3: The test statistic and its asymptotic distribution are

$$LR = n[\log(\tilde{\sigma}^2) - \log(\hat{\sigma}^2)] \sim \text{Asympt. } \chi_1^2,$$

where
$$\tilde{\sigma}^2 = \Sigma\tilde{u}_t^2/n,$$

and
$$\hat{\sigma}^2 = \Sigma\hat{u}_t^2/n,$$

where $\tilde{u}_t$ and $\hat{u}_t$ are the residuals from the restricted and the unrestricted regressions.

Step 4: Do not reject the null hypothesis if

$$\chi^2_{1-\frac{\alpha}{2},1} = \chi^2_{0.9750,1} \cong 0 < LR < \chi^2_{\frac{\alpha}{2},1} = \chi^2_{0.0250,1} = 5.0240,$$

otherwise reject it.

Step 5: The sample values from parts (i) and (ii) are

$$\tilde{\sigma}^2 = SSE_R/n = 1.50/23 = 0.0652,$$

and

$$\hat{\sigma}^2 = SSE/n = 1.40/23 = 0.0609.$$

Thus the value of the test statistic is

$$LR = 23[\log(0.0652) - \log(0.0609)] = 1.5868.$$

Step 6: Since the value of the test statistic falls in the acceptance region, do not reject the null hypothesis. There is evidence that the function exhibits constant returns to scale.

(iv) Using the Wald test

Step 1: The null and the alternative hypotheses are

$$H_o: g(\beta) = \beta_2 + \beta_3 - 1 = 0,$$

$$H_a: g(\beta) = \beta_2 + \beta_3 - 1 \neq 0.$$

Steps 2 & 3: The test statistic and its asymptotic distribution are

$$W = \frac{\hat{g}^2}{\text{Est. Var}(\hat{g})} = \frac{(\hat{\beta}_2 + \hat{\beta}_3 - 1)^2}{s^2_{\hat{\beta}_2+\hat{\beta}_3-1}} \sim \text{Asympt. } \chi^2_1.$$

Step 4: Do not reject the null hypothesis if

$$\chi^2_{1-\frac{\alpha}{2},1} = \chi^2_{0.9750,1} \cong 0 < W < \chi^2_{\frac{\alpha}{2},1} = \chi^2_{0.0250,1} = 5.0240,$$

otherwise reject it.

Step 5: The sample values from part (i) are

$$\hat{\beta}_2 + \hat{\beta}_3 - 1 = -0.10,$$

and

$$s^2_{\hat{\beta}_2+\hat{\beta}_3-1} = 0.0070.$$

Thus the value of the test statistic is

$$W = \frac{-1.10^2}{0.0070} = 1.4286.$$

Step 6: Since the value of the test statistic falls in the acceptance region, do not reject the null hypothesis. There is evidence that the production function exhibits constant returns to scale.

(v) Using the Lagrange multiplier test

Step 1: The null and the alternative hypotheses are

$$H_o\colon \beta_2 + \beta_3 - 1 = 0,$$

$$H_a\colon \beta_2 + \beta_3 - 1 \neq 0.$$

Steps 2 & 3: The test statistic and its asymptotic distribution are

$$LM = (\hat{\underline{\beta}} - \tilde{\underline{\beta}})'\underline{X}'\underline{X}(\hat{\underline{\beta}} - \tilde{\underline{\beta}})/\tilde{\sigma}^2 \sim \text{Asympt. } \chi_1^2.$$

Step 4: Do not reject the null hypothesis if

$$\chi^2_{1-\frac{\alpha}{2},1} = \chi^2_{0.9750,1} \cong 0 < LM < \chi^2_{\frac{\alpha}{2},1} = \chi^2_{0.0250,1} = 5.0240,$$

otherwise reject it.

Step 5: The sample values from part (ii) are

$$\tilde{\beta}_2 = 0.75,$$

$$\tilde{\beta}_3 = 1 - \tilde{\beta}_2 = 0.25,$$

and

$$(\hat{\underline{\beta}} - \tilde{\underline{\beta}}) = \begin{bmatrix} 0.70 \\ 0.20 \end{bmatrix} - \begin{bmatrix} 0.75 \\ 0.25 \end{bmatrix} = \begin{bmatrix} -0.05 \\ -0.05 \end{bmatrix}.$$

Thus the value of the test statistic is

$$LM = \begin{bmatrix} -0.05 & -0.05 \end{bmatrix} \begin{bmatrix} 12 & 8 \\ 8 & 12 \end{bmatrix} \begin{bmatrix} -0.05 \\ -0.05 \end{bmatrix} /0.0652 = 1.5337.$$

Step 6: Since the value of the test statistic falls in the acceptance region, do not reject the null hypothesis. There is evidence that the production function exhibits constant returns to scale.

11-4-c.

Referring to part (ii), we have

$$\tilde{\beta}_2 = 0.75,$$

and

$$\tilde{\beta}_3 = 1 - \tilde{\beta}_2 = 0.25.$$

Further,

$$s^2 = SSE_R/(n - 2) = 1.50/21 = 0.0714,$$

and

$$s^2_{\tilde{\beta}_2} = s^2/\Sigma(x'_{i2} - x'_{i3})^2 = 0.0714/8,$$

or

$$s^2_{\tilde{\beta}_2} = 0.0089.$$

Note that since

$$\tilde{\beta}_3 = 1 - \tilde{\beta}_2,$$

the variances, and hence the standard errors of $\tilde{\beta}_2$ and $\tilde{\beta}_3$ are the same. Therefore

$$s_{\tilde{\beta}_2} = s_{\tilde{\beta}_3} = 0.0945.$$

Now

$$SSE_R = 1.50,$$

and

$$SST = 10.00.$$

Thus

$$R^2 = 1 - SSE_R/SST = 1 - 1.50/10.00,$$

or

$$R^2 = 0.85.$$

11-5-a.

Differentiating

$$S = \sum_{t=2}^{n} [Y_t - a\gamma - \beta\gamma X_t - (1 - \gamma)Z_t]^2,$$

where

$$Z_t = Y_{t-1},$$

with respect to parameters a, β, and γ, setting the derivatives equal to zero, and putting a "^" on the parameters to denote their estimated values, we obtain

$$\partial S/\partial a \equiv -2\hat{\gamma}\Sigma[Y_t - \hat{a}\hat{\gamma} - \hat{\beta}\hat{\gamma}X_t - (1 - \hat{\gamma})Z_t] = 0,$$

$$\partial S/\partial \beta \equiv -2\hat{\gamma}\Sigma[Y_t - \hat{a}\hat{\gamma} - \hat{\beta}\hat{\gamma}X_t - (1 - \hat{\gamma})Z_t]X_t = 0,$$

and

$$\partial S/\partial \gamma \equiv -2\hat{\beta}\Sigma[Y_t - \hat{a}\hat{\gamma} - \hat{\beta}\hat{\gamma}X_t - (1 - \hat{\gamma})Z_t]X_t$$

$$+ 2\Sigma[Y_t - \hat{a}\hat{\gamma} - \hat{\beta}\hat{\gamma}X_t - (1 - \hat{\gamma})Z_t]Z_t = 0,$$

or equivalently

$$\Sigma[Y_t - \hat{a}\hat{\gamma} - \hat{\beta}\hat{\gamma}X_t - (1 - \hat{\gamma})Z_t] = 0,$$

$$\Sigma[Y_t - \hat{a}\hat{\gamma} - \hat{\beta}\hat{\gamma}X_t - (1 - \hat{\gamma})Z_t]X_t = 0,$$

and

$$\Sigma[Y_t - \hat{a}\hat{\gamma} - \hat{\beta}\hat{\gamma}X_t - (1 - \hat{\gamma})Z_t]Z_t = 0.$$

Let $\tilde{\beta}_1 = \hat{a}\hat{\gamma}$, $\tilde{\beta}_2 = \hat{\beta}\hat{\gamma}$, and $\tilde{\beta}_3 = (1 - \hat{\gamma})$. Then the standard least squares results are

$$\begin{bmatrix} \tilde{\beta}_2 \\ \tilde{\beta}_3 \end{bmatrix} = \begin{bmatrix} m_{XX} & m_{XZ} \\ m_{ZX} & m_{ZZ} \end{bmatrix}^{-1} \begin{bmatrix} m_{XY} & m_{ZY} \end{bmatrix} = \frac{1}{\Delta} \begin{bmatrix} m_{XY}m_{ZZ} - m_{ZY}m_{XZ} \\ m_{ZY}m_{XX} - m_{XY}m_{XZ} \end{bmatrix},$$

where

$$\Delta = m_{XX}m_{ZZ} - m_{XZ}^2,$$

and

$$\tilde{\beta}_1 = \bar{Y} - \tilde{\beta}_2\bar{X} - \tilde{\beta}_3\bar{Z},$$

where

$$\bar{Z} = \sum_{t=2}^{n} Y_{t-1}/(n - 1).$$

Since $\tilde{\beta}_1 = \hat{\alpha}\hat{\gamma}$, and $\tilde{\beta}_3 = (1 - \hat{\gamma})$, it follows that

$$\hat{\alpha} = \tilde{\beta}_1/(1 - \tilde{\beta}_3).$$

The estimated variance of $\hat{\alpha}$ using the approximation formula (11.29), section (11-2) of the text,[1] is

$$\text{Est. Var}(\hat{\alpha}) \cong \frac{\text{Est. Var}(\tilde{\beta}_1)}{(1 - \tilde{\beta}_3)^2} + \frac{\tilde{\beta}_1^2\text{Est. Var}(\tilde{\beta}_3)}{(1 - \tilde{\beta}_3)^4} + \frac{2\tilde{\beta}_1\text{Est. Cov}(\tilde{\beta}_1,\tilde{\beta}_3)}{(1 - \tilde{\beta}_3)^3},$$

or equivalently

$$\text{Est. Var}(\hat{\alpha}) \cong \frac{\text{Est. Var}(\tilde{\beta}_1) + \hat{\alpha}^2\text{Est. Var}(\tilde{\beta}_3) + 2\hat{\alpha}\text{Est. Cov}(\tilde{\beta}_1,\tilde{\beta}_3)}{\hat{\gamma}^2},$$

where

$$\text{Est. Var-Cov}\begin{bmatrix}\tilde{\beta}_1\\ \tilde{\beta}_2\\ \tilde{\beta}_3\end{bmatrix} = s^2\begin{bmatrix} n & \Sigma X_t & \Sigma Z_t \\ \Sigma X_t & \Sigma X_t^2 & \Sigma X_t Z_t \\ \Sigma Z_t & \Sigma Z_t X_t & \Sigma Z_t^2 \end{bmatrix}^{-1},$$

where

$$s^2 = (m_{YY} - \tilde{\beta}_2 m_{XY} - \tilde{\beta}_3 m_{ZY})/(n - 3).$$

---

[1]P. 486.

11-5-b.

Consider the log-likelihood function for $Y_2, \ldots, Y_n$ conditional on Y_1

$$L = [\frac{-(n - 1)}{2}]\log(2\pi\sigma^2) - \Sigma\epsilon_t^2/2\sigma^2,$$

where (t = 2, ..., n), and

$$\epsilon_t = Y_t - a\gamma - \beta\gamma X_t - (1 - \gamma)Y_{t-1}.$$

Differentiating L with respect to a, β, and γ, we obtain

$$\partial L/\partial a = \gamma\Sigma\epsilon_t/\sigma^2,$$

$$\partial L/\partial\beta = \gamma\Sigma\epsilon_t X_t/\sigma^2,$$

$$\partial L/\partial\gamma = \Sigma\epsilon_t V_t/\sigma^2,$$

where

$$V_t = a + \beta X_t - Y_{t-1}.$$

The second derivatives of L with respect to a, β, and γ are

$$\partial^2 L/\partial a^2 = -n\gamma^2/\sigma^2,$$

$$\partial^2 L/\partial\beta^2 = -\gamma^2\Sigma X_t^2/\sigma^2,$$

$$\partial^2 L/\partial\gamma^2 = -\Sigma V_t^2/\sigma^2,$$

$$\partial^2 L/\partial a\partial\beta = -\gamma^2\Sigma X_t/\sigma^2,$$

$$\partial^2 L/\partial a\partial\gamma = \Sigma\epsilon_t/\sigma^2 - \gamma\Sigma V_t/\sigma^2,$$

$$\partial^2 L/\partial\beta\partial\gamma = \Sigma\epsilon_t X_t/\sigma^2 - \gamma\Sigma V_t X_t/\sigma^2.$$

The asymptotic variances and covariances of the MLE's of the unknown parameters a, β, and γ can be determined by reference to the inverse of the information matrix

$$\begin{bmatrix} -E(\frac{\partial^2 L}{\partial \alpha^2}) & -E(\frac{\partial^2 L}{\partial \alpha \partial \beta}) & -E(\frac{\partial^2 L}{\partial \alpha \partial \gamma}) \\ -E(\frac{\partial^2 L}{\partial \beta \partial \alpha}) & -E(\frac{\partial^2 L}{\partial \beta^2}) & -E(\frac{\partial^2 L}{\partial \beta \partial \gamma}) \\ -E(\frac{\partial^2 L}{\partial \gamma \partial \alpha}) & -E(\frac{\partial^2 L}{\partial \gamma \partial \beta}) & -E(\frac{\partial^2 L}{\partial \gamma^2}) \end{bmatrix}^{-1} = \sigma^2 \begin{bmatrix} n\gamma^2 & \gamma^2 \Sigma X_t & \gamma \Sigma V_t \\ \gamma^2 \Sigma X_t & \gamma^2 \Sigma X_t^2 & \gamma \Sigma V_t X_t \\ \gamma \Sigma V_t & \gamma \Sigma V_t X_t & \Sigma V_t^2 \end{bmatrix}^{-1}$$

The formula for the asymptotic variance of $\hat{\alpha}$ using the information matrix is

$$\text{Asympt. Var}(\hat{\alpha}) = \sigma^2 \gamma^2 [\Sigma X_t^2 \Sigma V_t^2 - (\Sigma V_t X_t)^2]/|I|,$$

where $|I|$ is the determinant of the information matrix. In order to derive the formula for the estimated variance of $\hat{\alpha}$, we should substitute the MLE's of α, β, γ, and σ^2 in the above formula. However, the non-linear least squares estimators of the four unknown parameters derived in part (a), i.e., $\hat{\alpha}$, $\hat{\beta}$, $\hat{\gamma}$, and s^2, are equivalent to the MLE's. Thus

$$s_{\hat{\alpha}}^2 = s^2 \hat{\gamma}^2 [\Sigma X_t^2 \Sigma \hat{V}_t^2 - (\Sigma \hat{V}_t X_t)^2]/|\hat{I}| ,$$

where

$$\hat{V}_t = \hat{\alpha} + \hat{\beta} X_t - Y_{t-1},$$

and $|\hat{I}|$ is the determinant of the information matrix when the unknown parameters are replaced by their estimates. The two formulas of the estimated variance of $\hat{\alpha}$, one using the approximation formula and the other based on the ML information matrix, are equivalent. (The equivalency of the two is not shown here.)

11-6.

The *Box-Cox transformation* is estimated as

$$Y_i^* = \underset{(0.0434)}{2.0329} + \underset{(0.0150)}{0.5647}X_i^* + e_i, \qquad R^2 = 0.9841,$$

where

$$Y_i^* = \frac{Y_i^{\hat{\lambda}} - 1}{\hat{\lambda}},$$

and

$$X_i^* = \frac{X_i^{\hat{\lambda}} - 1}{\hat{\lambda}},$$

where

$$\hat{\lambda} = -0.0740,$$

and search over value of λ is carried to an accuracy of 0.001.

In order to conduct the PE test using the approach of MacKinnon *et. al.*, consider

$$Y_i = \alpha + \beta X_i + \theta_0[\widehat{\log}(Y_i) - \log(\tilde{Y}_i)] + \epsilon_i,$$

where $\tilde{Y}_i$ and $\widehat{\log}(Y_i)$ are the i-th fitted values of

$$Y_i = \alpha + \beta X_i + \epsilon_{0i},$$

and

$$\log(Y_i) = \gamma + \delta \log(X_i) + \epsilon_{1i},$$

respectively, using the ordinary least squares method. In order to conduct the PE test using the approach of Bera and McAleer, section (11-3) of the text,[1] consider

$$Y_i = \alpha + \beta X_i + \theta_0 \tilde{\eta}_{1i} + \epsilon_i,$$

[1] P. 521, n. 29.

where $\tilde{\eta}_{1i}$ is the least squares residual of the following model

$$\log(\tilde{Y}_i) = \gamma + \delta\log(X_i) + \eta_{1i},$$

where $\tilde{Y}_i$ is the same as above.

Step 1: The null and the alternative hypotheses are

$$H_o\colon \theta_0 = 0 \qquad (Y_i = \alpha + \beta X_i + \epsilon_{0i}),$$

$$H_a\colon \theta_0 \neq 0 \qquad [\log(Y_i) = \gamma + \delta\log(X_i) + \epsilon_{1i}].$$

Steps 2 & 3: The test statistic and its distribution are

$$t = \frac{\hat{\theta}_0}{s_{\hat{\theta}_0}} \sim t_{n-3}.$$

Step 4: Do not reject the null hypothesis if

$$|t| < t_{\alpha/2,n-3} = t_{0.0250,22} = 2.0740,$$

otherwise reject it.

Step 5: The value of the test statistic using the approach of MacKinnon *et. al.* is

$$t = \frac{1.4080}{0.3847} = 3.6600.$$

and that of the Bera and McAleer's approach is

$$t = \frac{-1.9133}{0.6764} = -2.8285.$$

Step 6: Since the value of the test statistic of either approach falls in the rejection region, reject the null hypothesis. There is evidence that the linear specification is wrong.

In order to allow for the possibility that the log-linear specification may be wrong, reverse H_o and H_a. Using the approach of MacKinnon *et. al.*, consider

$$\log(Y_i) = \gamma + \delta\log(X_i) + \theta_1\{\tilde{Y}_i - \exp[\hat{\log}(Y_i)]\} + \epsilon_i,$$

where $\tilde{Y}_i$ and $\hat{\log}(Y_i)$ are the same as above. Using the Bera and McAleer's approach, consider

$$\log(Y_i) = \gamma + \delta\log(X_i) + \theta_1\hat{\eta}_{0i} + \epsilon_i,$$

where $\hat{\eta}_{0i}$ is the least squares residual of the following model

$$\exp[\hat{\log}(Y_i)] = \alpha + \beta X_i + \eta_{0i},$$

where $\hat{\log}(Y_i)$ is the same as above.

Step 1: The null and the alternative hypotheses are

$$H_o\colon \theta_1 = 0 \qquad [\log(Y_i) = \gamma + \delta\log(X_i) + \epsilon_{1i}],$$

$$H_a\colon \theta_1 \neq 0 \qquad (Y_i = \alpha + \beta X_i + \epsilon_{0i}).$$

Steps 2 & 3: The test statistic and its distribution are

$$t = \frac{\hat{\theta}_1}{s_{\hat{\theta}_1}} \sim t_{n-3}.$$

Step 4: Do not reject the null hypothesis if

$$|t| < t_{\alpha/2,n-3} = t_{0.0250,22} = 2.0740,$$

otherwise reject it.

Step 5: The value of the test statistic using the approach of MacKinnon *et. al.* is

$$t = \frac{-0.1941}{0.1237} = -1.5685,$$

and that of the Bera and McAleer's approach is

$$t = \frac{0.1501}{0.0987} = 1.5213.$$

Step 6: Since the value of the test statistic of either approach falls in the acceptance region, do not reject the null hypothesis. There is evidence that the log-linear specification may be correct.

11-7-a.

In order to conduct the segmented regression test, variable F is arranged in order of magnitude where sub-samples 1, 2, and 3 contain 6, 7, and 6 observations, respectively. Further,

$$I_t = \beta_1 + \beta_2 F_{t-1} + \beta_3 K_{t-1}$$
$$+ \gamma_1 Z_{t1} + \gamma_2 F_{t-1} Z_{t1} + \gamma_3 Z_{t2} + \gamma_4 F_{t-1} Z_{t2} + \epsilon_t,$$

where

$$Z_{tj} = \begin{cases} 1 & \text{if observation } t \text{ belongs to sub-sample } j, \\ 0 & \text{otherwise,} \end{cases}$$

where (j = 1, 2).

Step 1: The null and the alternative hypotheses are

$$H_o: E(I_t) = \beta_1 + \beta_2 F_{t-1} + \beta_3 K_{t-1},$$
$$H_a: H_o \text{ is not true.}$$

Steps 2 & 3: The test statistic and its distribution are

$$F = \frac{(SSR_Q - SSR_K)/(Q - K)}{SSE_Q/(n - Q)} \sim F_{Q-K,n-Q},$$

where Q = 7 and K = 3.

Step 4: Do not reject the null hypothesis if

$$F < F_{\alpha,Q-K,n-Q} = F_{0.05,4,12} = 3.26,$$

otherwise reject it.

Step 5: The value of the test statistic is

$$F = \frac{(908{,}030 - 897{,}970)/(7 - 3)}{100{,}150/(19 - 7)} = 0.3013.$$

Step 6: Since the value of the test statistic falls in the acceptance region, do not reject the null hypothesis. There is no evidence that the model is not linear.

If the variable K is arranged in the order of magnitude where the sub-samples 1, 2, and 3 contain 6, 7, and 6 observations, respectively, the value of the test statistic is

$$F = \frac{(947,210 - 897,970)/(7 - 3)}{60,965/(19 - 7)} = 2.4230,$$

which leads to the same conclusion.

11-7-b.

In order to conduct the "rainbow" test consider

Step 1: The null and the alternative hypotheses are

$$H_o\colon E(I_t) = \beta_1 + \beta_2 F_{t-1} + \beta_3 K_{t-1},$$

$$H_a\colon H_o \text{ is not true.}$$

Steps 2 & 3: The test statistic and its distribution are

$$F = \frac{(SSE - SSE_D)/(n - m)}{SSE_D/(m - K)} \sim F_{n-m,m-K},$$

where m = 9 is the number of approximately one half middle observations (fifth to thirteenth) whose h_{ii} are smaller than the rest, and K = 3.

Step 4: Do not reject the null hypothesis if

$$F < F_{\alpha,n-m,m-K} = F_{0.05,10,6} = 4.06,$$

otherwise reject it.

Step 5: The value of the test statistic is

$$F = \frac{(110,210 - 37,782)/(19 - 9)}{37,782/(9 - 3)} = 1.1502.$$

Step 6: Since the value of the test statistic falls in the acceptance region, do not reject the null hypothesis. There is no evidence that any relevant explanatory variables have been omitted or that the model is not linear.

11-7-c.

In order to conduct the RESET test, consider

$$I_t = \beta_1 + \beta_2 F_{t-1} + \beta_3 K_{t-1} + \beta_4 F_{t-1}^2 + \beta_5 K_{t-1}^2$$

$$+ \beta_6 F_{t-1}^3 + \beta_7 K_{t-1}^3 + \beta_8 F_{t-1}^4 + \beta_9 K_{t-1}^4 + \epsilon_t.$$

Step 1: The null and the alternative hypotheses are

$$H_o: E(I_t) = \beta_1 + \beta_2 F_{t-1} + \beta_3 K_{t-1},$$

$$H_a: H_o \text{ is not true.}$$

Steps 2 & 3: The test statistic and its distribution are

$$F = \frac{(SSR_Q - SSR_K)/(Q - K)}{SSE_Q/(n - Q)} \sim F_{Q-K,n-Q},$$

where Q = 9 and K = 3.

Step 4: Do not reject the null hypothesis if

$$F < F_{\alpha,Q-K,n-Q} = F_{0.05,6,10} = 3.22,$$

otherwise reject it.

Step 5: The value of the test statistic is

$$F = \frac{(964{,}180 - 897{,}970)/(9 - 3)}{43{,}996/(19 - 9)} = 2.5082.$$

Step 6: Since the value of the test statistic falls in the acceptance region, do not reject the null hypothesis. There is no evidence that any relevant explanatory variables have been omitted or that the model is not linear.

11-8.

Let $\mu_1 = -\delta_1$ and $\mu_2 = -\delta_2$, so that the model can be written as

$$Y_t - \mu_1 Y_{t-1} - \mu_2 Y_{t-2} = a + \beta X_t + \epsilon_t - \mu_1 \epsilon_{t-1} - \mu_2 \epsilon_{t-2},$$

or

$$f(L)Y_t = a + \beta X_t + f(L)\epsilon_t,$$

where L is the lag operator and

$$f(L) = 1 - \mu_1 L - \mu_2 L^2.$$

Then we have

$$Y_t = \frac{a}{f(L)} + \frac{\beta X_t}{f(L)} + \epsilon_t = a^* + \beta X_t^* + \epsilon_t,$$

where

$$a^* = \frac{a}{f(L)} = \frac{a}{1 - \mu_1 - \mu_2},$$

and

$$X_t^* = \frac{X_t}{f(L)}.$$

Now

$$X_t = f(L)X_t^* = X_t^* - \mu_1 X_{t-1}^* - \mu_2 X_{t-2}^*,$$

or

$$X_t^* = X_t + \mu_1 X_{t-1}^* + \mu_2 X_{t-2}^*.$$

Successive substitution for the lagged values of X* enables us to express X_t^* in terms of current and lagged values of X. The initial conditions X_0^* and X_{-1}^* can be treated as unknown parameters, say θ_1 and θ_2, respectively. Then we have

$$X_1^* = X_1 + \mu_1\theta_1 + \mu_2\theta_2,$$

$$X_2^* = X_2 + \mu_1 X_1^* + \mu_2\theta_1,$$

$$X_3^* = X_3 + \mu_1 X_2^* + \mu_2 X_1^*,$$

$$\vdots$$

$$X_t^* = X_t + \mu_1 X_{t-1}^* + \mu_2 X_{t-2}^*.$$

In general, we may write

$$X_t^* = W_{0t} + \theta_1 W_{1t} + \theta_2 W_{2t},$$

where

$$W_{01} = X_1,$$

$$W_{02} = X_2 + \mu_1 W_{01},$$

$$W_{03} = X_3 + \mu_1 W_{02} + \mu_2 W_{01},$$

$$\vdots$$

$$W_{0t} = X_t + \mu_1 W_{0,t-1} + \mu_2 W_{0,t-2},$$

further,

$$W_{11} = \mu_1,$$

$$W_{12} = \mu_1 W_{11} + \mu_2,$$

$$W_{13} = \mu_1 W_{12} + \mu_2 W_{11},$$

$$\vdots$$

$$W_{1t} = \mu_1 W_{1,t-1} + \mu_2 W_{1,t-2},$$

and

$$W_{21} = \mu_2,$$

$$W_{22} = \mu_1 W_{21},$$

$$W_{23} = \mu_1 W_{22} + \mu_2 W_{21},$$

$$\vdots$$

$$W_{2t} = \mu_1 W_{2,t-1} + \mu_2 W_{2,t-2}.$$

Then the model

$$Y_t = a^* + \beta X_t^* + \epsilon_t,$$

can be presented as

$$Y_t = a/(1 - \mu_1 - \mu_2) + \beta W_{0t} + \beta\theta_1 W_{1t} + \beta\theta_2 W_{2t} + \epsilon_t,$$

where each of the W's involves the unknown parameters μ_1 and μ_2. The parameters of the model can be estimated by MLE, searching over various values of μ_1 and μ_2.

Alternatively, consider

$$Y_t - \epsilon_t = a + \beta X_t - \delta_1(Y_{t-1} - \epsilon_{t-1}) - \delta_2(Y_{t-2} - \epsilon_{t-2}),$$

or

$$Y_t^* = a + \beta X_t - \delta_1 Y_{t-1}^* - \delta_2 Y_{t-2}^*,$$

where (t = 1, ..., n). Lagging the above by one period and substituting the result into the model, we get

$$Y_t^* = a(1 - \delta_1) + \beta(X_t - \delta_1 X_{t-1}) + (\delta_1^2 - \delta_2)Y_{t-2}^* + \delta_1\delta_2 Y_{t-3}^*.$$

Upon successive lagging and substitution, we obtain

$$Y_t^* = a \sum_{i=0}^{n-1} \lambda_i + \beta \sum_{i=0}^{n-1} \lambda_i X_{t-i} - \lambda_t Y_0^* - \delta_2 \lambda_{t-1} Y_{-1}^*,$$

where

$$\lambda_0 = 1, \qquad \lambda_1 = -\delta_1,$$

and

$$\lambda_j = -\delta_1 \lambda_{j-1} - \delta_2 \lambda_{j-2} \qquad (j \geq 2).$$

Treating initial terms $Y_0^* = (Y_0 - \epsilon_0)$ and $Y_{-1}^* = (Y_{-1} - \epsilon_{-1})$ as unknown parameters and substituting $(Y_t - \epsilon_t)$ for Y_t^*, we obtain

$$Y_t = a\sum_{i=0}^{n-1}\lambda_i + \beta\sum_{i=0}^{n-1}\lambda_i X_{t-i} - \lambda_t Y_0^* - \delta_2\lambda_{t-1}Y_{-1}^* + \epsilon_t,$$

or in matrix notation

$$\mathbf{y} = \mathbf{Z}\gamma + \epsilon,$$

where $\mathbf{y} = \begin{bmatrix} y_1 \\ y_2 \\ \vdots \\ y_n \end{bmatrix}, \quad \gamma = \begin{bmatrix} a \\ \beta \\ Y_0^* \\ Y_{-1}^* \end{bmatrix}, \quad \epsilon = \begin{bmatrix} \epsilon_1 \\ \epsilon_2 \\ \vdots \\ \epsilon_n \end{bmatrix},$

$$\mathbf{Z} = \begin{bmatrix} \lambda_0 & \lambda_0 X_1 & \lambda_1 & -\delta_2\lambda_0 \\ \lambda_0+\lambda_1 & \lambda_0 X_2+\lambda_1 X_1 & \lambda_2 & -\delta_2\lambda_1 \\ \vdots & \vdots & \vdots & \vdots \\ \sum_{i=0}^{n-1}\lambda_i & \sum_{i=0}^{n-1}\lambda_i X_{t-i} & \lambda_n & -\delta_2\lambda_{n-1} \end{bmatrix},$$

and $\epsilon \sim \mathbf{N}(\mathbf{0}, \sigma^2\mathbf{I}).$

To obtain consistent MLE's of the coefficients, maximize the log-likelihood function

$$L = (\frac{-n}{2})\log(2\pi\sigma^2) - (\mathbf{y} - \mathbf{Z}\gamma)'(\mathbf{y} - \mathbf{Z}\gamma)/2\sigma^2,$$

with respect to a, β, Y_0^*, and Y_{-1}^* by searching over values of δ_1 and δ_2.

11-9-a.

The aggregate consumption function is estimated using the polynomial distributed lag formulation with the length of the lag of four periods (m = 4) and the degree of polynomial of two (p = 2).

$$C_t = \underset{(6.8313)}{-34.3150} + \underset{(0.1196)}{0.0716}L_t + \underset{(0.0918)}{0.6847}Y_t + \underset{(0.0457)}{0.3595}Y_{t-1}$$

$$+ \underset{(0.0575)}{0.1157}Y_{t-2} - \underset{(0.0360)}{0.0468}Y_{t-3} - \underset{(0.0643)}{0.1278}Y_{t-4} + e_t.$$

11-9-b.

The aggregate consumption function is estimated using the LaGuerre lag formulation with thè length of lag of infinite periods (m = ∞) and the degree of polynomial of two (p = 2). In this model the weights are given by

$$w_i = (\lambda_0 + \lambda_1 i + \lambda_2 i^2)\mu^i,$$

where (i = 0, 1, ...), and ($0 \le \mu < 1$). Then the model can be written as

$$C_t = \beta_1 + \beta_2 L_t + \sum_{i=0}^{\infty} w_i Y_{t-i} + \epsilon_t,$$

or

$$C_t = \beta_1 + \beta_2 L_t + \sum_{i=0}^{\infty} (\lambda_0 + \lambda_1 i + \lambda_2 i^2)\mu^i Y_{t-i} + \epsilon_t.$$

Upon expanding the above, we get

$$C_t = \beta_1 + \beta_2 L_t + \lambda_0 \sum_{i=0}^{\infty} \mu^i Y_{t-i} + \lambda_1 \sum_{i=0}^{\infty} i\mu^i Y_{t-i} + \lambda_2 \sum_{i=0}^{\infty} i^2 \mu^i Y_{t-i} + \epsilon_t.$$

Truncating the infinite sums and decomposing the remainder into "initial condition" terms, we obtain

$$C_t = \beta_1 + \beta_2 L_t + \lambda_0 \sum_{i=0}^{t-1} \mu^i Y_{t-i} + \lambda_1 \sum_{i=0}^{t-1} i\mu^i Y_{t-i} + \lambda_2 \sum_{i=0}^{t-1} i^2 \mu^i Y_{t-i}$$

$$+ \theta_0 \mu^t + \theta_1 t\mu^t + \theta_2 t^2 \mu^t + \epsilon_t.$$

The above relation is estimated by searching over value of μ in the interval of zero to one to an accuracy of 0.01. The results are as follows

$$\hat{\mu} = 0.7100,$$

$$\hat{\beta}_1 = 14.6300, \qquad \hat{\beta}_2 = -0.1058,$$

$$\hat{\lambda}_0 = 0.7027, \qquad \hat{\lambda}_1 = -0.2945, \qquad \hat{\lambda}_2 = 0.0208,$$

and

$$\hat{\theta}_0 = 248.0100, \qquad \hat{\theta}_1 = -163.9200, \qquad \hat{\theta}_2 = 15.7520.$$

Therefore, the estimated weights are

$$\hat{w}_0 = \hat{\lambda}_0 = 0.7027,$$

$$\hat{w}_1 = (\hat{\lambda}_0 + \hat{\lambda}_1 + \hat{\lambda}_2)\hat{\mu} = 0.3046,$$

$$\hat{w}_2 = (\hat{\lambda}_0 + 2\hat{\lambda}_1 + 4\hat{\lambda}_2)\hat{\mu}^2 = 0.0993,$$

$$\hat{w}_3 = (\hat{\lambda}_0 + 3\hat{\lambda}_1 + 9\hat{\lambda}_2)\hat{\mu}^3 = 0.0023,$$

$$\hat{w}_4 = (\hat{\lambda}_0 + 4\hat{\lambda}_1 + 16\hat{\lambda}_2)\hat{\mu}^4 = -0.0362,$$

etc., so that the LaGuerre lag estimate of the aggregate consumption function is

$$C_t = 14.6300 - 0.1058L_t + 0.7027Y_t + 0.3046Y_{t-1}$$

$$+ 0.0993Y_{t-2} + 0.0023Y_{t-3} - 0.0362Y_{t-4} + \cdots + e_t.$$

11-9-c.

The aggregate consumption function is estimated using the Shiller lag formulation with the length of the lag of four periods (m = 4) and the degree of polynomial of two (p = 2). The Shiller lag model is based on stochastic prior information

$$w_i - 3w_{i-1} + 3w_{i-2} - w_{i-3} = v_i \qquad (i = 3, 4),$$

where

$$v_i \sim N(0, \sigma_v^2),$$

and, *a priori*, sum of w's is considered to be unity. However, since each disturbance term of the original observations (ϵ) has a variance equal to σ^2, while that of additional observations (v) has a variance equal to σ_v^2, the additional observations bring in heteroskedasticity. This can be corrected by multiplying both sides of the above stochastic prior information by σ/σ_v to get

$$(w_i - 3w_{i-1} + 3w_{i-2} - w_{i-3})\sigma/\sigma_v = v_i\sigma/\sigma_v,$$

where $$\mathrm{Var}(v_i\sigma/\sigma_v) = \sigma^2.$$

In the absence of prior knowledge about the values of σ and σ_v, we use their estimates, s = 1.2937, and s_v = 1/2, where s is the standard error of the OLS estimate of the aggregate consumption function, and

$$s_v^2 = 64(1)^2/4^4 = 1/4.$$

The Shiller lag estimate of the function, then, is

$$C_t = \underset{(6.7172)}{-35.0700} + \underset{(0.1206)}{0.0436}L_t + \underset{(0.1112)}{0.7445}Y_t + \underset{(0.0913)}{0.2935}Y_{t-1}$$

$$+ \underset{(0.0768)}{0.1213}Y_{t-2} + \underset{(0.0970)}{0.0278}Y_{t-3} - \underset{(0.0846)}{0.1794}Y_{t-4} + e_t.$$

11-10.

Consider $\alpha_j^* = (\alpha_j + a)$, and $\beta_j^* = (\beta_j + b)$, where a and b are constants, and (j = 1, 2, 3). Denoting the new probabilities by π_{ij}^*, we obtain

$$\pi_{ij}^* = \frac{\exp(\alpha_j^* + \beta_j^* X_i)}{\sum_j \exp(\alpha_j^* + \beta_j^* X_i)}$$

$$= \frac{\exp(\alpha_j + a + \beta_j X_i + bX_i)}{\sum_j \exp(\alpha_j + a + \beta_j X_i + bX_i)} = \frac{\exp(\alpha_j + \beta_j X_i)}{\sum_j \exp(\alpha_j + \beta_j X_i)} = \pi_{ij},$$

which means that the trichotomous logit model is invariant to re-parametrization. Thus if the model is re-parametrized so that the third category is the reference category, the probabilities are not affected, however, we require that

$$\alpha_3^* = \beta_3^* = 0.$$

This means that

$$\alpha_3^* = \alpha_3 + a = 0, \qquad \beta_3^* = \beta_3 + b = 0,$$

or

$$a = -\alpha_3, \qquad b = -\beta_3.$$

Thus

$$\alpha_1^* = -\alpha_3, \qquad \beta_1^* = -\beta_3,$$

$$\alpha_2^* = \alpha_2 - \alpha_3, \qquad \beta_2^* = \beta_2 - \beta_3.$$

Now suppose $\hat{\alpha}_k$ and $\hat{\beta}_k$, (k = 2, 3), are MLE's of α_k and β_k, respectively. Then the MLE's of α_h^* and β_h^*, denoted by $\hat{\alpha}_h^*$ and $\hat{\beta}_h^*$, (h = 1, 2), respectively, would be

$$\hat{\alpha}_1^* = -\hat{\alpha}_3, \qquad \hat{\beta}_1^* = -\hat{\beta}_3,$$

and

$$\hat{\alpha}_2^* = \hat{\alpha}_2 - \hat{\alpha}_3, \qquad \hat{\beta}_2^* = \hat{\beta}_2 - \hat{\beta}_3.$$

11-11.

Step 1: The null and the alternative hypotheses are

$$H_o: \beta = 0,$$

$$H_a: \beta \neq 0.$$

Steps 2 & 3: The test statistic and its asymptotic distribution are

$$\chi^2 = -2[L(\hat{\omega}) - L(\hat{\Omega})] \sim \text{Asympt. } \chi^2_1,$$

where $L(\hat{\Omega})$ and $L(\hat{\omega})$ are the maximum values of the log-likelihood function with and without restricting β to be 0, respectively.

Step 4: Do not reject the null hypothesis if

$$\chi^2_{1-\frac{\alpha}{2},1} = \chi^2_{0.9750,1} \cong 0 < \chi^2 < \chi^2_{\frac{\alpha}{2},1} = \chi^2_{0.0250,1} = 5.0240,$$

otherwise reject it.

Step 5: The sample values under the null hypothesis (H_o) are

$$\hat{\alpha} = 0.3365,$$

and

$$L(\hat{\Omega}) = -8.1503,$$

and under the alternative hypothesis (H_a) are

$$\hat{\alpha} = -4.0003, \qquad \hat{\beta} = 0.0317,$$

and

$$L(\hat{\omega}) = -6.7037.$$

Thus the value of the test statistic is

$$\chi^2 = -2[-8.1503 - (-6.7037)] = 2.8933.$$

Step 6: Since the value of the test statistic falls in the acceptance region, do not reject the null hypothesis. There is no evidence that the income is not a relevant variable.

11-12-a.

In order to obtain consistent estimates of α and β, we should maximize the following log-likelihood function with respect to α, β, and σ^2.

$$L = \sum_{i=1}^{n} \{(1 - Z_i)\log[F(\frac{\kappa_1 - \alpha - \beta X_i}{\sigma})]$$

$$+ Z_i[(\frac{-1}{2})\log(2\pi\sigma^2) - (Y_i - \alpha - \beta X_i)^2/2\sigma^2]\},$$

where F is the cumulative distribution function of the standard normal variable, and

$$Z_i = \begin{cases} 1 & \text{if } Y_i \geq \kappa_1, \\ 0 & \text{if } Y_i < \kappa_1. \end{cases}$$

11-12-b.

In order to obtain consistent estimates of α and β, we should maximize the following log-likelihood function with respect to α, β, and σ^2.

$$L = \sum_{i=1}^{n} \{(1 - Z_i)\log[F(\frac{\kappa_1^* - \alpha - \beta X_i}{\sigma})]$$

$$+ Z_i[(\frac{-1}{2})\log(2\pi\sigma^2) - (Y_i - \alpha - \beta X_i)^2/2\sigma^2]\},$$

where κ_1^* is the minimum of Y_i, and

$$Z_i = \begin{cases} 1 & \text{if } Y_i \geq \kappa_1^*, \\ 0 & \text{if } Y_i < \kappa_1^*. \end{cases}$$

11-12-c.

In order to obtain consistent estimates of α and β, we should maximize the following log-likelihood function with respect to α, β, and σ^2.

$$L = \sum_{i=1}^{n} \left((1 - Z_i)\{\log[F(\frac{\kappa_1^* - \alpha - \beta X_i}{\sigma})] + \log[F(\frac{\kappa_2^* - \alpha - \beta X_i}{\sigma})]\} + Z_i[(\frac{-1}{2})\log(2\pi\sigma^2) - (Y_i - \alpha - \beta X_i)^2/2\sigma^2] \right),$$

where κ_1^* and κ_2^* are the minimum and the maximum of Y_i, respectively, and

$$Z_i = \begin{cases} 1 & \text{if } \kappa_1^* < Y_i < \kappa_2^*, \\ 0 & \text{otherwise.} \end{cases}$$

11-13.

The estimated model based on the Tobit model specification is

$$Y_i = -192.9300 + 1.7279X_i + e_i.$$

11-14.

In order to conduct the test of stability of the coefficients of the consumption function, the 26 chronological observations are divided into four mutually exclusive groups, where

$$m_1 = 7, \quad m_2 = 6, \quad m_3 = 6, \quad \text{and} \quad m_4 = 7.$$

Note that

$$n_1 = 7, \quad n_2 = 13, \quad n_3 = 19, \quad \text{and} \quad n_4 = 26.$$

Step 1: The null and the alternative hypotheses are

$$H_o\colon \beta_{tj} = \beta_{sj},$$

$$H_a\colon H_o \text{ is not true,}$$

where (t, s = 1, ..., 26) and (j = 1, 2, 3).

Steps 2 & 3: The test statistic and its distribution are

$$F_g = \frac{(SSE_g - SSE_{g-1})/m_g}{SSE_{g-1}/(n_{g-1} - K)} \sim F_{m_g, n_{g-1}-K},$$

where (g = 2, 3, 4), and K = 3.

Step 4: Do not reject the null hypothesis if

$$F_2 < F_{\alpha,m_2,n_1-K} = F_{0.05,6,4} = 6.16,$$

$$F_3 < F_{\alpha,m_3,n_2-K} = F_{0.05,6,10} = 3.22,$$

and

$$F_4 < F_{\alpha,m_4,n_3-K} = F_{0.05,7,16} = 2.66,$$

otherwise reject it.

Step 5: The values of the test statistic are

$$F_2 = \frac{(SSE_2 - SSE_1)/6}{SSE_1/(7 - 3)} = \frac{(23.0920 - 7.3714)/6}{7.3714/4} = 1.4218,$$

$$F_3 = \frac{(SSE_3 - SSE_2)/6}{SSE_2/(13 - 3)} = \frac{(40.2110 - 23.0920)/6}{23.0920/10} = 1.2356,$$

and

$$F_4 = \frac{(SSE_4 - SSE_3)/7}{SSE_3/(19 - 3)} = \frac{(83.5230 - 40.2110)/7}{40.2110/16} = 2.4620.$$

Step 6: Since the values of the test statistic fall in the acceptance region, do not reject the null hypothesis. There is no evidence that the coefficients of the consumption function have not remained constant throughout the period.

11-15-a.

Consider the convergent parameter model. Lagging it by one period, multiplying it by λ, and subtracting the result from the model, we get

$$Y_t - \lambda Y_{t-1} = \alpha_t - \lambda\alpha_{t-1} + \beta(X_t - \lambda X_{t-1}).$$

Substituting for $(\alpha_t - \lambda\alpha_{t-1})$, we obtain

$$Y_t - \lambda Y_{t-1} = \alpha(1 - \lambda) + \beta(X_t - \lambda X_{t-1}) + u_t.$$

Now consider the standard regression model with an AR(1) disturbance. Using the Cochrane-Orcutt transformation, we have

$$Y_t - \rho Y_{t-1} = \alpha(1 - \rho) + \beta(X_t - \rho X_{t-1}) + u_t.$$

It is clear that the two models are observationally equivalent.

11-15-b.

Consider the convergent parameter model. Lagging it by one period, multiplying it by λ, and subtracting the result from the model, we get

$$Y_t - \lambda Y_{t-1} = \alpha_t - \lambda\alpha_{t-1} + \beta(X_t - \lambda X_{t-1}) + \epsilon_t - \lambda\epsilon_{t-1}.$$

Substituting for $(\alpha_t - \lambda\alpha_{t-1})$, we obtain

$$Y_t - \lambda Y_{t-1} = \alpha(1 - \lambda) + \beta(X_t - \lambda X_{t-1}) + \epsilon_t^*,$$

where $$\epsilon_t^* = u_t + \epsilon_t - \lambda\epsilon_{t-1}.$$

Now consider the standard regression model with an MA(1) disturbance $w_t^* = (w_t - \theta w_{t-1})$ represented as

$$Y_t = \gamma_0 + \gamma_1 X_t + \gamma_2 X_{t-1} + \gamma_3 Y_{t-1} + w_t^*.$$

The two models will be observationally equivalent if the two disturbances ϵ_t^* and w_t^*, which are normally distributed (since we assume normal distribution for ϵ, u, and w), have the same mean, the same variance, and the same auto-covariances. The first condition is automatically satisfied since

$$E(\epsilon_t^*) = E(w_t^*) = 0.$$

For the second condition, we require that

$$\mathrm{Var}(\epsilon_t^*) = \mathrm{Var}(w_t^*),$$

or equivalently

$$(1) \qquad \sigma_u^2 + \sigma_\epsilon^2 + \lambda^2\sigma_\epsilon^2 = \sigma_w^2 + \theta^2\sigma_w^2,$$

since

$$E(\epsilon_t\epsilon_s) = E(\epsilon_t u_t) = E(\epsilon_t u_s) = E(w_t w_s) = 0 \qquad (t \neq s).$$

For the third condition, we require that

$$\mathrm{Cov}(\epsilon_t^*, \epsilon_{t-1}^*) = \mathrm{Cov}(w_t^*, w_{t-1}^*),$$

or equivalently

$$(2) \qquad -\lambda\sigma_\epsilon^2 = -\theta\sigma_w^2,$$

since

$$\mathrm{Cov}(\epsilon_t^*, \epsilon_s^*) = \mathrm{Cov}(w_t^*, w_s^*) = 0 \qquad (s < t - 2).$$

Upon substituting (2) into (1), we obtain a quadratic form in θ in terms of λ, σ_ϵ^2, and σ_u^2, as follows

$$\theta^2 - [\sigma_u^2/\lambda\sigma_\epsilon^2 + (1 + \lambda^2)/\lambda]\theta + 1 = 0,$$

or

$$\theta^2 - C\theta + 1 = 0,$$

with two roots

$$(3) \qquad \theta = (C \pm \sqrt{C^2 - 4})/2.$$

Thus the two models are observationally equivalent if (3) is satisfied. Note that a necessary condition is that $|C| \geq 2$.

11-16-a.

For the first stage we substitute X_i^* into Y_i and X_i to get

$$Y_i = \beta\pi_1 Z_{i1} + \varepsilon_i = \gamma Z_{i1} + \epsilon_i,$$

and
$$X_i = \pi_1 Z_{i1} + u_i.$$

Now we obtain the LSE's of γ and π_1, say $\hat{\gamma}$ and $\hat{\pi}_1$, as follows

$$\hat{\gamma} = \Sigma Z_{i1}Y_i/\Sigma Z_{i1}^2,$$

and
$$\hat{\pi}_1 = \Sigma Z_{i1}X_i/\Sigma Z_{i1}^2,$$

and estimate σ^2 and σ_u^2 by s^2 and s_u^2, respectively, defined as

$$s^2 = \Sigma(Y_i - \hat{\gamma}Z_{i1})^2/(n - 1),$$

and
$$s_u^2 = \Sigma(X_i - \hat{\pi}_1 Z_{i1})^2/(n - 1).$$

For the second stage we minimize

$$S = \Sigma(Y_i - \beta\pi_1 Z_{i1})^2/s^2 + \Sigma(X_i - \pi_1 Z_{i1})^2/s_u^2,$$

with respect to β and π_1. Differentiating S with respect to β and π_1, equating each derivative to zero, and putting a "~" on the parameter to indicate that the resulting equations are satisfied by the LSE's of the parameters rather than their true values, we obtain

$$\Sigma(Y_i - \tilde{\beta}\tilde{\pi}_1 Z_{i1})Z_{i1} = 0,$$

and
$$\Sigma(X_i - \tilde{\pi}_1 Z_{i1})Z_{i1} = 0.$$

Solving for $\tilde{\beta}$ and $\tilde{\pi}_1$, we get

$$\tilde{\beta} = \Sigma Z_{i1}Y_i/\tilde{\pi}_1\Sigma Z_{i1}^2,$$

and
$$\tilde{\pi}_1 = \Sigma Z_{i1}X_i/\Sigma Z_{i1}^2.$$

Substituting for $\tilde{\pi}_1$ from the second equation into the first, we obtain

$$\tilde{\beta} = \Sigma Z_{i1}Y_i/\Sigma Z_{i1}X_i \qquad \text{Q.E.D.}$$

In order to prove consistency of $\tilde{\beta}$, consider

$$\tilde{\beta} = \frac{\Sigma Z_{i1}Y_i}{\Sigma Z_{i1}X_i} = \frac{\Sigma Z_{i1}(\beta\pi_1 Z_{i1} + \epsilon_i)}{\Sigma Z_{i1}(\pi_1 Z_{i1} + u_i)} = \frac{\beta\pi_1 \Sigma Z_{i1}^2 + \Sigma Z_{i1}\epsilon_i}{\pi_1 \Sigma Z_{i1}^2 + \Sigma Z_{i1}u_i}.$$

Further,

$$\text{plim}(\tilde{\beta}) = \frac{\beta\pi_1 \text{plim}(\Sigma Z_{i1}^2/n) + \text{plim}(\Sigma Z_{i1}\epsilon_i/n)}{\pi_1 \text{plim}(\Sigma Z_{i1}^2/n) + \text{plim}(\Sigma Z_{i1}u_i/n)} = \beta,$$

since $\Sigma Z_{i1}^2/n$ is a consistent estimator of the population variance of Z_{i1}, which is a finite number different from zero, and $\Sigma Z_{i1}\epsilon_i/n$ and $\Sigma Z_{i1}u_i/n$ are consistent estimators of the population covariances of Z_i and ϵ_i, and Z_i and u_i, respectively, which are zero. Thus $\tilde{\beta}$ is a consistent estimator of β. Now in order to derive a consistent estimator of the variance of $\tilde{\beta}$, we note that $\tilde{\beta}$ is the instrumental variables estimator of β in the model

$$Y_i = \beta X_i - \beta u_i + \epsilon_i,$$

where Z_1 is used as the instrumental variable for X. Employing the formula (9.26a), section (9-1) of the text,[1] a consistent estimator of the variance of $\tilde{\beta}$ is

$$\text{Est. Var}(\tilde{\beta}) = s^2 \Sigma Z_{i1}^2/(\Sigma Z_{i1}X_i)^2,$$

where

$$s^2 = \Sigma(Y_i - \tilde{\beta}X_i)^2/(n - 1).$$

---

[1]P. 360.

11-16-b.

If

$$X_i^* = \pi_1 Z_{i1} + \pi_2 Z_{i2},$$

then

$$Y_i = \beta\pi_1 Z_{i1} + \beta\pi_2 Z_{i2} + \epsilon_i,$$

and

$$X_i = \pi_1 Z_{i1} + \pi_2 Z_{i2} + u_i.$$

Now

$$\begin{aligned}\tilde{\beta} &= \frac{\Sigma Z_{i1} Y_i}{\Sigma Z_{i1} X_i} \\ &= \frac{\Sigma Z_{i1}(\beta\pi_1 Z_{i1} + \beta\pi_2 Z_{i2} + \epsilon_i)}{\Sigma Z_{i1}(\pi_1 Z_{i1} + \pi_2 Z_{i2} + u_i)} \\ &= \frac{\beta\pi_1 \Sigma Z_{i1}^2 + \beta\pi_2 \Sigma Z_{i1} Z_{i2} + \Sigma Z_{i1}\epsilon_i}{\pi_1 \Sigma Z_{i1}^2 + \pi_2 \Sigma Z_{i1} Z_{i2} + \Sigma Z_{i1} u_i}.\end{aligned}$$

Therefore

$$\text{plim}(\tilde{\beta}) = \frac{\beta\pi_1 \text{plim}(\frac{\Sigma Z_{i1}^2}{n}) + \beta\pi_2 \text{plim}(\frac{\Sigma Z_{i1} Z_{i2}}{n}) + \text{plim}(\frac{\Sigma Z_{i1}\epsilon_i}{n})}{\pi_1 \text{plim}(\frac{\Sigma Z_{i1}^2}{n}) + \pi_2 \text{plim}(\frac{\Sigma Z_{i1} Z_{i2}}{n}) + \text{plim}(\frac{\Sigma Z_{i1} u_i}{n})},$$

or

$$\text{plim}(\tilde{\beta}) = \beta,$$

since $\Sigma Z_{i1} Z_{i2}/n$ is a consistent estimator of the population covariance of Z_{i1} and Z_{i2}, which is a finite number. Thus $\tilde{\beta}$ as defined in part (a) is *still* consistent.

11-17.

The LSE of β_2, say $\hat{\beta}_2$, in the model

(1) $$Y_i = \beta_1 + \beta_2 X_{i2} + \beta_3^* Z_i + \epsilon_i^*,$$

where $$Z_i = \gamma + \delta X_{i3} + u_i,$$

is

(2) $$\hat{\beta}_2 = \frac{m_{2Y}m_{ZZ} - m_{ZY}m_{2Z}}{m_{22}m_{ZZ} - m_{2Z}^2}.$$

If we substitute for Y_i from (1) into (2), we obtain

(3) $$\hat{\beta}_2 = \beta_2 + \frac{\beta_3(m_{23}m_{ZZ} - m_{2Z}m_{3Z})}{m_{22}m_{ZZ} - m_{2Z}^2} + \frac{m_{2\epsilon}m_{ZZ} - m_{Z\epsilon}m_{2Z}}{m_{22}m_{ZZ} - m_{2Z}^2}.$$

Dividing the numerator and the denominator of (3) by n^2 and taking probability limit of its both sides, we obtain

(4) $$\text{plim}(\hat{\beta}_2) = \beta_2 + \frac{\beta_3[\text{plim}(\frac{m_{23}}{n})\text{plim}(\frac{m_{ZZ}}{n}) - \text{plim}(\frac{m_{2Z}}{n})\text{plim}(\frac{m_{3Z}}{n})]}{\text{plim}(\frac{m_{22}}{n})\text{plim}(\frac{m_{ZZ}}{n}) - \text{plim}(\frac{m_{2Z}}{n})^2},$$

since

$$\text{plim}(m_{2\epsilon}/n) = \text{plim}(m_{Z\epsilon}/n) = 0.$$

Consider the individual probability limits

$$\text{plim}(m_{23}/n) = \text{plim}(\Sigma x_{i2}' x_{i3}'/n) = \sigma_{23},$$

$$\text{plim}(m_{ZZ}/n) = \text{plim}(\Sigma z_i'^2/n)$$

$$= \text{plim}[\Sigma(\delta x_{i3}' + u_i')^2/n]$$

$$= \delta^2 \text{plim}(\Sigma x_{i3}'^2/n) + 2\delta \text{plim}(\Sigma x_{i3}' u_i'/n) + \text{plim}(\Sigma u_i'^2/n)$$

$$= \delta^2 \sigma_{33} + \sigma_u^2,$$

$$\text{plim}(m_{2Z}/n) = \text{plim}(\Sigma x'_{i2}z'_i/n)$$

$$= \text{plim}[\Sigma x'_{i2}(\delta x'_{i3} + u'_i)/n]$$

$$= \delta\text{plim}(\Sigma x'_{i2}x'_{i3}/n) + \text{plim}(\Sigma x'_{i2}u'_i/n)$$

$$= \delta\sigma_{23},$$

$$\text{plim}(m_{3Z}/n) = \text{plim}(\Sigma x'_{i3}z'_i/n)$$

$$= \text{plim}[\Sigma x'_{i3}(\delta x'_{i3} + u'_i)/n]$$

$$= \delta\text{plim}(\Sigma x'^2_{i3}/n) + \text{plim}(x'_{i3}u'_i/n)$$

$$= \delta\sigma_{33},$$

further,

$$\text{plim}(m_{22}/n) = \text{plim}(\Sigma x'^2_{i2}/n) = \sigma_{22},$$

and

$$\text{plim}(m_{2Z}/n)^2 = [\text{plim}(m_{2Z}/n)]^2 = \delta^2\sigma^2_{23}.$$

Substituting the above results into (4), we get

$$\text{(5)} \qquad \text{plim}(\hat{\beta}_2) = \beta_2 + \frac{\beta_3[\sigma_{23}(\delta^2\sigma_{33} + \sigma^2_u) - \delta^2\sigma_{33}\sigma_{23}]}{\sigma_{22}(\delta^2\sigma_{33} + \sigma^2_u) - \delta^2\sigma^2_{23}}.$$

Simplifying (5), we obtain the asymptotic bias of $\hat{\beta}_2$ as

$$\text{Asympt. } B(\hat{\beta}_2) = \text{plim}(\hat{\beta}_2 - \beta_2) = \frac{\beta_3\sigma_{23}\sigma^2_u}{\delta^2\sigma_{22}\sigma_{33}(1 - r^2_{23}) + \sigma_{22}\sigma^2_u},$$

where

$$r^2_{23} = \sigma^2_{23}/\sigma_{22}\sigma_{33},$$

is the squared population coefficient of correlation between X_2 and X_3.

Now the LSE of β_2, say $\tilde{\beta}_2$, in the model

$$Y_i = \beta_1 + \beta_2 X_{i2} + \epsilon_i^{**},$$

is

$$\tilde{\beta}_2 = \frac{m_{2Y}}{m_{22}}. \tag{6}$$

If we substitute for Y_i from (1) into (6), we obtain

$$\tilde{\beta}_2 = \beta_2 + \frac{\beta_3 m_{23} + m_{2\epsilon}}{m_{22}}. \tag{7}$$

Dividing the numerator and the denominator of (7) by n and taking probability limit of its both sides, we obtain

$$\text{plim}(\tilde{\beta}_2) = \beta_2 + \frac{\beta_3\sigma_{23}}{\sigma_{22}},$$

or the asymptotic bias of $\tilde{\beta}_2$ is

$$\text{Asympt. B}(\tilde{\beta}_2) = \text{plim}(\tilde{\beta}_2 - \beta_2) = \frac{\beta_3\sigma_{23}}{\sigma_{22}}.$$

Consider the ratio of the asymptotic biases of $\tilde{\beta}_2$ and $\hat{\beta}_2$, as follows

$$\frac{\text{Asympt. B}(\tilde{\beta}_2)}{\text{Asympt. B}(\hat{\beta}_2)} = \frac{\beta_3\sigma_{23}/\sigma_{22}}{\beta_3\sigma_{23}\sigma_u^2/[\delta^2\sigma_{22}\sigma_{33}(1 - r_{23}^2) + \sigma_{22}\sigma_u^2]},$$

or

$$\frac{\text{Asympt. B}(\tilde{\beta}_2)}{\text{Asympt. B}(\hat{\beta}_2)} = 1 + \frac{\delta^2\sigma_{33}(1 - r_{23}^2)}{\sigma_u^2} \geq 1.$$

Thus the stronger the population correlation between X_2 and X_3, the closer the ratio to unity. If $r_{23} = 1$, the asymptotic biases will be equal.

11-18.

Consider the disequilibrium model. Substituting for the demand and the supply in the price equation, we get

$$P_t - P_{t-1} = \delta(\alpha_1 + \beta_1 P_t + \gamma_1 X_{t1} + u_{t1} - \alpha_2 - \beta_2 P_t - \gamma_2 X_{t2} - u_{t2}).$$

Upon simplifying, we obtain

$$(1 - \delta\beta_1 + \delta\beta_2)P_t = \delta(\alpha_1 - \alpha_2) + P_{t-1} + \delta\gamma_1 X_{t1} - \delta\gamma_2 X_{t2} + \delta(u_{t1} - u_{t2}),$$

or equivalently

$$P_t = \alpha^{**} + \beta^{**}P_{t-1} + \gamma_1^{**}X_{t1} + \gamma_2^{**}X_{t2} + u_t^{**},$$

where

$$\alpha^{**} = \frac{\delta(\alpha_1 - \alpha_2)}{1 - \delta\beta_1 + \delta\beta_2}, \qquad \beta^{**} = \frac{1}{1 - \delta\beta_1 + \delta\beta_2},$$

$$\gamma_1^{**} = \frac{\delta\gamma_1}{1 - \delta\beta_1 + \delta\beta_2}, \qquad \gamma_2^{**} = \frac{-\delta\gamma_2}{1 - \delta\beta_1 + \delta\beta_2},$$

and

$$u_t^{**} = \frac{\delta(u_{t1} - u_{t2})}{1 - \delta\beta_1 + \delta\beta_2}.$$

Consider the "partial adjustment" model. Equating the demand and the supply equations, we obtain

$$\alpha_1 + \beta_1 P_t^* + \gamma_1 X_{t1} + u_{t1} = \alpha_2 + \beta_2 P_t^* + \gamma_2 X_{t2} + u_{t2},$$

or

$$P_t^* = \frac{\alpha_2 - \alpha_1}{\beta_1 - \beta_2} - \frac{\gamma_1 X_{t1}}{\beta_1 - \beta_2} + \frac{\gamma_2 X_{t2}}{\beta_1 - \beta_2} - \frac{u_{t1} - u_{t2}}{\beta_1 - \beta_2}.$$

Substituting the above in the price equation, we get

$$P_t - P_{t-1} = (1 - \mu)\left(\frac{\alpha_2 - \alpha_1}{\beta_1 - \beta_2} - \frac{\gamma_1 X_{t1}}{\beta_1 - \beta_2} + \frac{\gamma_2 X_{t2}}{\beta_1 - \beta_2} - \frac{u_{t1} - u_{t2}}{\beta_1 - \beta_2} - P_{t-1}\right).$$

Upon simplifying, we obtain

$$P_t = \frac{(1-\mu)(a_2 - a_1)}{\beta_1 - \beta_2} + \mu P_{t-1} - \frac{(1-\mu)\gamma_1 X_{t1}}{\beta_1 - \beta_2} + \frac{(1-\mu)\gamma_2 X_{t2}}{\beta_1 - \beta_2} - \frac{(1-\mu)(u_{t1} - u_{t2})}{\beta_1 - \beta_2},$$

or equivalently

$$P_t = a^* + \beta^* P_{t-1} + \gamma_1^* X_{t1} + \gamma_2^* X_{t2} + u_t^*,$$

where

$$a^* = \frac{(1-\mu)(a_2 - a_1)}{\beta_1 - \beta_2}, \qquad \beta^* = \mu,$$

$$\gamma_1^* = \frac{-(1-\mu)\gamma_1}{\beta_1 - \beta_2}, \qquad \gamma_2^* = \frac{(1-\mu)\gamma_2}{\beta_1 - \beta_2},$$

and $$u_t^* = \frac{-(1-\mu)(u_{t1} - u_{t2})}{\beta_1 - \beta_2}.$$

The two models will be observationally equivalent if

$$u_t^{**} = u_t^*,$$

which implies

$$\mu = \frac{1}{1 - \delta(\beta_1 - \beta_2)}.$$

Consider the identifiability of the disequilibrium model. Since if $D_t < S_t$, then $D_t = Q_t$, we get the following two relations

$$Q_t = a_1 + \beta_1 P_t + \gamma_1 X_{t1} + u_{t1},$$

and $$P_t - P_{t-1} = \delta(Q_t - a_2 - \beta_2 P_t - \gamma_2 X_{t2} - u_{t2}),$$

or

$$P_t = \frac{-a_2\delta}{1 + \delta\beta_2} + \frac{\delta Q_t}{1 + \delta\beta_2} - \frac{\gamma_2 \delta X_{t2}}{1 + \delta\beta_2} + \frac{P_{t-1}}{1 + \delta\beta_2} + u_{t2}^{**},$$

where

$$u_{t2}^{**} = \frac{-\delta u_{t2}}{1 + \delta\beta_2}.$$

The joint distribution of Q_t and P_t when $D_t < S_t$ is a multivariate normal with the following logarithmic function

$$\log[f_D(Q_t,P_t)] = (\frac{-1}{2})\log(2\pi) - (\frac{1}{2})\log|\Sigma| + \log(J_D) - \mathbf{u}_t'\Sigma^{-1}\mathbf{u}_t/2,$$

where $\mathbf{u}_t = \begin{bmatrix} u_{t1} \\ u_{t2}^{**} \end{bmatrix}$, $\Sigma = \mathbf{E}(\mathbf{u}_t\mathbf{u}_t')$, and $J_D = \begin{vmatrix} 1 & -\beta_1 \\ \frac{-\delta}{1 + \delta\beta_2} & 1 \end{vmatrix}$.

Similarly, since if $S_t < D_t$, then $S_t = Q_t$, we get the following two relations

$$Q_t = a_2 + \beta_2 P_t + \gamma_2 X_{t2} + u_{t2},$$

and $$P_t - P_{t-1} = \delta(a_1 + \beta_1 P_t + \gamma_1 X_{t1} + u_{t1} - Q_t),$$

or

$$P_t = \frac{a_1\delta}{1 - \delta\beta_1} - \frac{\delta Q_t}{1 - \delta\beta_1} + \frac{\gamma_1\delta X_{t2}}{1 - \delta\beta_1} + \frac{P_{t-1}}{1 - \delta\beta_1} + u_{t1}^{**},$$

where

$$u_{t1}^{**} = \frac{\delta u_{t1}}{1 - \delta\beta_1}.$$

The joint distribution of Q_t and P_t when $S_t < D_t$ is a multivariate normal with the following logarithmic function

$$\log[f_S(Q_t,P_t)] = (\frac{-1}{2})\log(2\pi) - (\frac{1}{2})\log|\Omega| + \log(J_S) - \mathbf{v}_t'\Omega^{-1}\mathbf{v}_t/2,$$

where $\mathbf{v}_t = \begin{bmatrix} u_{t2} \\ u_{t1}^{**} \end{bmatrix}$, $\Omega = \mathbf{E}(\mathbf{v}_t\mathbf{v}_t')$, and $J_S = \begin{vmatrix} 1 & -\beta_2 \\ \frac{\delta}{1 - \delta\beta_1} & 1 \end{vmatrix}$.

Now the log-likelihood function for the observables Q_t and P_t is

$$L = \sum_t \{(Z_t)\log[f_D(Q_t,P_t)] + (1 - Z_t)\log[f_S(Q_t,P_t)]\},$$

where $$Z_t = \begin{cases} 1 & \text{if } D_t < S_t \text{ (and thus } Q_t = D_t\text{)}, \\ 0 & \text{if } S_t < D_t \text{ (and thus } Q_t = S_t\text{)}. \end{cases}$$

Maximum likelihood estimators of all unknown parameters may be obtained by maximizing L.[1] Since MLE's are consistent, and since identifiability of unknown parameters is a necessary condition for consistency, it follows that the disequilibrium model is generally identifiable. Now consider identifiability of the "partial adjustment" model. From the four equations of the model involving unobservable variables P_t^*, D_t, and S_t, we obtain only one relation involving observable variables, namely

$$P_t = \alpha^* + \beta^* P_{t-1} + \gamma_1^* X_{t1} + \gamma_2^* X_{t2} + u_t^*,$$

where $$\alpha^* = \frac{(1 - \mu)(\alpha_2 - \alpha_1)}{\beta_1 - \beta_2}, \qquad \beta^* = \mu,$$

$$\gamma_1^* = \frac{-(1 - \mu)\gamma_1}{\beta_1 - \beta_2}, \qquad \gamma_2^* = \frac{(1 - \mu)\gamma_2}{\beta_1 - \beta_2},$$

and $$u_t^* = \frac{-(1 - \mu)(u_{t1} - u_{t2})}{\beta_1 - \beta_2}.$$

From the four consistent estimates of α^*, β^*, γ_1^*, and γ_2^*, we may not be able to estimate the seven parameters α_1, α_2, β_1, β_2, γ_1, γ_2, and μ. Thus the model is not necessarily identifiable.

---

[1]G. S. Maddala, *Limited Dependent and Qualitative Variables in Econometrics* (Cambridge, England: Cambridge University Press, 1983), pp. 306-7.

11-19.

Let $\hat{\beta}_1$ and $\hat{\beta}_2$ be LSE's of β_1 and β_2 of the second model, where

$$\hat{\beta}_1 = (X_1'M_2X_1)^{-1}X_1'M_2y,$$

and

$$\hat{\beta}_2 = (X_2'M_1X_2)^{-1}X_2'M_1y,$$

where

$$M_r = I - X_r(X_r'X_r)^{-1}X_r', \qquad (r = 1, 2).$$

Using model two, we have

$$y = X_1\hat{\beta}_1 + X_2\hat{\beta}_2 + \hat{e},$$

$$X_1'\hat{e} = X_2'\hat{e} = \hat{e}'X_1 = \hat{e}'X_2 = 0,$$

and

$$s^2 = \frac{\hat{e}'\hat{e}}{n - K_1 - K_2} = \frac{SSE_{II}}{n - K_1 - K_2}.$$

Let $\tilde{\beta}_1$ be the LSE of β_1 of the first model, where

$$\tilde{\beta}_1 = (X_1'X_1)^{-1}X_1'y.$$

Substituting the second model into $\tilde{\beta}_1$, we obtain

$$\begin{aligned}\tilde{\beta}_1 &= (X_1'X_1)^{-1}X_1'(X_1\hat{\beta}_1 + X_2\hat{\beta}_2 + \hat{e}) \\ &= \hat{\beta}_1 + (X_1'X_1)^{-1}X_1'X_2\hat{\beta}_2 + (X_1'X_1)^{-1}X_1'\hat{e} \\ &= \hat{\beta}_1 + (X_1'X_1)^{-1}X_1'X_2\hat{\beta}_2,\end{aligned}$$

or

$$\tilde{\beta}_1 - \hat{\beta}_1 = (X_1'X_1)^{-1}X_1'X_2\hat{\beta}_2.$$

Further,

$$(\tilde{\beta}_1 - \hat{\beta}_1)'\mathbf{X}_1'\mathbf{X}_1(\tilde{\beta}_1 - \hat{\beta}_1) = \hat{\beta}_2'\mathbf{X}_2'\mathbf{X}_1(\mathbf{X}_1'\mathbf{X}_1)^{-1}\mathbf{X}_1'\mathbf{X}_2\hat{\beta}_2,$$

and

$$\hat{\beta}_2'\mathbf{X}_2'\mathbf{X}_1(\tilde{\beta}_1 - \hat{\beta}_1) = \hat{\beta}_2'\mathbf{X}_2'\mathbf{X}_1(\mathbf{X}_1'\mathbf{X}_1)^{-1}\mathbf{X}_1'\mathbf{X}_2\hat{\beta}_2.$$

Now

$$\begin{aligned}
SSE_I &= (\mathbf{y} - \mathbf{X}_1\tilde{\beta}_1)'(\mathbf{y} - \mathbf{X}_1\tilde{\beta}_1) \\
&= (\mathbf{X}_1\hat{\beta}_1 + \mathbf{X}_2\hat{\beta}_2 + \hat{\mathbf{e}} - \mathbf{X}_1\tilde{\beta}_1)'(\mathbf{X}_1\hat{\beta}_1 + \mathbf{X}_2\hat{\beta}_2 + \hat{\mathbf{e}} - \mathbf{X}_1\tilde{\beta}_1) \\
&= [-\mathbf{X}_1(\tilde{\beta}_1 - \hat{\beta}_1) + \mathbf{X}_2\hat{\beta}_2 + \hat{\mathbf{e}}]'[-\mathbf{X}_1(\tilde{\beta}_1 - \hat{\beta}_1) + \mathbf{X}_2\hat{\beta}_2 + \hat{\mathbf{e}}] \\
&= (\tilde{\beta}_1 - \hat{\beta}_1)'\mathbf{X}_1'\mathbf{X}_1(\tilde{\beta}_1 - \hat{\beta}_1) - 2\hat{\beta}_2'\mathbf{X}_2'\mathbf{X}_1(\tilde{\beta}_1 - \hat{\beta}_1) \\
&\quad - 2\hat{\mathbf{e}}'\mathbf{X}_1(\tilde{\beta}_1 - \hat{\beta}_1) + 2\hat{\mathbf{e}}'\mathbf{X}_2\hat{\beta}_2 + \hat{\beta}_2'\mathbf{X}_2'\mathbf{X}_2\hat{\beta}_2 + \hat{\mathbf{e}}'\hat{\mathbf{e}}.
\end{aligned}$$

Substituting for these from above, we get

$$SSE_I = -\hat{\beta}_2'\mathbf{X}_2'\mathbf{X}_1(\mathbf{X}_1'\mathbf{X}_1)^{-1}\mathbf{X}_1'\mathbf{X}_2\hat{\beta}_2 + \hat{\beta}_2'\mathbf{X}_2'\mathbf{X}_2\hat{\beta}_2 + SSE_{II},$$

$$SSE_I = \hat{\beta}_2'\mathbf{X}_2'[\mathbf{I} - \mathbf{X}_1(\mathbf{X}_1'\mathbf{X}_1)^{-1}\mathbf{X}_1']\mathbf{X}_2\hat{\beta}_2 + SSE_{II},$$

$$SSE_I = \hat{\beta}_2'\mathbf{X}_2'\mathbf{M}_1\mathbf{X}_2\hat{\beta}_2 + SSE_{II},$$

or

$$SSE_I - SSE_{II} = \hat{\beta}_2'\mathbf{X}_2'\mathbf{M}_1\mathbf{X}_2\hat{\beta}_2.$$

Thus

$$K_2 \geq \hat{\beta}_2'\mathbf{X}_2'\mathbf{M}_1\mathbf{X}_2\hat{\beta}_2/s^2,$$

$$K_2 \geq (SSE_I - SSE_{II})/s^2,$$

$$K_2 \geq \frac{SSE_I - SSE_{II}}{SSE_{II}/(n - K_1 - K_2)},$$

or

$$\frac{(SSE_I - SSE_{II})/K_2}{SSE_{II}/(n - K_1 - K_2)} \leq 1 \qquad \text{Q.E.D.}$$

11-20.

The problem of testing the appropriateness of a logit versus a probit model is one of testing *non-linear, non-nested* hypothesis. As indicated in the section (11-10) of the text,[1] suitable tests are Cox test or its variants. Note that not all the tests in model choice are applicable to non-linear model selection.

For dichotomous dependent variables since the logistic and cumulative normal distributions are very close in the mid-range but the former has slightly heavier tails, the results are not likely to be very different using the logit or probit model, unless the data are heavily concentrated in the tails. When the dependent variable is polytomous, there are major differences between the two models.

In order to choose between a logit and a probit model we propose the following testing procedure, adopted from Fomby *et. al.*[2]

Step 1: The null and the alternative hypotheses are

$$H_o: E(Y_i) = F_1(\mathbf{x}\beta) = 1/[1 + \exp(-\mathbf{x}\beta)],$$

$$H_a: E(Y_i) = F_2(\mathbf{x}\beta) = \int_{-\infty}^{\mathbf{x}\beta} (1/\sqrt{2\pi})\exp(-z_i^2/2)dz_i,$$

where $\mathbf{x}\rightarrow 1\text{x}K$, $\beta\rightarrow K\text{x}1$, and Z is the standardized normal.

---

[1]P. 596.

[2]T. B. Fomby, R. C. Hill, and S. R. Johnson, *Advanced Econometric Methods* (New York: Springer-Verlag, 1984), p. 419.

Steps 2 & 3: The test statistic and its asymptotic distribution are

$$Z = C/s_C \sim \text{Asympt. } N(0, 1),$$

where

$$C = \hat{L}_1 - \hat{L}_2 - (n)\text{plim}[(\hat{L}_1 - \hat{L}_2)/n],$$

$$L_j = \sum_{i=1}^{n} \{(Y_i)\log[F_j(\mathbf{x}\beta)] + (1 - Y_i)\log[1 - F_j(\mathbf{x}\beta)]\},$$

where (j = 1, 2), $\hat{L}_1$ and $\hat{L}_2$ are evaluated under H_o and H_a, respectively, $\text{plim}[(\hat{L}_1 - \hat{L}_2)/n]$ is evaluated under H_o using maximum likelihood estimation, and s_C is the estimated standard error of C, where the variance of C is defined as

$$\text{Var}(C) = \text{Var}(L_1 - L_2) - n\Sigma'(I^*)^{-1}\Sigma,$$

where

$$\Sigma = \frac{\partial \text{plim}[(\hat{L}_1 - \hat{L}_2)/n]}{\partial \beta}$$

and

$$I^* = -\text{plim}[(\frac{\partial^2 L_1}{\partial \beta \partial \beta'})/n],$$

is the asymptotic information matrix under the null hypothesis.

Step 4: Do not reject the null hypothesis if

$$|z| < z_{\alpha/2},$$

otherwise reject it.

Step 5: Evaluation. Calculate the value of the test statistic.

Step 6: Conclusion. Make a statistical inference.

CHAPTER 12

12-1-a.

Consider

$$Y_{it} = a + \beta X_{it} + \epsilon_{it} \qquad (i = 1, 2, \ldots, N;\ t = 1, 2),$$

where
$$E(\epsilon_{it}\epsilon_{jt}) = 0 \qquad (i \neq j),$$

$$E(\epsilon_{it}^2) = \sigma_i^2,$$

$$\epsilon_{i2} = \rho\epsilon_{i1} + u_{i2},$$

where
$$E(\epsilon_{i1}u_{j2}) = 0 \qquad \text{for all } i, j,$$

$$u_{it} \sim N(0, \sigma_{ui}^2),$$

$$\epsilon_{i1} \sim N[0, \sigma_{ui}^2/(1 - \rho^2)].$$

Now

$$E(\epsilon'\epsilon) = \begin{bmatrix} \sigma_1^2 \mathbf{V} & \mathbf{0} & \cdots & \mathbf{0} \\ \mathbf{0} & \sigma_2^2 \mathbf{V} & \cdots & \mathbf{0} \\ \vdots & \vdots & & \vdots \\ \mathbf{0} & \mathbf{0} & \cdots & \sigma_N^2 \mathbf{V} \end{bmatrix} = \Omega,$$

where
$$\mathbf{V} = \begin{bmatrix} 1 & \rho \\ \rho & 1 \end{bmatrix}, \qquad \mathbf{0} = \begin{bmatrix} 0 & 0 \\ 0 & 0 \end{bmatrix}.$$

12-1-b.

In order to obtain consistent estimates of the element of Ω, first apply OLS method to all 2N observations, and calculate the corresponding residuals e_{it}. These residuals are then used to obtain a consistent estimator of ρ, say $\hat{\rho}$, employing the formula

$$\hat{\rho} = \Sigma e_{i2}e_{i1}/\Sigma e_{i1}^2,$$

where (i = 1, ..., N). Since T = 2 is small, $\hat{\rho}$ may exceed one in absolute value. To avoid this we may use

$$\hat{\rho} = \Sigma e_{i2}e_{i1}/\sqrt{\Sigma e_{i2}^2 \Sigma e_{i1}^2}.$$

Next using $\hat{\rho}$ we transform the model according to "Prais-Winsten transformation" as follows

$$Y_{it}^* = \alpha + \beta X_{it}^* + u_{it}^*,$$

where $\quad Y_{i1}^* = \sqrt{1 - \hat{\rho}^2}Y_{i1}, \qquad Y_{i2}^* = Y_{i2} - \hat{\rho}Y_{i1},$

and $\quad X_{i1}^* = \sqrt{1 - \hat{\rho}^2}X_{i1}, \qquad X_{i2}^* = X_{i2} - \hat{\rho}X_{i1}.$

Now apply the OLS method to the above transformed model using the 2N observations. The resulting regression residuals, say $\hat{u}_{it}^*$, can be used to estimate the variances of u_{it}, i.e., σ_{ui}^2, as

$$s_{ui}^2 = (\hat{u}_{i1}^{*2} + \hat{u}_{i2}^{*2})/2.$$

Since $\sigma_i^2 = \sigma_{ui}^2/(1 - \rho^2)$, a consistent estimator of σ_i^2, say s_i^2, is

$$s_i^2 = s_{ui}^2/(1 - \hat{\rho}^2),$$

since $\hat{\rho}$ and s_{ui}^2 are consistent estimators of ρ and σ_{ui}^2, respectively. Thus a consistent estimator of Ω, say $\hat{\Omega}$, is

$$\hat{\Omega} = \begin{bmatrix} s_1^2\hat{V} & 0 & \cdots & 0 \\ 0 & s_2^2\hat{V} & \cdots & 0 \\ \vdots & \vdots & & \vdots \\ 0 & 0 & \cdots & s_N^2\hat{V} \end{bmatrix},$$

where $\hat{V} = \begin{bmatrix} 1 & \hat{\rho} \\ \hat{\rho} & 1 \end{bmatrix}, \quad \mathbf{0} = \begin{bmatrix} 0 & 0 \\ 0 & 0 \end{bmatrix}.$

12-1-c.

In order to use the OLS method to obtain asymptotically efficient estimates of the regression coefficients, we perform a double transformation - one designed to remove autocorrelation and the other heteroskedasticity. The Prais-Winsten transformation described in part (**b**) removed the first. In order to remove heteroskedasticity, we divide both sides of the transformed model by s_{ui}, which leads to

$$Y^*_{it}/s_{ui} = \alpha/s_{ui} + \beta X^*_{it}/s_{ui} + u^*_{it}/s_{ui}.$$

The disturbance u^*_{it}/s_{ui} is asymptotically non-autocorrelated and homoskedastic. The above model can then be estimated by the OLS method using all of the 2N pooled observations.

If there is any information about the variances of the household disturbances, for instance, $\sigma_i^2 = \sigma^2 X_i^2$, this should be incorporated in the estimation procedure. Above we have proceeded as if no such information were available.

12-2.

First, calculate the LSE of β, say $\hat{\beta}$

$$\hat{\beta} = (x'x)^{-1}x'y$$

$$= \left[\begin{bmatrix} x_1' & x_2' \end{bmatrix} \begin{bmatrix} x_1 \\ x_2 \end{bmatrix} \right]^{-1} \begin{bmatrix} x_1' & x_2' \end{bmatrix} \begin{bmatrix} y_1 \\ y_2 \end{bmatrix}$$

$$= (x_1'y_1 + x_2'y_2)/(x_1'x_1 + x_2'x_2)$$

$$= (10 + 8)/(10 + 10)$$

$$= 0.90,$$

yielding the following residuals

$$e_1 = y_1 - x_1\hat{\beta}, \qquad \text{and} \qquad e_2 = y_2 - x_2\hat{\beta}.$$

Next estimate the elements of the Ω matrix using these residuals as follows

$$s_{11} = e_1'e_1/(T - 1)$$

$$= (y_1'y_1 - 2x_1'y_1\hat{\beta} + x_1'x_1\hat{\beta}^2)/(T - 1)$$

$$= [13.90 - 2(10)0.90 + 10(0.90^2)]/(21 - 1)$$

$$= 0.20,$$

$$s_{12} = s_{21}$$

$$= e_1'e_2/(T - 1)$$

$$= (y_1'y_2 - x_1'y_2\hat{\beta} - x_2'y_1\hat{\beta} + x_1'x_2\hat{\beta}^2)/(T - 1)$$

$$= [11.92 - 8(0.90) - 8(0.90) + 8(0.90^2)]/(21 - 1)$$

$$= 0.20,$$

and

$$s_{22} = \mathbf{e}_2'\mathbf{e}_2/(T - 1)$$

$$= (\mathbf{y}_2'\mathbf{y}_2 - 2\mathbf{x}_2'\mathbf{y}_2\hat{\beta} + \mathbf{x}_2'\mathbf{x}_2\hat{\beta}^2)/(T - 1)$$

$$= [12.30 - 2(8)0.90 + 10(0.90^2)]/(21 - 1)$$

$$= 0.30.$$

Thus the $\hat{\Omega}$ matrix and its inverse are

$$\hat{\Omega} = \begin{bmatrix} 0.20\mathbf{I} & 0.20\mathbf{I} \\ 0.20\mathbf{I} & 0.30\mathbf{I} \end{bmatrix}, \quad \text{and} \quad \hat{\Omega}^{-1} = \begin{bmatrix} 15\mathbf{I} & -10\mathbf{I} \\ -10\mathbf{I} & 10\mathbf{I} \end{bmatrix}.$$

Now the feasible Aitken estimator of β, say $\tilde{\beta}$, is

$$\tilde{\beta} = (\mathbf{x}'\hat{\Omega}^{-1}\mathbf{x})^{-1}\mathbf{x}'\hat{\Omega}^{-1}\mathbf{y}$$

$$= \left[\begin{bmatrix} \mathbf{x}_1' & \mathbf{x}_2' \end{bmatrix} \begin{bmatrix} 15\mathbf{I} & -10\mathbf{I} \\ -10\mathbf{I} & 10\mathbf{I} \end{bmatrix} \begin{bmatrix} \mathbf{x}_1 \\ \mathbf{x}_2 \end{bmatrix} \right]^{-1} \begin{bmatrix} \mathbf{x}_1' & \mathbf{x}_2' \end{bmatrix} \begin{bmatrix} 15\mathbf{I} & -10\mathbf{I} \\ -10\mathbf{I} & 10\mathbf{I} \end{bmatrix} \begin{bmatrix} \mathbf{y}_1 \\ \mathbf{y}_2 \end{bmatrix}$$

$$= \frac{15\mathbf{x}_1'\mathbf{y}_1 - 10\mathbf{x}_1'\mathbf{y}_2 - 10\mathbf{x}_2'\mathbf{y}_1 + 10\mathbf{x}_2'\mathbf{y}_2}{15\mathbf{x}_1'\mathbf{x}_1 - 10\mathbf{x}_1'\mathbf{x}_2 - 10\mathbf{x}_2'\mathbf{x}_1 + 10\mathbf{x}_2'\mathbf{x}_2}$$

$$= \frac{15(10) - 10(8) - 10(8) + 10(8)}{15(10) - 10(8) - 10(8) + 10(10)}$$

$$= 0.7778,$$

and its estimated variance and standard error are

$$s^2_{\tilde{\beta}} = (\mathbf{x}'\hat{\Omega}^{-1}\mathbf{x})^{-1}$$

$$= 1/(15\mathbf{x}_1'\mathbf{x}_1 - 10\mathbf{x}_1'\mathbf{x}_2 - 10\mathbf{x}_2'\mathbf{x}_1 + 10\mathbf{x}_2'\mathbf{x}_2)$$

$$= 0.0111,$$

$$s_{\tilde{\beta}} = 0.1054.$$

12-3-a.

First, calculate the LSE's of β_1 and β_2

$$\hat{\beta}_1 = \mathbf{x}_1'\mathbf{y}_1/\mathbf{x}_1'\mathbf{x}_1 = 10/10 = 1,$$

and

$$\hat{\beta}_2 = \mathbf{x}_2'\mathbf{y}_2/\mathbf{x}_2'\mathbf{x}_2 = 8/10 = 0.80,$$

yielding the following residuals

$$\mathbf{e}_1 = \mathbf{y}_1 - \mathbf{x}_1\hat{\beta}_1, \quad \text{and} \quad \mathbf{e}_2 = \mathbf{y}_2 - \mathbf{x}_2\hat{\beta}_2.$$

Next estimate the elements of Ω using these residuals as follows

$$\begin{aligned} s_{11} &= \mathbf{e}_1'\mathbf{e}_1/(T - 1) \\ &= (\mathbf{y}_1'\mathbf{y}_1 - 2\mathbf{x}_1'\mathbf{y}_1\hat{\beta}_1 + \mathbf{x}_1'\mathbf{x}_1\hat{\beta}_1^2)/(T - 1) \\ &= [12 - 2(10)(1) + 10(1)]/(21 - 1) \\ &= 0.10, \end{aligned}$$

$$\begin{aligned} s_{12} &= s_{21} \\ &= \mathbf{e}_1'\mathbf{e}_2/(T - 1) \\ &= (\mathbf{y}_1'\mathbf{y}_2 - \mathbf{x}_1'\mathbf{y}_2\hat{\beta}_1 - \mathbf{x}_2'\mathbf{y}_1\hat{\beta}_2 + \mathbf{x}_1'\mathbf{x}_2\hat{\beta}_1\hat{\beta}_2)/(T - 1) \\ &= [10 - 8(1) - 8(0.80) + 8(1)(0.80)]/(21 - 1) \\ &= 0.10, \end{aligned}$$

$$\begin{aligned} s_{22} &= \mathbf{e}_2'\mathbf{e}_2/(T - 1) \\ &= (\mathbf{y}_2'\mathbf{y}_2 - 2\mathbf{x}_2'\mathbf{y}_2\hat{\beta}_2 + \mathbf{x}_2'\mathbf{x}_2\hat{\beta}_2^2)/(T - 1) \\ &= [12.40 - 2(8)(0.80) + 10(0.64)]/(21 - 1) \\ &= 0.30. \end{aligned}$$

Thus the $\hat{\Omega}$ matrix and its inverse are

$$\hat{\Omega} = \begin{bmatrix} 0.10I & 0.10I \\ 0.10I & 0.30I \end{bmatrix}, \quad \text{and} \quad \hat{\Omega}^{-1} = \begin{bmatrix} 15I & -5I \\ -5I & 5I \end{bmatrix}.$$

Now the feasible Aitken estimator of β, say $\tilde{\beta}$, is

$$\tilde{\beta} = (X'\hat{\Omega}^{-1}X)^{-1}X'\hat{\Omega}^{-1}y,$$

or

$$\begin{bmatrix} \tilde{\beta}_1 \\ \tilde{\beta}_2 \end{bmatrix} = \left[\begin{bmatrix} x_1' & 0 \\ 0 & x_2' \end{bmatrix}\begin{bmatrix} 15I & -5I \\ -5I & 5I \end{bmatrix}\begin{bmatrix} x_1 & 0 \\ 0 & x_2 \end{bmatrix}\right]^{-1}\begin{bmatrix} x_1' & 0 \\ 0 & x_2' \end{bmatrix}\begin{bmatrix} 15I & -5I \\ -5I & 5I \end{bmatrix}\begin{bmatrix} y_1 \\ y_2 \end{bmatrix}$$

$$= \begin{bmatrix} 15x_1'x_1 & -5x_1'x_2 \\ -5x_2'x_1 & 5x_2'x_2 \end{bmatrix}^{-1}\begin{bmatrix} 15x_1'y_1 - 5x_1'y_2 \\ 5x_2'y_2 - 5x_2'y_1 \end{bmatrix}$$

$$= \begin{bmatrix} 150 & -40 \\ -40 & 50 \end{bmatrix}^{-1}\begin{bmatrix} 150-40 \\ 40-40 \end{bmatrix}$$

$$= \begin{bmatrix} 0.9322 \\ 0.7458 \end{bmatrix},$$

and its estimated variance-covariance and standard error are

$$\textbf{Est. Var-Cov}(\tilde{\beta}) = (X'\hat{\Omega}^{-1}X)^{-1},$$

or

$$\text{Est.}\begin{bmatrix} \mathrm{Var}(\tilde{\beta}_1) & \mathrm{Cov}(\tilde{\beta}_1,\tilde{\beta}_2) \\ \mathrm{Cov}(\tilde{\beta}_2,\tilde{\beta}_1) & \mathrm{Var}(\tilde{\beta}_2) \end{bmatrix} = \begin{bmatrix} 0.0085 & 0.0064 \\ 0.0064 & 0.0254 \end{bmatrix},$$

and

$$\text{Est. Standard Error}\begin{bmatrix} \tilde{\beta}_1 \\ \tilde{\beta}_2 \end{bmatrix} = \begin{bmatrix} 0.0921 \\ 0.1594 \end{bmatrix}.$$

12-3-b.

The MLE of β, say $\check{\beta}$, can be obtained by iteration of the process in part (a) until convergence is reached. The calculations are presented in table 12-1.

TABLE 12-1

Iteration	$\hat{\beta}_1$	$\hat{\beta}_2$	s_{11}	s_{12}	s_{22}
1st	1.000000	0.800000	0.100000	0.100000	0.300000
2nd	0.932203	0.745763	0.102298	0.106895	0.301471
3rd	0.925634	0.737834	0.102765	0.107799	0.301932
4th	0.924867	0.736949	0.102823	0.107701	0.301988
5th	0.924776	0.736846	0.102830	0.107718	0.301994
6th	0.924766	0.736834	0.102830	0.107720	0.301995
7th	0.924764	0.736833	0.102830	0.107720	0.301995
8th	0.924764	0.736833			

Thus the MLE of β is

$$\begin{bmatrix} \check{\beta}_1 \\ \check{\beta}_2 \end{bmatrix} = \begin{bmatrix} 0.924764 \\ 0.736833 \end{bmatrix},$$

and its estimated variance-covariance and estimated standard error are

$$\textbf{Est. Var-Cov}(\check{\beta}) = (\mathbf{X}'\check{\Omega}^{-1}\mathbf{X})^{-1},$$

where

$$\check{\Omega} = \begin{bmatrix} 0.102830 & 0.107720 \\ 0.107720 & 0.301995 \end{bmatrix},$$

or

$$\text{Est.} \begin{bmatrix} \text{Var}(\check{\beta}_1) & \text{Cov}(\check{\beta}_1,\check{\beta}_2) \\ \text{Cov}(\check{\beta}_2,\check{\beta}_1) & \text{Var}(\check{\beta}_2) \end{bmatrix} = \begin{bmatrix} 0.0085 & 0.0071 \\ 0.0071 & 0.0248 \end{bmatrix},$$

and

$$\text{Est. Standard Error} \begin{bmatrix} \check{\beta}_1 \\ \check{\beta}_2 \end{bmatrix} = \begin{bmatrix} 0.0920 \\ 0.1576 \end{bmatrix}.$$

12-4.

Consider

$$\underline{y} = \underline{X}\underline{\beta} + \underline{\epsilon},$$

where

$$\underline{y} = \begin{bmatrix} \underline{y}_1 \\ \underline{y}_2 \\ \underline{y}_3 \end{bmatrix}, \quad \underline{\beta} = \begin{bmatrix} \beta_1 \\ \beta_2 \\ \beta_3 \end{bmatrix}, \quad \underline{\epsilon} = \begin{bmatrix} \underline{\epsilon}_1 \\ \underline{\epsilon}_2 \\ \underline{\epsilon}_3 \end{bmatrix},$$

$$\underline{X} = \begin{bmatrix} \underline{x}_1 & 0 & 0 \\ 0 & \underline{x}_2 & 0 \\ 0 & 0 & \underline{x}_3 \end{bmatrix},$$

and

$$E(\underline{\epsilon}\underline{\epsilon}') = \Omega.$$

Further, consider

$$\underline{y}^* = \underline{X}^*\underline{\beta}^* + \underline{\epsilon}^*,$$

where

$$\underline{y}^* = \begin{bmatrix} \underline{y}_1 \\ \underline{y}_2 \end{bmatrix}, \qquad \underline{\beta}^* = \begin{bmatrix} \beta_1 \\ \beta_2 \end{bmatrix}, \qquad \underline{\epsilon}^* = \begin{bmatrix} \underline{\epsilon}_1 \\ \underline{\epsilon}_2 \end{bmatrix},$$

and

$$\underline{X}^* = \begin{bmatrix} \underline{x}_1 & 0 \\ 0 & \underline{x}_2 \end{bmatrix}.$$

Now let $\tilde{\underline{\beta}}' = \begin{bmatrix} \tilde{\beta}_1 & \tilde{\beta}_2 & \tilde{\beta}_3 \end{bmatrix}$ and $\tilde{\underline{\beta}}^{*\prime} = \begin{bmatrix} \tilde{\beta}_1^* & \tilde{\beta}_2^* \end{bmatrix}$ be the GLS estimators of $\underline{\beta}$ and $\underline{\beta}^*$, respectively. Let $\tilde{b}_3$ be any linear unbiased estimator of β_3. Form $\underline{b}' = \begin{bmatrix} \tilde{\beta}_1^* & \tilde{\beta}_2^* & \tilde{b}_3 \end{bmatrix}$,

where

$$\text{Var-Cov}(\tilde{\underline{\beta}}) = (\underline{X}'\Omega^{-1}\underline{X})^{-1},$$

and

$$\text{Var-Cov}(\underline{b}) = \Sigma,$$

Since $\tilde{\underline{\beta}}$ is BLUE, and hence efficient, and since

$$\text{Var-Cov}(\underline{b}) - \text{Var-Cov}(\tilde{\underline{\beta}}) = \Sigma - (\underline{X}'\Omega^{-1}\underline{X})^{-1},$$

is a semi-definite positive matrix, it follows that

$$\text{Var}(\tilde{\beta}_1^*) - \text{Var}(\tilde{\beta}_1) \geq 0,$$

or

$$\frac{\text{Var}(\tilde{\beta}_1^*)}{\text{Var}(\tilde{\beta}_1)} \geq 1.$$

12-5.

There are n seemingly unrelated equations

$$V_{1t} = a_1 + \beta_1 P_{1t} + \gamma_1 V_t + \epsilon_{1t},$$

$$V_{2t} = a_2 + \beta_2 P_{2t} + \gamma_2 V_t + \epsilon_{2t},$$

$$\vdots$$

$$V_{nt} = a_n + \beta_n P_{nt} + \gamma_n V_t + \epsilon_{nt},$$

where (t = 1, ..., T), and

$$\Omega = \begin{bmatrix} \sigma_{11}I & \sigma_{12}I & \cdots & \sigma_{1n}I \\ \sigma_{21}I & \sigma_{22}I & \cdots & \sigma_{2n}I \\ \vdots & \vdots & & \vdots \\ \sigma_{n1}I & \sigma_{n2}I & \cdots & \sigma_{nn}I \end{bmatrix} = \begin{bmatrix} \sigma_{11} & \sigma_{12} & \cdots & \sigma_{1n} \\ \sigma_{21} & \sigma_{22} & \cdots & \sigma_{2n} \\ \vdots & \vdots & & \vdots \\ \sigma_{n1} & \sigma_{n2} & \cdots & \sigma_{nn} \end{bmatrix} \otimes I = \Sigma \otimes I,$$

where I is an identity matrix of dimension T. However, the condition $\Sigma\epsilon_{it} = 0$ causes the Σ, and hence the Ω, to be singular. To see this consider n = 2. Here we have

$$\epsilon_{1t} + \epsilon_{2t} = 0,$$

where

$$E(\epsilon_{1t}^2) = \sigma_{11}, \qquad E(\epsilon_{2t}^2) = \sigma_{22}.$$

Therefore

$$E(\epsilon_{1t}\epsilon_{2t}) = E(\epsilon_{1t})(-\epsilon_{1t}) = -\sigma_{11},$$

and

$$E(\epsilon_{1t}\epsilon_{2t}) = E(-\epsilon_{2t})(\epsilon_{2t}) = -\sigma_{22},$$

which imply $\sigma_{11} = \sigma_{22} = \sigma^2$. Thus

$$\Sigma = \begin{bmatrix} \sigma^2 & -\sigma^2 \\ -\sigma^2 & \sigma^2 \end{bmatrix} = \sigma^2 \begin{bmatrix} 1 & -1 \\ -1 & 1 \end{bmatrix}.$$

Further, for n = 3, we have

$$\epsilon_{1t} + \epsilon_{2t} + \epsilon_{3t} = 0,$$

where

$$E(\epsilon_{1t}^2) = \sigma_{11}, \qquad E(\epsilon_{2t}^2) = \sigma_{22}, \qquad E(\epsilon_{3t}^2) = \sigma_{33}.$$

Thus

$$E(\epsilon_{1t}\epsilon_{2t}) = E(\epsilon_{1t})(-\epsilon_{1t} - \epsilon_{3t}) = -\sigma_{11} - E(\epsilon_{1t}\epsilon_{3t}),$$

$$E(\epsilon_{1t}\epsilon_{3t}) = E(-\epsilon_{2t} - \epsilon_{3t})(\epsilon_{3t}) = -\sigma_{33} - E(\epsilon_{2t}\epsilon_{3t}),$$

and

$$E(\epsilon_{2t}\epsilon_{3t}) = E(\epsilon_{2t})(-\epsilon_{1t} - \epsilon_{2t}) = -\sigma_{22} - E(\epsilon_{1t}\epsilon_{2t}).$$

One possible solution to the above system of three simultaneous equations is

$$\sigma_{11} = \sigma_{22} = \sigma_{33} = \sigma^2,$$

and

$$E(\epsilon_{1t}\epsilon_{2t}) = E(\epsilon_{1t}\epsilon_{3t}) = E(\epsilon_{2t}\epsilon_{3t}) = -\sigma^2/2.$$

Thus

$$\Sigma = \begin{bmatrix} \sigma^2 & -\sigma^2/2 & -\sigma^2/2 \\ -\sigma^2/2 & \sigma^2 & -\sigma^2/2 \\ -\sigma^2/2 & -\sigma^2/2 & \sigma^2 \end{bmatrix} = \sigma^2 \begin{bmatrix} 1 & -1/2 & -1/2 \\ -1/2 & 1 & -1/2 \\ -1/2 & -1/2 & 1 \end{bmatrix}.$$

Therefore, we can generalize for n equations

$$\Sigma = \sigma^2 \begin{bmatrix} 1 & 1/(1-n) & \cdots & 1/(1-n) \\ 1/(1-n) & 1 & \cdots & 1/(1-n) \\ \vdots & \vdots & & \vdots \\ 1/(1-n) & 1/(1-n) & \cdots & 1 \end{bmatrix}.$$

It is readily seen that Σ, and hence Ω, are singular since sum of each row or column is zero. Therefore, the inverse of Σ, and hence that of Ω, do not exist. This means that there is a functional dependency among n equations or one of them is redundant.

In order to obtain an asymptotically efficient estimates of the regression coefficients we must omit one equation and use an estimation method. Note that maximum likelihood (ML) method is the only one which is invariant to normalization. Thus if ML method is used, it does not make any difference which equation is omitted. However, if other methods of estimation are employed we obtain different results depending on the choice of equation to be omitted.

Now, omitting the first equation and using ML method, the log-likelihood function will be

$$L = [\frac{-(n - 1)T}{2}]\log(2\pi) - (\tfrac{1}{2})\log|\Omega^*| - (\mathbf{y} - \mathbf{X}\delta)'\Omega^{*-1}(\mathbf{y} - \mathbf{X}\delta)/2,$$

where

$$\Omega^* = \Sigma^*\otimes\mathbf{I},$$

where Σ^* is the same as Σ except that the first row and the first column are omitted,

$$y' = \begin{bmatrix} v_2 & v_3 & \cdots & v_n \end{bmatrix},$$

and

$$X = \begin{bmatrix} 1 & p_2 & v & 0 & 0 & 0 & \cdots & 0 & 0 & 0 \\ 0 & 0 & 0 & 1 & p_3 & v & \cdots & 0 & 0 & 0 \\ \vdots & \vdots & \vdots & \vdots & \vdots & \vdots & & \vdots & \vdots & \vdots \\ 0 & 0 & 0 & 0 & 0 & 0 & \cdots & 1 & p_n & v \end{bmatrix},$$

where v_j, p_j, $(j = 2, \ldots, n)$, v, 1, and 0 are column vectors of T elements, and

$$\delta' = \begin{bmatrix} a_2 & \beta_2 & \gamma_2 & a_3 & \beta_3 & \gamma_3 & \cdots & a_n & \beta_n & \gamma_n \end{bmatrix}.$$

Now asymptotically efficient estimates of the regression coefficient δ, say $\hat{\delta}$, can be obtained by maximizing the likelihood function. The restrictions

$$\Sigma a_i = 0, \qquad \Sigma \beta_i P_{it} = 0,$$

and

$$\Sigma \gamma_i = 1,$$

are satisfied by setting the first equation as the residual equation, i.e.,

$$\hat{a}_1 = -\hat{a}_2 - \cdots - \hat{a}_n,$$

$$\hat{\beta}_1 = (-\hat{\beta}_2 P_{2t} - \cdots - \hat{\beta}_n P_n)/P_{1t},$$

and

$$\hat{\gamma}_1 = 1 - \hat{\gamma}_2 - \cdots - \hat{\gamma}_n.$$

12-6-a.

Consider the two equations and their one period lag

(1) $$\epsilon_1(t) = \rho_{11}\epsilon_1(t-1) + \rho_{12}\epsilon_2(t-1) + v_1(t),$$

(2) $$\epsilon_1(t-1) = \rho_{11}\epsilon_1(t-2) + \rho_{12}\epsilon_2(t-2) + v_1(t-1),$$

(3) $$\epsilon_2(t) = \rho_{21}\epsilon_1(t-1) + \rho_{22}\epsilon_2(t-1) + v_2(t),$$

(4) $$\epsilon_2(t-1) = \rho_{21}\epsilon_1(t-2) + \rho_{22}\epsilon_2(t-2) + v_2(t-1).$$

Substituting (4) into (1) and simplifying, we obtain

(5) $$\epsilon_1(t) = \rho_{11}\epsilon_1(t-1) + \rho_{12}\rho_{21}\epsilon_1(t-2) + \rho_{12}\rho_{22}\epsilon_2(t-2) + v_1(t) + \rho_{12}v_2(t-1).$$

Multiplying (2) by ρ_{22} and substituting the result into (5)

(6) $$\epsilon_1(t) = (\rho_{11} + \rho_{22})\epsilon_1(t-1) + (\rho_{12}\rho_{21} - \rho_{11}\rho_{22})\epsilon_1(t-2) + v_1(t) - \rho_{22}v_1(t-1) + \rho_{12}v_2(t-1).$$

Comparing (6) with the first equation in part (a), we get

$$a_{11} = \rho_{11} + \rho_{22},$$

$$a_{12} = \rho_{12}\rho_{21} - \rho_{11}\rho_{22},$$

and $$\zeta_1(t) = v_1(t) - \rho_{22}v_1(t-1) + \rho_{12}v_2(t-1).$$

Now substituting (2) into (3) and simplifying, we obtain

(7) $$\epsilon_2(t) = \rho_{11}\rho_{21}\epsilon_1(t-2) + \rho_{22}\epsilon_2(t-1) + \rho_{12}\rho_{21}\epsilon_2(t-2) + \rho_{21}v_1(t-1) + v_2(t).$$

Multiplying (4) by ρ_{11}, substituting the result into (7), and simplifying, we get

(8) $$\epsilon_2(t) = (\rho_{11} + \rho_{22})\epsilon_2(t-1) + (\rho_{12}\rho_{21} - \rho_{11}\rho_{22})\epsilon_2(t-2) + \rho_{12}v_1(t-1) + v_2(t) - \rho_{11}v_2(t-1).$$

Comparing (8) with the second equation in part (a), we obtain

$$a_{21} = \rho_{11} + \rho_{22},$$

$$a_{22} = \rho_{12}\rho_{21} - \rho_{11}\rho_{22},$$

and $$\zeta_2(t) = \rho_{12}v_1(t-1) + v_2(t) - \rho_{11}v_2(t-1).$$

The point of this exercise is to show that a system of M seemingly unrelated regressions with vector-autoregressive disturbances is equivalent to that of M seemingly unrelated regressions with autoregressive disturbance of order M in each equation of the system. Since the number of equations under consideration is frequently arbitrary, the implied order of autoregression of the disturbances becomes equally arbitrary.

12-6-b.

Consider the disturbances and the variance-covariance matrix

$$\epsilon = \begin{bmatrix} \epsilon_1 \\ \epsilon_2 \\ \vdots \\ \epsilon_T \end{bmatrix}, \quad \text{and} \quad E(\epsilon\epsilon') = \begin{bmatrix} \Sigma_{11} & \Sigma_{12} & \cdots & \Sigma_{1T} \\ \Sigma_{21} & \Sigma_{22} & \cdots & \Sigma_{2T} \\ \vdots & \vdots & & \vdots \\ \Sigma_{T1} & \Sigma_{T2} & \cdots & \Sigma_{TT} \end{bmatrix} = \Omega,$$

where $$\epsilon_t = \begin{bmatrix} \epsilon_1(t) \\ \epsilon_2(t) \end{bmatrix} \qquad (t = 1, \ldots, T),$$

$$\Sigma_{tt} = E(\epsilon_t\epsilon_t') = \begin{bmatrix} E[\epsilon_1(t)\epsilon_1(t)] & E[\epsilon_1(t)\epsilon_2(t)] \\ E[\epsilon_2(t)\epsilon_1(t)] & E[\epsilon_2(t)\epsilon_2(t)] \end{bmatrix},$$

and $$\Sigma_{ts} = E(\epsilon_t \epsilon_s') = \begin{bmatrix} E[\epsilon_1(t)\epsilon_1(s)] & E[\epsilon_1(t)\epsilon_2(s)] \\ E[\epsilon_2(t)\epsilon_1(s)] & E[\epsilon_2(t)\epsilon_2(s)] \end{bmatrix}.$$

In order to find Σ_{tt} and Σ_{ts}, consider

$$\begin{bmatrix} \epsilon_1(t) \\ \epsilon_2(t) \end{bmatrix} = \begin{bmatrix} \rho_{11} & \rho_{12} \\ \rho_{21} & \rho_{22} \end{bmatrix} \begin{bmatrix} \epsilon_1(t-1) \\ \epsilon_2(t-1) \end{bmatrix} + \begin{bmatrix} v_1(t) \\ v_2(t) \end{bmatrix},$$

or in matrix notation

$$\epsilon_t = R\epsilon_{t-1} + v_t.$$

Upon successive lagging and substitution, we obtain

$$\epsilon_t = \sum_{i=0}^{\infty} R^i L^i v_t,$$

where L is the lag operator. Now

$$E(\epsilon_t \epsilon_t') = E[\sum_{i=0}^{\infty} R^i L^i v_t L^i v_t' (R^i)'].$$

Given the appropriate mathematical conditions are satisfied when taking the mathematical expectations, we get

$$\Sigma_{tt} = \sum_{i=0}^{\infty} R^i \begin{bmatrix} \sigma_{v1}^2 & 0 \\ 0 & \sigma_{v2}^2 \end{bmatrix} (R^i)',$$

and $$\Sigma_{ts} = \sum_{i=t-s}^{\infty} R^i \begin{bmatrix} \sigma_{v1}^2 & 0 \\ 0 & \sigma_{v2}^2 \end{bmatrix} (R^{i-t+s})',$$

where $$\sigma_{vj}^2 = E[v_j(t)]^2 \qquad (j = 1, 2).$$

12-7-a.

Let **P** denote a lower triangular matrix defined as

$$\mathbf{P} = \begin{bmatrix} \mathbf{I} & 0 & 0 \\ a_1\mathbf{I} & a_2\mathbf{I} & 0 \\ a_3\mathbf{I} & a_4\mathbf{I} & a_5\mathbf{I} \end{bmatrix},$$

where a_i, $(i = 1, \ldots, 5)$, are constants to be determined. For the transformation to yield the desired result, we require that

$$\begin{bmatrix} 1 & 0 & 0 \\ a_1 & a_2 & 0 \\ a_3 & a_4 & a_5 \end{bmatrix} \begin{bmatrix} \epsilon_{1t} \\ \epsilon_{2t} \\ \epsilon_{3t} \end{bmatrix} = \begin{bmatrix} v_{1t} \\ v_{2t} \\ v_{3t} \end{bmatrix},$$

such that

1. $E(v_{it}) = 0 \qquad (i = 1, 2, 3),$
2. $\mathrm{Var}(v_{it}) = \sigma_{11},$
3. $\mathrm{Cov}(v_{it}, v_{jt}) = 0 \qquad (i \neq j).$

Condition (1) is automatically satisfied. Conditions (2) and (3) require that

$$\mathrm{Var}(v_{1t}) = \mathrm{Var}(\epsilon_{1t}) = \sigma_{11},$$

$$\mathrm{Var}(v_{2t}) = \mathrm{Var}(a_1\epsilon_{1t} + a_2\epsilon_{2t}) = \sigma_{11},$$

$$\mathrm{Var}(v_{3t}) = \mathrm{Var}(a_3\epsilon_{1t} + a_4\epsilon_{2t} + a_5\epsilon_{3t}) = \sigma_{11},$$

$$\mathrm{Cov}(v_{1t}, v_{2t}) = \mathrm{Cov}(\epsilon_{1t}, a_1\epsilon_{1t} + a_2\epsilon_{2t}) = 0,$$

$$\mathrm{Cov}(v_{1t}, v_{3t}) = \mathrm{Cov}(\epsilon_{1t}, a_3\epsilon_{1t} + a_4 e_{2t} + a_5\epsilon_{3t}) = 0,$$

$$\mathrm{Cov}(v_{2t}, v_{3t}) = \mathrm{Cov}(a_1\epsilon_{1t} + a_2\epsilon_{2t}, a_3\epsilon_{1t} + a_4 e_{2t} + a_5\epsilon_{3t}) = 0,$$

or

$$a_1^2\sigma_{11} + a_2^2\sigma_{22} + 2a_1a_2\sigma_{12} = \sigma_{11},$$

$$a_3^2\sigma_{11} + a_4^2\sigma_{22} + a_5^2\sigma_{33} + 2a_3a_4\sigma_{12} + 2a_3a_5\sigma_{13} + 2a_4a_5\sigma_{23} = \sigma_{11},$$

$$a_1\sigma_{11} + a_2\sigma_{12} = 0,$$

$$a_3\sigma_{11} + a_4\sigma_{12} + a_5\sigma_{13} = 0,$$

$$a_1a_3\sigma_{11} + (a_1a_4 + a_2a_3)\sigma_{12} + a_1a_5\sigma_{13} + a_2a_4\sigma_{22} + a_2a_5\sigma_{23} = 0.$$

Solving the first and the third equations simultaneously, we get

$$a_1 = \pm\sqrt{(1 - \rho_{12}^2)/(1 - \rho_{12}^2)},$$

and

$$a_2 = \mp\sqrt{\sigma_{11}/\sigma_{22}(1 - \rho_{12}^2)},$$

where the sign of a_1 is opposite that of a_2, and

$$\rho_{12}^2 = \sigma_{12}^2/\sigma_{11}\sigma_{22}.$$

Solving the three remaining equations simultaneously, we obtain

$$a_3 = \pm[\sigma_{12}(\sigma_{11}\sigma_{23} - \sigma_{12}\sigma_{13}) + \sigma_{11}\sigma_{22}\sigma_{13}(1 - \rho_{12}^2)]/\Delta,$$

$$a_4 = \mp\sigma_{11}(\sigma_{11}\sigma_{23} - \sigma_{12}\sigma_{13})/\Delta,$$

and

$$a_5 = \mp\sigma_{11}^2\sigma_{22}(1 - \rho_{12}^2)/\Delta,$$

where the sign of a_3 is opposite those of a_4 and a_5,

$$\rho_{13}^2 = \sigma_{13}^2/\sigma_{11}\sigma_{33},$$

and

$$\Delta = \sqrt{\sigma_{11}^3\sigma_{22}^2\sigma_{33}(1 - \rho_{12}^2)^2[(1 - \rho_{13}^2) - \frac{(\sigma_{11}\sigma_{23} - \sigma_{12}\sigma_{13})^2}{\sigma_{11}^2\sigma_{22}\sigma_{33}(1 - \rho_{12}^2)}]}.$$

12-7-b.

The LSE of β_2, say $\hat{\beta}_2$, is

(1) $$\hat{\beta}_2 = (X_2'X_2)^{-1}X_2'y_2.$$

The Aitken estimator of the set of two regressions is

(2) $$\tilde{\beta} = (X'\Omega^{-1}X)^{-1}X'\Omega^{-1}y,$$

where $$y = \begin{bmatrix} y_1 \\ y_2 \end{bmatrix}, \qquad X = \begin{bmatrix} X_1 & 0 \\ 0 & X_2 \end{bmatrix}, \qquad \Omega^{-1} = \frac{1}{\Delta}\begin{bmatrix} \sigma_{22}I & -\sigma_{12}I \\ -\sigma_{12}I & \sigma_{11}I \end{bmatrix},$$

and $$\Delta = \sigma_{11}\sigma_{22} - \sigma_{12}^2.$$

Substituting the above into $\tilde{\beta}$ in (2), we obtain

(3) $$\sigma_{22}X_1'X_1\tilde{\beta}_1 - \sigma_{12}X_1'X_2\tilde{\beta}_2 = \sigma_{22}X_1'y_1 - \sigma_{12}X_1'y_2,$$

(4) $$\sigma_{11}X_2'X_2\tilde{\beta}_2 - \sigma_{12}X_2'X_1\tilde{\beta}_1 = \sigma_{11}X_2'y_2 - \sigma_{12}X_2'y_1.$$

Consider y_1, y_2, ϵ_1, and ϵ_2 are each nx1, $\beta_1 \to$Gx1, $\beta_2 \to$Kx1, and $X_1 = \begin{bmatrix} X_2 & Z \end{bmatrix}$, where $X_1 \to$nxG, $X_2 \to$nxK, and $Z \to$nx(G-K). Substituting for X_1 in (3), we obtain the following two sets of equations

(5) $$\sigma_{22}X_2'\begin{bmatrix} X_2 & Z \end{bmatrix}\tilde{\beta}_1 - \sigma_{12}X_2'X_2\tilde{\beta}_2 = \sigma_{22}X_2'y_1 - \sigma_{12}X_2'y_2,$$

(6) $$\sigma_{22}Z'\begin{bmatrix} X_2 & Z \end{bmatrix}\tilde{\beta}_1 - \sigma_{12}Z'X_2\tilde{\beta}_2 = \sigma_{22}Z'y_1 - \sigma_{12}Z'y_2,$$

where (5) and (6) contain K and (G - K) equations, respectively. Substituting for X_1 in (4), we obtain a set of K equations

(7) $$\sigma_{11}X_2'X_2\tilde{\beta}_2 - \sigma_{12}X_2'\begin{bmatrix} X_2 & Z \end{bmatrix}\tilde{\beta}_1 = \sigma_{11}X_2'y_2 - \sigma_{12}X_2'y_1.$$

Solving the system of 2K simultaneous equations in (5) and (7) by multiplying the former by σ_{12} and the latter by σ_{22} and adding the two resulting equations, we obtain

$$\sigma_{11}\sigma_{22}X_2'X_2\tilde{\beta}_2 - \sigma_{12}^2X_2'X_2\tilde{\beta}_2 = \sigma_{11}\sigma_{22}X_2'y_2 - \sigma_{12}^2X_2'y_2,$$

or

$$\tilde{\beta}_2 = (X_2'X_2)^{-1}X_2'y_2,$$

which is the same as the LSE of β_2 in (1).

12-7-c.

Step 1: The null and the alternative hypotheses are

$$H_o: \beta_1 - \beta_2 = 0,$$

$$H_a: \beta_1 - \beta_2 \neq 0.$$

Steps 2 & 3: The test statistic and its distribution are

$$t = (\tilde{\beta}_1 - \tilde{\beta}_2)/s_{\tilde{\beta}_1-\tilde{\beta}_2} \sim t_{n-2},$$

where $\tilde{\beta}$ is the feasible Aitken estimator of β.

Step 4: Do not reject the null hypothesis if

$$|t| < t_{a/2,n-2} = t_{0.0050,38} = 2.5760,$$

otherwise reject it.

Step 5: In order to find sample values, first calculate the LSE's of β_1 and β_2 as follows

$$\hat{\beta}_1 = x_1'y_1/x_1'x_1 = 4/10 = 0.40,$$

and $$\hat{\beta}_2 = x_2'y_2/x_2'x_2 = 0/5 = 0.00,$$

yielding the following residuals

$$e_1 = y_1 - x_1\hat{\beta}_1, \qquad \text{and} \qquad e_2 = y_2 - x_2\hat{\beta}_2.$$

Next estimate the elements of the Ω matrix using these residuals as follows

$$s_{11} = e_1'e_1/T$$

$$= (y_1'y_1 - 2x_1'y_1\hat{\beta}_1 + x_1'x_1\hat{\beta}_1^2)/T$$

$$= [100 - 2(4)(0.40) + 10(0.16)]/20$$

$$= 4.92,$$

further,

$$s_{12} = s_{21}$$

$$= e_1'e_2/T$$

$$= (y_1'y_2 - x_1'y_2\hat{\beta}_1 - x_2'y_1\hat{\beta}_2 + x_1'x_2\hat{\beta}_1\hat{\beta}_2)/T$$

$$= [20 - 0(0.40) - 1(0) + (-2)(0.40)(0)]/20$$

$$= 1,$$

and

$$s_{22} = e_2'e_2/T$$

$$= (y_2'y_2 - 2x_2'y_2\hat{\beta}_2 + x_2'x_2\hat{\beta}_2^2)/T$$

$$= [150 - 2(0)(0) + 5(0)]/20$$

$$= 7.50.$$

Thus the $\hat{\Omega}$ matrix and its inverse are

$$\hat{\Omega} = \begin{bmatrix} 4.92I & 1.00I \\ 1.00I & 7.50I \end{bmatrix}, \quad \text{and} \quad \hat{\Omega}^{-1} = \frac{1}{35.90}\begin{bmatrix} 7.50I & -1.00I \\ -1.00I & 4.92I \end{bmatrix}.$$

Now the feasible Aitken estimator of β is

$$\tilde{\beta} = (X'\hat{\Omega}^{-1}X)^{-1}X'\hat{\Omega}^{-1}y,$$

or

$$\begin{bmatrix} \tilde{\beta}_1 \\ \tilde{\beta}_2 \end{bmatrix} = \begin{bmatrix} 7.50x_1'x_1 & -1.00x_1'x_2 \\ -1.00x_2'x_1 & 4.92x_2'x_2 \end{bmatrix}^{-1} \begin{bmatrix} 7.50x_1'y_1 - x_1'y_2 \\ 4.92x_2'y_2 - x_2'y_1 \end{bmatrix}$$

$$= \begin{bmatrix} 75.00 & 2.00 \\ 2.00 & 24.60 \end{bmatrix}^{-1} \begin{bmatrix} 30-0 \\ 0-1 \end{bmatrix}$$

$$= \begin{bmatrix} 0.4020 \\ -0.0733 \end{bmatrix},$$

and its estimated variance-covariance is

$$\textbf{Est. Var-Cov}(\tilde{\beta}) = (\mathbf{X}'\hat{\Omega}^{-1}\mathbf{X})^{-1},$$

or

$$\text{Est.} \begin{bmatrix} \text{Var}(\tilde{\beta}_1) & \text{Cov}(\tilde{\beta}_1, \tilde{\beta}_2) \\ \text{Cov}(\tilde{\beta}_2, \tilde{\beta}_1) & \text{Var}(\tilde{\beta}_2) \end{bmatrix} = \begin{bmatrix} 0.4797 & -0.0390 \\ -0.0390 & 1.4625 \end{bmatrix}.$$

Therefore

$$\tilde{\beta}_1 - \tilde{\beta}_2 = 0.4020 - (-0.0733) = 0.4753,$$

$$s^2_{\tilde{\beta}_1 - \tilde{\beta}_2} = 0.4797 - 2(-0.0390) + 1.4625 = 2.0202,$$

and

$$s_{\tilde{\beta}_1 - \tilde{\beta}_2} = 1.4213.$$

Thus the value of the test statistic is

$$t = 0.4753/1.4213 = 0.3344.$$

Step 6: Since the value of the test statistic falls in the acceptance region, do not reject the null hypothesis. There is no evidence that the two regression coefficients are not the same.

CHAPTER 13

13-1.

The Keynesian model may be written in matrix form as

$$\begin{bmatrix} 1 & -\beta \\ -1 & 1 \end{bmatrix} \begin{bmatrix} C_t \\ Y_t \end{bmatrix} + \begin{bmatrix} -a & 0 \\ 0 & -1 \end{bmatrix} \begin{bmatrix} 1 \\ I_t \end{bmatrix} = \begin{bmatrix} \epsilon_t \\ 0 \end{bmatrix}.$$

Consider the identification status of the first equation. For the order condition we have

$$K^{**} = G^{\Delta} - 1 = 1,$$

and for the rank condition[1] we have

$$\Delta = \begin{bmatrix} -1 \end{bmatrix},$$

and $$\text{rank}(\Delta) = G - 1 = 1,$$

which means that the first equation is exactly identified.

---

[1]The rank condition of

$$\text{rank}(\Pi_{\Delta^{**}}) \le G^{\Delta} - 1,$$

is equivalent to

$$\text{rank}(\Delta) \le G - 1,$$

since

$$\text{rank}(\Pi_{\Delta^{**}}) = \text{rank}(\Delta) - G^{\Delta\Delta},$$

and $$G^{\Delta} = G - G^{\Delta\Delta}.$$

ILS method. Consider the reduced form of the model

$$\begin{bmatrix} C_t \\ Y_t \end{bmatrix} = \begin{bmatrix} 1 & -\beta \\ -1 & 1 \end{bmatrix}^{-1} \begin{bmatrix} \alpha & 0 \\ 0 & 1 \end{bmatrix} \begin{bmatrix} 1 \\ I_t \end{bmatrix} + \begin{bmatrix} 1 & -\beta \\ -1 & 1 \end{bmatrix}^{-1} \begin{bmatrix} \epsilon_t \\ 0 \end{bmatrix},$$

or

$$\begin{bmatrix} C_t \\ Y_t \end{bmatrix} = \frac{1}{1 - \beta} \begin{bmatrix} \alpha & \beta \\ \alpha & 1 \end{bmatrix} \begin{bmatrix} 1 \\ I_t \end{bmatrix} + \frac{1}{1 - \beta} \begin{bmatrix} \epsilon_t \\ \epsilon_t \end{bmatrix}.$$

Therefore the reduced form of the consumption equation is

$$C_t = \frac{\alpha}{1 - \beta} + \frac{\beta I_t}{1 - \beta} + \frac{\epsilon_t}{1 - \beta},$$

or

$$C_t = \gamma_1 + \gamma_2 I_t + \epsilon_t^*.$$

The least squares estimator of γ_2, say $\hat{\gamma}_2$, is

$$\hat{\gamma}_2 = \frac{\Sigma i_t' c_t'}{\Sigma i_t'^2}.$$

Since $\gamma_2 = \beta/(1 - \beta)$, solving for the ILS estimator of β, say $\tilde{\beta}$, we obtain

$$\tilde{\beta} = \frac{\Sigma i_t' c_t'}{\Sigma i_t'(i_t' + c_t')} = \frac{\Sigma i_t' c_t'}{\Sigma i_t' y_t'}.$$

2SLS method. Consider the reduced form equation of Y_t

$$Y_t = \frac{\alpha}{1 - \beta} + \frac{I_t}{1 - \beta} + \frac{\epsilon_t}{1 - \beta},$$

or

$$Y_t = \gamma_3 + \gamma_4 I_t + \epsilon_t^*.$$

For the first stage of the 2SLS method, we find

$$\hat{Y}_t = \hat{\gamma}_3 + \hat{\gamma}_4 I_t,$$

or

$$\hat{y}_t' = \hat{\gamma}_4 i_t',$$

where $\hat{\gamma}_3$ and $\hat{\gamma}_4$ are the OLS of γ_3 and γ_4, respectively, and $\hat{\gamma}_4$ is defined as

$$\hat{\gamma}_4 = \frac{\Sigma i_t' y_t'}{\Sigma i_t'^2}.$$

For the second stage use $\hat{Y}_t$ as an instrument for Y_t and apply OLS to the first structural form equation. The 2SLS estimator of β, say $\check{\beta}$, is

$$\check{\beta} = \frac{\Sigma \hat{y}_t' c_t'}{\Sigma \hat{y}_t' y_t'} = \frac{\Sigma \hat{\gamma}_4 i_t' c_t'}{\Sigma \hat{\gamma}_4 i_t' y_t'} = \frac{\Sigma i_t' c_t'}{\Sigma i_t' y_t'},$$

which is identical to the ILS estimator of β.

LIML method. This method calls for maximizing the likelihood function for the observations on the endogenous variables included in the equation to be estimated. In this case the included endogenous variables are C_t and Y_t, where the former is in the structural form and the latter is in the reduced form, i.e.,

$$C_t = \alpha + \beta Y_t + \epsilon_t,$$

and

$$Y_t = \frac{\alpha}{1 - \beta} + \frac{I_t}{1 - \beta} + \frac{\epsilon_t}{1 - \beta}.$$

However, the variance-covariance matrix of the disturbances of the two equations is singular. One way to deal with this problem is to substitute the second structural form equation, which is an identity, into the first before setting up the likelihood function, which results in

$$C_t = \alpha + \beta(C_t + I_t) + \epsilon_t,$$

or

$$\epsilon_t = (1 - \beta)C_t - \alpha - \beta I_t.$$

The *Jacobian* of the transformation from ϵ's to C's is

$$\left|\frac{\partial \epsilon}{\partial C}\right| = (1 - \beta)^T.$$

By an extension of Theorem 19 (the "change of variable" theorem), section (7-3) of the text,[1] the likelihood function is

$$f(C_1, \ldots, C_T) = \left|\frac{\partial \epsilon}{\partial C}\right| f(\epsilon_1, \ldots, \epsilon_T)$$

$$= (1 - \beta)^T f(\epsilon_1, \ldots, \epsilon_T)$$

$$= (1 - \beta)^T f(\epsilon_1)\cdots f(\epsilon_T),$$

since ϵ's are normally and independently distributed. The log-likelihood function is then given as

$$L = \log[f(C_1, \ldots, C_T)] = (T)\log(1 - \beta) + \Sigma\log[f(\epsilon_t)],$$

where $(t = 1, \ldots, T)$, or

$$L = (T)\log(1 - \beta) - (\tfrac{T}{2})\log(2\pi\sigma^2) - \Sigma[(1 - \beta)C_t - a - \beta I_t]^2/2\sigma^2.$$

Differentiating L with respect to a, β, and σ^2, setting them equal to zero, and putting a "ˇ" on the parameters to be estimated, we get

$$(1) \quad \frac{\partial L}{\partial a} \equiv (\frac{1}{\check{\sigma}^2})\Sigma[(1 - \check{\beta})C_t - \check{a} - \check{\beta}I_t] = 0,$$

$$(2) \quad \frac{\partial L}{\partial \beta} \equiv \frac{-T}{1 - \check{\beta}} + (\frac{1}{\check{\sigma}^2})\Sigma[(1 - \check{\beta})C_t - \check{a} - \check{\beta}I_t](C_t + I_t) = 0,$$

$$(3) \quad \frac{\partial L}{\partial \sigma^2} \equiv \frac{-T}{2\check{\sigma}^2} + (\frac{1}{2\check{\sigma}^4})\Sigma[(1 - \check{\beta})C_t - \check{a} - \check{\beta}I_t]^2 = 0.$$

Solving for $\check{a}$ from (1), we obtain

$$\check{a} = (1 - \check{\beta})\bar{C} - \check{\beta}\bar{I}.$$

---

[1] P. 220.

Substituting for $\check{\alpha}$ into (2) and (3), we get

$$\frac{-T}{1-\check{\beta}} + \left(\frac{1}{\check{\sigma}^2}\right)\Sigma[(1-\check{\beta})c_t' - \check{\beta}i_t'](C_t + I_t) = 0,$$

or

$$(4) \qquad \frac{-T}{1-\check{\beta}} + \left(\frac{1}{\check{\sigma}^2}\right)\Sigma[(1-\check{\beta})c_t' - \check{\beta}i_t'](c_t' + i_t') = 0,$$

and

$$(5) \qquad \frac{-T}{2\check{\sigma}^2} + \left(\frac{1}{2\check{\sigma}^4}\right)\Sigma[(1-\check{\beta})c_t' - \check{\beta}i_t']^2 = 0.$$

Solving for $\check{\sigma}^2$ from (5), we obtain

$$(6) \qquad \check{\sigma}^2 = \Sigma[(1-\check{\beta})c_t' - \check{\beta}i_t']^2/T.$$

Substituting (6) into (4), we get

$$\frac{-T}{1-\check{\beta}} + \frac{T\Sigma[(1-\check{\beta})c_t' - \check{\beta}i_t'](c_t' + i_t')}{\Sigma[(1-\check{\beta})c_t' - \check{\beta}i_t']^2} = 0.$$

Solving for $\check{\beta}$, we obtain

$$\check{\beta} = \frac{\Sigma i_t'c_t'}{\Sigma i_t'c_t' + \Sigma i_t'^2} = \frac{\Sigma i_t'c_t'}{\Sigma i_t'(c_t' + i_t')} = \frac{\Sigma i_t'c_t'}{\Sigma i_t'y_t'},$$

which is identical to the ILS and the 2SLS estimators of β.

FIML method. This method calls for the usual application of the maximum likelihood principle to all stochastic equations of the system simultaneously. However, the presence of an identity in the system will cause the variance-covariance matrix of the structural disturbances to be singular. One way to deal with this problem is to substitute the identity into the stochastic equation before setting up the likelihood function, which is exactly the same as the LIML method described above. Thus the four methods of estimation are identical.

13-2.

Consider the OLS estimator of β_{12}

$$\hat{\beta}_{12} = \frac{\Sigma y'_{2t} y'_{1t}}{\Sigma y'^{2}_{2t}},$$

and its asymptotic variance

$$\text{Asympt. Var}[\sqrt{T}(\hat{\beta}_{12} - \beta_{12})] = \frac{\sigma_{11}}{\text{plim}(\Sigma y'^{2}_{2t}/T)}.$$

In order to obtain the ILS estimator of β_{12}, consider the model written in matrix form

$$\begin{bmatrix} 1 & -\beta_{12} \\ 0 & 1 \end{bmatrix} \begin{bmatrix} Y_{1t} \\ Y_{2t} \end{bmatrix} + \begin{bmatrix} -\gamma_{11} & 0 \\ -\gamma_{21} & -\gamma_{22} \end{bmatrix} \begin{bmatrix} 1 \\ X_t \end{bmatrix} = \begin{bmatrix} u_{1t} \\ u_{2t} \end{bmatrix},$$

and the identification status of the first equation. For the order condition we have

$$K^{**} = G^{\Delta} - 1 = 1,$$

and for the rank condition we have

$$\Delta = \begin{bmatrix} -\gamma_{22} \end{bmatrix},$$

and

$$\text{rank}(\Delta) = G - 1 = 1,$$

which means that the first equation is exactly identified. The reduced form of the model is

$$\begin{bmatrix} Y_{1t} \\ Y_{2t} \end{bmatrix} = \begin{bmatrix} \gamma_{11}+\gamma_{21}\beta_{12} & \gamma_{22}\beta_{12} \\ \gamma_{21} & \gamma_{22} \end{bmatrix} \begin{bmatrix} 1 \\ X_t \end{bmatrix} + \begin{bmatrix} u_{1t}+\beta_{12}u_{2t} \\ u_{2t} \end{bmatrix}.$$

Therefore the reduced form equations are

$$Y_{1t} = \gamma_{11} + \gamma_{21}\beta_{12} + \gamma_{22}\beta_{12}X_t + u_{1t} + \beta_{12}u_{2t},$$

or

$$Y_{1t} = \pi_{11} + \pi_{12}X_t + u_t^*,$$

and

$$Y_{2t} = \gamma_{21} + \gamma_{22}X_t + u_{2t}.$$

Consider the OLS estimators of π_{12} and γ_{22} as follows

$$\hat{\pi}_{12} = \Sigma x_t' y_{1t}' / \Sigma x_t'^2,$$

and

$$\hat{\gamma}_{22} = \Sigma x_t' y_{2t}' / \Sigma x_t'^2.$$

Since $\pi_{12} = \gamma_{22}\beta_{12}$, the ILS estimator of β_{12} is

$$\tilde{\beta}_{12} = \frac{\hat{\pi}_{12}}{\hat{\gamma}_{22}} = \frac{\Sigma x_t' y_{1t}'}{\Sigma x_t' y_{2t}'},$$

and its asymptotic variance is

$$\text{Asympt. Var}[\sqrt{T}(\tilde{\beta}_{12} - \beta_{12})] = \frac{\sigma_{11}\text{plim}(\Sigma x_t'^2/T)}{[\text{plim}(\Sigma x_t' y_{2t}'/T)]^2}.$$

Now

$$\frac{\text{Asympt. Var}[\sqrt{T}(\hat{\beta}_{12} - \beta_{12})]}{\text{Asympt. Var}[\sqrt{T}(\tilde{\beta}_{12} - \beta_{12})]}$$

$$= \frac{[\text{plim}(\Sigma x_t' y_{2t}'/T)]^2}{\text{plim}(\Sigma x_t'^2/T)\text{plim}(\Sigma y_{2t}'^2/T)} = \text{plim}(R^2_{XY_2}) \le 1,$$

since $R^2_{XY_2}$ is the coefficient of determination of X and Y_2. Therefore

$$\text{Asympt. Var}(\tilde{\beta}_{12}) \ge \text{Asympt. Var}(\hat{\beta}_{12}).$$

13-3-a.

Tintner's model of the American meat market may be written in matrix form as

$$\begin{bmatrix} 1 & -a_1 \\ 1 & -b_1 \end{bmatrix} \begin{bmatrix} Y_{1t} \\ Y_{2t} \end{bmatrix} + \begin{bmatrix} -a_0 & -a_2 & 0 & 0 \\ -b_0 & 0 & -b_2 & -b_3 \end{bmatrix} \begin{bmatrix} 1 \\ X_{1t} \\ X_{2t} \\ X_{3t} \end{bmatrix} = \begin{bmatrix} u_{1t} \\ u_{2t} \end{bmatrix}.$$

Consider the identification status of the demand equation. For the order condition we have

$$K^{**} = 2 > G^{\Delta} - 1 = 1,$$

and for the rank condition we have

$$\Delta = \begin{bmatrix} -b_2 & -b_3 \end{bmatrix},$$

and

$$\text{rank}(\Delta) = G - 1 = 1,$$

which means that the demand equation is over-identified. Consider the identification status of the supply equation. For the order condition we have

$$K^{**} = G^{\Delta} - 1 = 1,$$

and for the rank condition we have

$$\Delta = \begin{bmatrix} -a_2 \end{bmatrix},$$

and

$$\text{rank}(\Delta) = G - 1 = 1,$$

which means that the supply equation is exactly identified.

13-3-b.

Substituting the specification into the supply equation, we get

$$Y_{1t} = b_0 + b_1 Y_{2t} + b_3 Z_t + u_{2t},$$

where

$$Z_t = KX_{2t} + X_{3t}.$$

Now the model may be written in matrix form as

$$\begin{bmatrix} 1 & -a_1 \\ 1 & -b_1 \end{bmatrix} \begin{bmatrix} Y_{1t} \\ Y_{2t} \end{bmatrix} + \begin{bmatrix} -a_0 & -a_2 & 0 \\ -b_0 & 0 & -b_3 \end{bmatrix} \begin{bmatrix} 1 \\ X_{1t} \\ Z_t \end{bmatrix} = \begin{bmatrix} u_{1t} \\ u_{2t} \end{bmatrix}.$$

Consider the identification status of the demand equation. For the order condition we have

$$K^{**} = G^{\Delta} - 1 = 1,$$

and for the rank condition we have

$$\Delta = \begin{bmatrix} -b_3 \end{bmatrix},$$

and

$$\text{rank}(\Delta) = G - 1 = 1,$$

which means that the demand equation becomes exactly identified. Consider the identification status of the supply equation. For the order condition we have

$$= G^{\Delta} - 1 = 1,$$

and for the rank condition we have

$$\Delta = \begin{bmatrix} -a_2 \end{bmatrix},$$

and

$$\text{rank}(\Delta) = G - 1 = 1,$$

which means that the supply equation remains exactly identified.

13-3-c.

After adding the term a_3X_{4t} to the demand equation, the model may be written in matrix form as

$$\begin{bmatrix} 1 & -a_1 \\ 1 & -b_1 \end{bmatrix} \begin{bmatrix} Y_{1t} \\ Y_{2t} \end{bmatrix} + \begin{bmatrix} -a_0 & -a_2 & 0 & 0 & -a_3 \\ -b_0 & 0 & -b_2 & -b_3 & 0 \end{bmatrix} \begin{bmatrix} 1 \\ X_{1t} \\ X_{2t} \\ X_{3t} \\ X_{4t} \end{bmatrix} = \begin{bmatrix} u_{1t} \\ u_{2t} \end{bmatrix}.$$

Consider the identification status of the demand equation. For the order condition we have

$$K^{**} = 2 > G^{\Delta} - 1 = 1,$$

and for the rank condition we have

$$\Delta = \begin{bmatrix} -b_2 & -b_3 \end{bmatrix},$$

and $$\text{rank}(\Delta) = G - 1 = 1,$$

which means that the demand equation remains over-identified. Consider the identification status of the supply equation. For the order condition we have

$$K^{**} = 2 > G^{\Delta} - 1 = 1,$$

and for the rank condition we have

$$\Delta = \begin{bmatrix} -a_2 & -a_3 \end{bmatrix},$$

and $$\text{rank}(\Delta) = G - 1 = 1,$$

which means that the supply equation becomes over-identified.

13-4-a.

The aggregate model of the economy may be written in matrix form as

$$\begin{bmatrix} 1 & -\alpha_2 & 0 & 0 \\ 0 & 0 & 1 & -\beta_2 \\ 0 & -1 & 0 & 1 \\ -1 & 0 & -1 & 1 \end{bmatrix} \begin{bmatrix} C_t \\ D_t \\ I_t \\ Y_t \end{bmatrix} + \begin{bmatrix} -\alpha_1 & 0 & 0 & 0 \\ -\beta_1 & 0 & 0 & -\beta_2 \\ 0 & 0 & -1 & 0 \\ 0 & -1 & 0 & 0 \end{bmatrix} \begin{bmatrix} 1 \\ G_t \\ T_t \\ Y_{t-1} \end{bmatrix} = \begin{bmatrix} u_{1t} \\ u_{2t} \\ 0 \\ 0 \end{bmatrix}.$$

Consider the identification status of the consumption equation. For the order condition we have

$$K^{**} = 3 > G^{\Delta} - 1 = 1,$$

and for the rank condition we have

$$\Delta = \begin{bmatrix} 1 & -\beta_2 & 0 & 0 & -\beta_3 \\ 0 & 1 & 0 & -1 & 0 \\ -1 & 1 & -1 & 0 & 0 \end{bmatrix},$$

and

$$\text{rank}(\Delta) = G - 1 = 3,$$

which means that the consumption equation is over-identified. Consider the identification status of the investment equation. For the order condition we have

$$K^{**} = 2 > G^{\Delta} - 1 = 1,$$

and for the rank condition we have

$$\Delta = \begin{bmatrix} 1 & -a_2 & 0 & 0 \\ 0 & -1 & 0 & -1 \\ -1 & 0 & -1 & 0 \end{bmatrix},$$

and

$$\text{rank}(\Delta) = G - 1 = 3,$$

which means that the investment equation is also over-identified.

13-4-b.

The 3SLS estimates of the consumption and the investment equations are

$$C_t = \underset{(2.2113)}{15.9640} + \underset{(0.0374)}{0.6516}D_t + e_{1t},$$

and

$$I_t = \underset{(8.2725)}{-12.0170} - \underset{(0.3945)}{0.5132}Y_t + \underset{(0.4206)}{0.7441}Y_{t-1} + e_{2t}.$$

13-5-a.

Substituting

$$C_t = a_1 + a_2 D_t + u_{1t},$$

$$I_t = \beta_1 + \beta_2 Y_t + \beta_3 Y_{t-1} + u_{2t},$$

and

$$D_t = Y_t - T_t,$$

into the identity

$$Y_t = C_t + I_t + G_t,$$

we obtain the fundamental dynamic equation

$$Y_t = \theta_0 + \theta_1 Y_{t-1} + \theta_2 G_t + \theta_3 T_t + \epsilon_t,$$

where

$$\theta_0 = \frac{\alpha_1 + \beta_1}{1 - \alpha_2 - \beta_2}, \qquad \theta_1 = \frac{\beta_3}{1 - \alpha_2 - \beta_2},$$

$$\theta_2 = \frac{1}{1 - \alpha_2 - \beta_2}, \qquad \theta_3 = \frac{-\alpha_2}{1 - \alpha_2 - \beta_2},$$

and

$$\epsilon_t = \frac{u_{1t} + u_{2t}}{1 - \alpha_2 - \beta_2}.$$

Upon substituting the estimated values of the parameters α_1, α_2, β_1, β_2, and β_3 from **(4-b)**, we obtain the estimated fundamental dynamic equation

$$Y_t = 4.5810 + 0.8636Y_{t-1} + 1.1606G_t - 0.7563T_t + e_t.$$

Consider the stability condition

$$-1 < \theta_1 = \frac{\beta_3}{1 - \alpha_2 - \beta_2} < 1.$$

Since the estimated θ_1 is equal to 0.8636, the estimated system is stable.

13-5-b.

Consider the fundamental dynamic equation derived in part (a). Upon successive substitution for Y_{t-1}, Y_{t-2}, ..., we obtain the final form of the equation

$$\begin{aligned} Y_t = {} & \theta_0(1 + \theta_1 + \theta_1^2 + \cdots) + \theta_1^t Y_0 \\ & + \theta_2(G_t + \theta_1 G_{t-1} + \theta_1^2 G_{t-2} + \cdots) \\ & + \theta_3(T_t + \theta_1 T_{t-1} + \theta_1^2 T_{t-2} + \cdots) \\ & + (\epsilon_t + \theta_1 \epsilon_{t-1} + \theta_1^2 \epsilon_{t-2} + \cdots). \end{aligned}$$

The coefficients of G's, i.e., θ_2, $\theta_2\theta_1$, $\theta_2\theta_1^2$, ..., are the dynamic multipliers of Y with respect to G. The estimated values of the multipliers are presented in table 13-1.

TABLE 13-1

Dynamic Multipliers of G on Y			
Lag	Multiplier	Lag	Multiplier
0	1.1606	11	0.2314
1	1.0024	12	0.1998
2	0.8657	13	0.1726
3	0.7476	14	0.1490
4	0.6456	15	0.1287
5	0.5576	16	0.1111
6	0.4816	17	0.0960
7	0.4159	18	0.0829
8	0.3592	19	0.0716
9	0.3102	20	0.0618
10	0.2679	21	0.0534
			8.1726

13-5-c.

The long-run (equilibrium) multiplier of Y with respect to G is

$$\theta_2(1 + \theta_1 + \theta_1^2 + \cdots) = \frac{\theta_2}{1 - \theta_1}.$$

Thus the estimated value of the long-run multiplier is

$$\frac{1.1606}{1 - 0.8636} = 8.5088.$$

13-6-a.

The dynamic model of the market for the commodity may be written in matrix form as

$$\begin{bmatrix} 1 & 0 & -\alpha_1 & 0 \\ 0 & 1 & -\beta_1 & 0 \\ 0 & 0 & 1 & 0 \\ 1 & -1 & 0 & -1 \end{bmatrix} \begin{bmatrix} S_t \\ D_t \\ P_t \\ Q_t \end{bmatrix} + \begin{bmatrix} -\alpha_0 & 0 & 0 & 0 \\ -\beta_0 & 0 & 0 & 0 \\ 0 & -1 & -m & m \\ 0 & 0 & -1 & 0 \end{bmatrix} \begin{bmatrix} 1 \\ P_{t-1} \\ Q_{t-1} \\ Q_{t-2} \end{bmatrix} = \begin{bmatrix} u_{1t} \\ u_{2t} \\ u_{3t} \\ 0 \end{bmatrix}.$$

Consider the identification status of the production equation. For the order condition we have

$$K^{**} = 3 > G^{\Delta} - 1 = 1,$$

and for the rank condition we have

$$\Delta = \begin{bmatrix} 1 & 0 & 0 & 0 & 0 \\ 0 & 0 & -1 & -m & m \\ -1 & -1 & 0 & -1 & 0 \end{bmatrix},$$

and $\text{rank}(\Delta) = G - 1 = 3,$

which means that the production equation is over-identified. Consider the identification status of the sales equation. For the order condition we have

$$K^{**} = 3 > G^{\Delta} - 1 = 1,$$

and for the rank condition we have

$$\Delta = \begin{bmatrix} 1 & 0 & 0 & 0 & 0 \\ 0 & 0 & -1 & -m & m \\ 1 & 1 & 0 & -1 & 0 \end{bmatrix},$$

and

$$\text{rank}(\Delta) = G - 1 = 3,$$

which means that the sales equation is also over-identified. Consider the identification status of the price equation. For the order condition we have

$$K^{**} = 1 > G^{\Delta} - 1 = 0,$$

and for the rank condition we have

$$\Delta = \begin{bmatrix} 1 & 0 & 0 & -\alpha_0 \\ 0 & 1 & 0 & -\beta_0 \\ 1 & -1 & -1 & 0 \end{bmatrix},$$

and

$$\text{rank}(\Delta) = G - 1 = 3,$$

which means that the price equation is also over-identified.

13-6-b.

In order to derive the time path of the end-of-period level of stock (Q_t), substitute for the production (S_t) and the sales (D_t) from the first two equations into the fourth equation of the model to get

(1) $S_t - D_t = \alpha_0 - \beta_0 + (\alpha_1 - \beta_1)P_t + u_{1t} - u_{2t} = Q_t - Q_{t-1}.$

Lagging (1) by one period and subtracting the result from it, we obtain

(2) $(\alpha_1 - \beta_1)(P_t - P_{t-1}) + v_t = Q_t - 2Q_{t-1} + Q_{t-2},$

where

$$v_t = u_{1t} - u_{2t} - u_{1,t-1} + u_{2,t-2}.$$

Substituting for the price differentials ($P_t - P_{t-1}$) from the third equation of the model into (2), we get

$$(\alpha_1 - \beta_1)[m(Q_{t-1} - Q_{t-2}) + u_{3t}] + v_t = Q_t - 2Q_{t-1} + Q_{t-2},$$

or

(3) $$Q_t - [2 + m(\alpha_1 - \beta_1)]Q_{t-1} + [1 + m(\alpha_1 - \beta_1)]Q_{t-2} = w_t,$$

where

$$w_t = v_t + (\alpha_1 - \beta_1)u_{3t}.$$

Disregarding the disturbance term w_t in (3), the time path of Q_t is found to be a second-order homogeneous difference equation. In order to derive the time path of the price (P_t), lag the fourth equation of the model by one period as follows

(4) $$S_{t-1} - D_{t-1} = Q_{t-1} - Q_{t-2},$$

and substitute for the quantity differentials ($Q_{t-1} - Q_{t-2}$) from (4) into the third equation of the model to obtain

(5) $$P_t - P_{t-1} = m(S_{t-1} - D_{t-1}) + u_{3t}.$$

Lagging (1) by one period and substituting the result into (5), we obtain

$$P_t - P_{t-1} = m[\alpha_0 - \beta_0 + (\alpha_1 - \beta_1)P_{t-1} + u_{1,t-1} - u_{2,t-1}] + u_{3t},$$

or

(6) $$P_t - [1 + m(\alpha_1 - \beta_1)]P_{t-1} = m(\alpha_0 - \beta_0) + \epsilon_t,$$

where

$$\epsilon_t = m(u_{1,t-1} - u_{2,t-1}) + u_{3t}.$$

Disregarding the disturbance term ϵ_t in (6), the time path of P_t is found to be a first-order non-homogeneous difference equation.

13-6-c.

The stability condition for P_t is

$$-1 \leq 1 + m(\alpha_1 - \beta_1) < 1,$$

or

$$-2 < m(\alpha_1 - \beta_1) < 0.$$

Since $\alpha_1 > 0$, $\beta_1 < 0$, and $m < 0$, the quantity $m(\alpha_1 - \beta_1)$ is necessarily negative. However, the stability condition requires the quantity to be greater than negative two (-2). For the stability condition of Q_t consider

$$Q_t - [2 + m(\alpha_1 - \beta_1)]Q_{t-1} + [1 + m(\alpha_1 - \beta_1)]Q_{t-2} = 0,$$

with the characteristic equation of

$$\lambda^2 - [2 + m(\alpha_1 - \beta_1)]\lambda + [1 + m(\alpha_1 - \beta_1)] = 0,$$

which has two roots

$$\lambda_1 = 1,$$

and

$$\lambda_2 = 1 + m(\alpha_1 - \beta_1).$$

If the time path of P_t is stable, i.e., if

$$-1 < 1 + m(\alpha_1 - \beta_1) < 1,$$

which implies

$$-1 < \lambda_2 < 1,$$

the first root ($\lambda_1 = 1$) will be the larger root and the time path of Q_t will be one of regular oscillations. Otherwise if the time path of P_t is not stable, the oscillations would be explosive.

13-6-d.

For the time path of P_t to be one of regular oscillations, the coefficient of P_{t-1} in (6) must be either equal to one or equal to negative one (-1). However, given the specifications of the model the coefficient is necessarily a negative quantity. Thus, for regular oscillations in the time path of P_t

$$1 + m(\alpha_1 - \beta_1) = -1,$$

or

$$m = -2/(\alpha_1 - \beta_1).$$

NOTES

NOTES

NOTES

NOTES

NOTES

NOTES

NOTES

NOTES

NOTES

NOTES

NOTES

NOTES